D0335222

IF ONLY
THEY
DIDN'T
SPEAK
ENGLISH

IF ONLY THEY DIDN'T SPEAK ENGLISH

Notes from
Trump's America

JON SOPEL

1 3 5 7 9 10 8 6 4 2

BBC Books, an imprint of Ebury Publishing
20 Vauxhall Bridge Road,
London SW1V 2SA

BBC Books is part of the Penguin Random House group of companies
whose addresses can be found at global.penguinrandomhouse.com

Penguin
Random House
UK

Copyright © Jon Sopel 2017

Jon Sopel has asserted his right to be identified as the author of this
Work in accordance with the Copyright, Designs and Patents Act 1988

First published by BBC Books in 2017

www.penguin.co.uk
A CIP catalogue record for this book is available from the British Library

Hardback ISBN 9781785942266
Trade Paperback ISBN 9781785942280

Typeset in India by Integra Software Services Pvt. Ltd, Pondicherry

Printed and bound in Great Britain by Clays Ltd, St Ives PLC

Penguin Random House is committed to a sustainable future for
our business, our readers and our planet. This book is made
from Forest Stewardship Council® certified paper.

MIX
Paper from
responsible sources
FSC® C018179

To Linda – who's shared this wonderful
American adventure (and Alfie, the miniature
German Schnauzer who came along too).
And to Max and Anna, our gorgeous grown-up
children who were left behind in London.

Contents

Foreword

Some books are the result of a blinding flash of inspiration; others have the gestation period of an elephant. This book – and how in tune with the 2016 madness and Donald Trump zeitgeist is this? – is the product of a tweet.

I had been on BBC Radio 2 with Simon Mayo, talking about some aspect of the presidential election campaign, when I received a tweet from a man purporting to be a literary agent. He said he'd like to talk to me as it seemed I could tell a story. Unusually, for Twitter, he turned out to be who he said he was. So I spoke to this charming and clever man, Rory Scarfe, and he suggested I scribble a few hundred words of what I would like to write about. This I thought would be enough to secure a big, fat literary contract. But no, he now wanted 15,000 words to show to publishers. And I thought, well that is simply not going to happen. Too busy with a presidential election to cover.

And this is where my wife, Linda, intervened. We were about to go to Barbados with our kids, who live and work in London, and assorted friends. I am not the best person

Leabharlanna Fhine Gall

at lying around on a sun lounger and, it is said, I can be annoying to others who are happy to do nothing but read books, listen to their music and soak up the sun. So I was told in no uncertain terms that instead of irritating everyone I should start work on the book. And each morning in this little piece of paradise, in the aptly named villa 'Eden' at Sugar Hill, I would sit in the gazebo and write. I also spent a good deal of last summer in the Hampshire garden of my oldest friend, Pete Morgan, trying to make progress. Linda has also been a source of brilliant ideas about how the book could be improved; what should be included and what left out.

That was the start. For getting it finished, and getting a whole bunch of half-formed ideas into a vaguely cogent shape, I need to thank a number of people. Most of all my editor, Yvonne Jacob at BBC Books, who has been a source of endless enthusiasm and encouragement, my brilliant colleague and friend from New York, Nick Bryant, who read the manuscript and offered really perceptive observations. BBC bosses get a bad rap, but I want to thank them for being so supportive in this endeavour – particularly Paul Danahar, the bureau chief in Washington, who would, on the rare quiet days, let me slip away to write. He was the person who, when we were discussing some extraordinary aspect of the campaign and the problem of explaining the craziness – and foreignness – of it to our British audience, said, 'If only they didn't speak English.' I thought to myself now that would one day make a great book title. Malcolm Balen in London tried to keep me 'free, fair and impartial' with what I have written. And then there's the team. My cameramen, John Landy and Ian Druce, and producers Lynsea Garrison, Sarah Svoboda and

Rozalia Hristova, who've been the 'band of brothers' (and sisters), and shared so many of the experiences that have formed the backbone of these succeeding chapters, deserve a huge thank you too. Without Jonathan Csapo to sort, fix and manage in the bureau I am not sure I would be able to function.

And of course this book is only possible because of all the people in all the places we've met and interviewed along the way.

Without this becoming like an Oscars speech, where the music wells up to drown out the person spending far too much time gushing at the microphone, I want to say one other thank you. The family across the street from us in Washington are the Powells – I mention them in the book. When we arrived they could not have been more welcoming to us. And they were a constant source of insight and stories – invariably over a negroni or two. As I was finishing the book, Elizabeth, at the age of 39, was diagnosed with – and died two months later from – a rare and aggressive form of lung cancer. As a family they are all that I love about America – positive, optimistic, kind, decent. So this is to Jeff and his two beautiful children, Eleanor and Charlie; and in memory of an exceptional woman.

Jon Sopel, July 2017
Washington DC

Introduction

We're going to play a game. I'm going to say a name and I want you to write down what comes to mind. OK. Let's start: New York. I reckon you're going to put skyscrapers, shopping, the Empire State Building, steam rising out of vents, cycling in Central Park, yellow taxis. Broadway. Bustle. Trump Tower – yup, I guess we can't ignore that any more. The soaring clarinet at the opening of Gershwin's 'Rhapsody in Blue', Sinatra belting out 'New York, New York' or Jay Z's 'concrete jungle where dreams are made of ...' in 'Empire State of Mind'. Or that scene when Harry met Sally in a diner, and any number of Woody Allen films – in fact his whole oeuvre. *Midnight Cowboy, King Kong, Fame* – and on and on and on.

And if I were to say LA, I bet you'd write tall palm trees, Sunset Boulevard, soft-top cars, ripped men on Muscle Beach, silicone-enhanced film stars in Beverly Hills, rollerbladers in Santa Monica, the Hollywood sign. And Miami? Steamy hot, Art Deco buildings, old Cuban men playing dominos, water, powerboats, wide beaches. Or the Grand Canyon? Las Vegas? San Francisco? Yellowstone? Chicago? Nashville?

Through music, literature, film and TV, and even through the food we eat and the clothes that we wear, we all have a highly developed sense of what America is; through our own visits we feel we know the country; and through our shared, tangled history we claim a special relationship.

But America in the election year of 2016 – and its extraordinary aftermath – felt about as foreign a country as you could imagine. It was fearful, angry and impatient for change. Journeying across the continent to cover the most turbulent race in recent history lifted a lid on seething resentments and profound anxieties. And most of that rage would find its embodiment in one unlikely person, who was brash, unpredictable – and, in the end, unstoppable.

And in my 30-plus years of being a journalist, I had never covered an election like it, nor witnessed anything like its bitter aftermath. The new president, having scaled the mountaintop, was not enjoying the view – he still had enemies to slay: Republicans who questioned him, the intelligence services, Democrats whom he had put to the sword. Even America's favourite actress, Meryl Streep, got a kicking for daring to question whether the new president was being divisive. He raged at suggestions that his inauguration had fewer people attending than Barack Obama's. He claimed that five million Americans had voted illegally for Hillary Clinton. And he went after the media with a rare ferocity and contempt.

I would even sample a little taste of it myself. There had never been anything like President Trump's first proper news conference in the East Room of the White House (and if the walls could speak, I suspect they'd have nodded sagely and said, 'You're right, we never have seen anything like it'). He lashed out at the media for half an hour, as being the most dishonest, loathsome perpetrators of fake news. He swatted away an earnest young orthodox Jew who dared to ask him about anti-Semitism. An African American reporter asked whether the president had plans to meet the Congressional Black Caucus. With a casual racism that shocked nearly all the journalists in the room he asked whether she would fix up a meeting – in other words, perhaps, all you black people know each other, you could sort it out for me. She demurred.

I was the only foreign journalist to get called. And I wanted to ask him about the problems he was having over his attempts to ban travellers from seven mainly Muslim countries. It should have been straightforward. It was not. Having spoken just one word, my English accent alerted him.

'Which news organisation are you from?'

'BBC News,' I replied.

'Here's another beauty,' says the president.

'That's a good line. We are free, impartial and fair.'

'Yeah. Sure.'

'Mr President ...'

'Just like CNN, right?' he asked sarcastically.

'On the travel ban – we could banter back and forth ...'

I eventually got to ask my question, and he replied. When I tried to ask a follow-up I was told to sit down, and then, a little menacingly, he added, 'I know who *you* are ...'

I have never seen politics done like this anywhere. And don't take that as in any way disapproving. It's not. This news conference was enormously entertaining. The whole 75 minutes went by in a flash. You had no idea what was going to happen next. And that's the way it has been for the past 18 months, and that's the way it is going to be for the foreseeable future. It was – and is – as foreign as foreign can be.

And can you imagine, back in March 2014 when I went through the selection board for the job as North America Editor, if I had said I think a reality TV star, property developer and golf-course owner called Trump with no political experience, who'd been married three times, was going to become America's 45th president, how they would have laughed. Equally, though, if I had said the Democratic Party was going to flirt heavily with choosing a socialist revolutionary as its candidate, the head of BBC News and the rest of the panel would have thought it was time to give Sopel a nice desk with no sharp edges and lots of foam furnishings around him where he could do no harm to himself – or the corporation.

I guess over the past 20 years I have travelled to the US an average of three or four times a year: sometimes for work, sometimes to see friends, sometimes to holiday. I had the best mid-life crisis one could ever hope for with five mates as we hired Harley-Davidsons and rode across Arizona, Nevada and California. I thought I knew this fabulous and complicated country. I didn't, and there were times in 2016 when I felt I knew it less well with each passing month.

America is surprising, varied and dynamic. American friends ask me what has been the most unexpected thing about living here. Easy: politeness and civility (admittedly Donald Trump is challenging that). Yes, the stats may say you're much more likely to die at the hands of some mad gunman than you would be in the UK (though it's still an infinitesimally small chance) – but the odds are much higher that you are going to be blown away by civility, decency and courtesy.

The work ethic of young people is off the charts. American kids in college are unbelievably focused – they don't do gap years; their summers are spent working hard to secure internships to add lustre to their CVs. And when they start work, wow, do they put in the hours – probably they work round the clock so they don't have to think about their hideous college loans that they are paying back at scandalous, usurious interest rates.

And there are things about the mundanities of life that you might expect. Yes, the portions of food are often way too big, sweet things are sweeter, salty things are saltier, and Americans drive enormous cars and have no idea how to parallel park. Television overall is much better in the UK (what else do you expect me to say?!), but some of the drama and some of the comedy is *way* better than what you'd get in Britain. Americans are obsessed by the weather – and rightly so. America gets a lot of weather, much of it extremely violent and dramatic. But these are the superficial differences that separate us; there are much deeper fissures too – and it's those fault lines that the coming chapters will seek to explore.

So let's go back to the game we started with, only this time play it the other way round. Get the average American to write down what comes into their mind when you say London – they will say fog. I can't tell you how often Americans have asked me, is it always foggy, damp and rainy in London? Personally I blame Ella Fitzgerald for singing so beautifully about 'a foggy day in London town'. They will know the Houses of Parliament (and how all those MPs will do nothing but shout at each other). They will know Buckingham Palace. They know about the royal family – that is the one bit of British news that will always break through (at parties I can feel the wave of disappointment come over people I meet who ask me if I know the Queen well, and I have to reply 'not terribly …'). They know Adele, David Beckham, Gordon Ramsay – even Jeremy Clarkson. And they love our sixties and seventies rock music. The Who, Jethro Tull, The Rolling Stones still do good business in the US.

But ask people about Manchester, Birmingham, Glasgow or Newcastle, about the Lake District or the Brecon Beacons, and I suspect not a lot will be written down.

The special relationship is something that concerns us far more than it does them. They like us. They like our quirks. They hate our weather. They love our accent. But for an awful lot of Americans Britain is a small island that they would really struggle to identify on a map of the globe. They know much less about us than we know about them – or think we do.

But America is at a moment where all the things we thought we knew for certain about this superpower, that have been there since the Second World War – are up in the air. This nation is at a turning point. Having lived here for the past few years and travelled from coast to coast – or 'from sea to shining sea' as the song 'America the Beautiful' would have it – there is a restlessness that is palpable. I've gone from the chill of the Great Lakes in the depths of winter to the steamy Deep South, reported from the most iconic cities to the most Hicksville towns where the tumbleweed blows through (in Midland, Texas, the wind was so strong that the tumbleweed overtook the car we were driving in). There is a common thread. A huge number of Americans feel their 'dream' is being torn away from them. Of the status quo, a piercing cry of 'enough' has gone up. Of the future, the demand is for 'change'. But what that will look like is anyone's guess; at the moment there are only vague shapes and ill-defined contours. The past 18 months have made predicting the future a complete fool's errand.

This complex, God-fearing, gun-loving, patriotic, government-hating gargantuan of a country wants to pull up the drawbridge and look after itself. And as to what the rest of the world thinks? Think Rhett Butler in *Gone with the Wind* – 'Frankly, my dear, I don't give a damn.'

You see, if only they didn't speak English in America, then we'd treat it as a foreign country – and possibly understand it a lot better.

Chapter 1

Anger

As Americans gathered to see out 2016 after one of the most momentous – and unexpected – years in the nation's history, ready to link arms, sing 'Auld Lang Syne' and drink a cup of kindness to 2017, Donald Trump had time for one last tweet. It read: 'Happy New Year to all, including my many enemies and those who have fought me and lost so badly they just don't know what to do. Love.'

Magnanimity was a commodity in short supply as Americans went about electing their 45th president.

It seemed a fitting end to a tumultuous and defining year in which one section of American society would look at the other as if they were from different tribes. The divisions were between black and white, young and old, rich and poor, urban and rural, educated and uneducated. In short, those who were doing well and that vast swathe of America who felt left behind. And it was this latter group whose fury and rage Donald Trump tapped into.

They were angry. Angry about wages. Angry about job insecurity. Angry about their savings. Angry about college fees. Angry about their loans. Angry about their healthcare. Angry there were plots to take away their guns. Angry about their kids' futures. Angry about illegal immigrants. Angry about the value of their homes. Angry with politics. Angry with politicians. Angry with Obama. Angry with Congress. Angry with Wall Street. Angry about America's place in the world. Angry about the rest of the world. Angry about the treatment of military veterans. Angry the country was going to hell in a handcart. Angry about just about everything and anything.

At times it seemed that it wasn't so much about blue collar or white collar – Americans were just hot under the collar. When you asked anyone what they thought about the state of the country, it seemed that every reply commenced with 'Don't get me started ...'

And in perfect harmony with the national mood, America went through the nastiest, most mean-spirited, poison-drenched, hate-filled, vituperative election, with a result as remarkable as any in the country's 240-year history. An election that pitched a pompous, braggadocious, thin-skinned, sexually boasting property billionaire and reality TV host, who was big on gut instinct but knew precious little about the detail of any policy, against a political insider of 30-plus years who knew Washington inside out, had the detail of everything at her fingertips, never more comfortable than when surrounded by nerdy policy wonks – but had a singular lack of capacity to connect with the public, or communicate clearly why she wanted to be president, other than that it was her entitlement and her turn. The boor versus the bore.

They were two candidates extraordinary in one other respect too. They were uniquely unpopular. Their disapproval ratings broke all records. In this country of 320 million talented, creative and brilliant people with rich reservoirs of experience to draw upon and varied backgrounds, America ended up with a choice of Trump versus Clinton; a decision not of 'who do I like the most', but 'who do I loathe the least'.

Donald J. Trump played by the Queensberry Rules in reverse. There was no belt below which he would not punch, no line he wouldn't cross. Gouging and holding were to be encouraged; the rabbit punch was the norm. And if the referee called him out, he'd whack the ref with an elbow in the ribs for being biased against him.

The former governor of New York, Mario Cuomo, once remarked that in politics you campaign in poetry and you govern in prose. Donald Trump campaigned with a flame-thrower in one hand and a flick knife in the other. Big groups like the media, Wall Street, Washington, the establishment would get the flamethrower treatment. Political opponents who stood in his way (Republican and Democrat) would get the switch-blade. His other favoured method was the drive-by killing by Twitter. He was the master of assassination in 140 characters. The scenes of carnage by the end looked like something out of *Reservoir Dogs*.

Covering the 2016 election was a very different experience to anything I had ever done. Not just for its unabashed nasti-ness, but for some of the subject matter too. I was in new territory. Call me sheltered, but in the course of covering politics I had never hitherto discussed penis size or a woman's vagina – but these were subjects that now had their moment in the sun. And they were interspersed with showers, sometimes 'golden showers'. There were earnest discussions with TV bulletin editors about what words could be used pre and post watershed. Could we say 'I moved on her like a bitch?', as Donald Trump proclaimed in that tape? 'Can we use the word "pussy"?' I had to ask one weekend editor. This was new territory for me.

Indeed the two most dramatic moments of the final weeks of the election came with the release of that *Access Hollywood* sex tape from 2005 in which Donald Trump seems to boast about being able to do whatever he likes to a woman because of his fame, and the FBI announcing 11 days from polling day that it was reopening its investigation into Hillary Clinton's emails. The latter was because, in the course of another inquiry, it had come across Clinton correspondence on the computer of someone being investigated for 'sexting', and sending pictures of his penis to unsuspecting recipients. His name was Anthony Weiner. And the former congressman was married to Mrs Clinton's closest aide, Huma Abedin. The suggestion was clear – there was more on this computer to interest the FBI than just Weiner's much selfied 'manhood'. And then there was the sex tape, on which Trump is heard boasting about grabbing a woman's genitals to someone called Bush. Where does a satirist go with that? Election 2016: all wiener and bush. You really couldn't make this stuff up. But it was all part of the lurid Technicolor circus that was election 2016.

And the candidates for the most illustrious crown in democratic politics went about winning by tearing chunks out of each other. The mostly insightful Republican pollster, Frank Luntz, had said to me at the Republican Convention in Cleveland in the summer of 2016, if this is an election about Hillary Clinton, Donald Trump wins, and if it's about Donald Trump, Hillary Clinton gets it.

Though Luntz may have been right about that, he is going to struggle to recover from his election-night tweet, which read: 'In case I wasn't clear enough from my previous tweets, Hillary Clinton will be the next President of the United States.' As predictions go it had strong echoes of poor Michael Fish, the BBC weatherman who, back in 1987, told viewers there was no hurricane coming. Only for Britain to wake up the next morning and find every tree knocked down across the land. America woke on the morning of 9 November to find that the political establishment had been completely uprooted by Whirlwind Donald.

But Luntz had been right in his original analysis. With Donald Trump and Hillary Clinton 'enjoying' such dire poll ratings the trick was to accept you were never going to be loved; better instead, therefore, to do everything to make your opponent more despised. Politicians in my experience are people who want to command the spotlight. In this election they wanted their unpopular rival to be under the microscope, squirming under the lights of a disapproving public.

Ten out of ten for effort to both candidates, but when it came to doing mean and nasty, no one could outdo 'the Donald'.

Covering the election of Barack Obama eight years earlier was not the same.

Culpeper is an old railway town in the foothills of the Blue Ridge mountains, surrounded by the richest and most lush rolling Virginia farmland. In 2008 it was one of the must-win states for Barack Obama, and Culpeper was a

Republican county within the state. I was there doing a big 'outside broadcast' from the coffee shop on Main Street, and as the results started to come in, so the emotions rose as it became clear that 'yes we can' was going to become 'yes he did'. I remember interviewing one elderly African American woman who wept as she told me, 'I really do feel free at last,' echoing the famous words of Martin Luther King. Just after she said it one of Gordon Brown's tough political operatives in London texted me to say, 'She's just made me cry my eyes out.'

Emotion is not unusual on election nights. But this was something else. I drove back into Washington in the small hours of the morning, and every time we got to a red light, people in other cars would get out to embrace each other: total strangers coming together to share a historic moment. The lights would turn green, they would get back in their vehicles and as they hit the next 'stop' sign they would do the same thing again with a different, random group of revellers. That next morning America seemed to have a giant smile on its face. Hope: the iconic word on the famous Obama poster had become the mood of a nation.

In 2016, 35 per cent of the residents of Culpeper voted for Hillary Clinton; 60.4 per cent for Donald Trump. 'Hope' had become 'Nope' as far as the Democrats were concerned; we were now in the age of rage.

On the night of the election in 2016 I was at Hillary Clinton's campaign HQ in New York, in the Hell's Kitchen area of the city. The Javits Center is a huge convention space, with one obvious eye-catching attraction for her team. It had a glass roof – and in her victory speech she would be able to look skywards and point to its metaphorical shattering, as the final glass ceiling to a woman's ambition, this woman's ambition. We the BBC, and the rest of the world's camera crews, were housed on a steeply raked tribune opposite where she would deliver those remarks. The shape of the stage had been elaborately carved so she would appear to be standing on a platform cut out in the shape of the map of America. Throughout the evening two men were posted to each corner of our broadcast 'riser' and they sat at machines with large conical funnels pointing upwards. These were the machines that would launch into the air millions of shards of shiny paper to recreate the effect of a glass ceiling shattering.

Their services were not called upon. At around two in the morning, when all hope had been lost, the two men manning the machines wandered off. And skulking onto the stage was Hillary Clinton's chief of staff, John Podesta. He told everyone to go home. If only those infernal machines could have shot up packets of Kleenex they would have done a roaring trade, as thousands of campaign workers and activists wept big, gulping, body-shaking, heartfelt tears. Painful it was to be surrounded by so much misery that night.

A few days before polling it had emerged that the Clinton campaign had applied for permission to hold a celebratory firework party along the Hudson River in New York. That evening one of the late-night comedians mused whether the fireworks would spell out the word 'hubris'. He was right. In Greek tragedy after hubris comes nemesis. And in Donald Trump, Hillary Clinton had found her nemesis.

This election cycle was not a time to be a conventional politician, offering small, incremental change to complex problems. Not a time to be merely nudging the status quo by one degree north or south. Not a time to be an obvious paid-up member of the establishment, with a dynastic name.

In 2016 the American public was in a sulphurous, belligerent, mutinous mood. The litany of complaints and grievances from the electorate demanded something more ground-shaking than some variation of 'more of the same', 'steady as she goes' and 'safe pair of hands'. The people wanted CHANGE (in block capital letters). Mainstream politics migrated to its more populist, exotic and unpredictable shores. The politician who was going to catch the eye at this moment in US history was ideally not going to be a politician. What was needed was a tribune of the people who would be their voice; someone who would tear at the consensus, who would offer big, brave alternatives, who would show there was a different way of doing business.

And so it was that a 70-year-old New York property tycoon, who had been born with a silver spoon in his mouth, who flew around in his own private jet, who had never known a day's hardship in his life, who had lived a playboy life and had managed to dodge national service when other young men his age were being shipped off to Vietnam, became the champion of the disaffected, white working class. He had five children from three different marriages (just imagine for a second what would have been said about an African American – like Barack Obama – running for president with that kind of past ... or, indeed, a woman running for the highest office with that backstory). He was happy to go on TV to rank women on a score of one to ten on their looks, and didn't care a jot if he caused offence or ruffled feathers. He was completely anathema to everything the Republican Party establishment wanted its candidate for 2016 to be.

He is the complete antithesis of anyone who could run for office in the UK. Can you imagine, for a second, a loud-mouthed billionaire, who brags about not paying tax, who sneers at women and the disabled, who puffs his chest with pride at his sexual conquests, becoming our next prime minister? In Britain the Trump private jet wouldn't be allowed to leave the political gate, let alone get onto the runway and soar into the sky.

As a young political correspondent at Westminster I covered the fall of Thatcher and the subsequent leadership election, which pitched the patrician Douglas Hurd against the wealthy Michael Heseltine and the south London boy, John Major. The contest became a farcical attempt to show which was the more humble. It was the 'lowlier than thou' campaign. Each man having to show that he was not the product of privilege or advantage or wealth. One of the reasons Tony Blair is despised by sections of the UK public is that he went out and made a lot of money when he stopped being prime minister (OK, yes – the Iraq War might have played a part too …).

Donald Trump hasn't had to bother with any of that. He is arrogant and brash and loaded. And despite this, perhaps *because* of this, he somehow became the Republican nominee for president. Midway through 2016 the party of Lincoln, Coolidge, Teddy Roosevelt, Eisenhower and Reagan became the party of Donald J. Trump. For the first time in America's history, there would be a candidate from one of the two main parties who had neither held elected office nor been a senior military commander. In a conventional job application, in the column marked 'relevant experience', the word 'none' would have been written.

Except in one important respect. In America people with money are venerated. Money equals success, and America loves winners. And the fact that he freely admits to doing everything he can to pay the least money possible to the IRS (the equivalent of the Inland Revenue) doesn't provoke disgust or disdain – for many it engenders admiration. 'Good for you, Donald,' they say – the thinking being that any money given to government will be spent badly and wantonly.

He also broke with a 50-year-long tradition by refusing to release his tax returns. One leaked document suggested that nearly two decades could have passed without him paying any federal income tax at all. He was questioned in the media repeatedly about it, but told the press to get lost (he actually said his returns could not be released while they were being audited, but tax experts repeatedly said that was not a barrier to releasing them), and said the public weren't interested in his tax returns. He was partially right. His supporters didn't care, even if his opponents thought it to be an outrage.

Trump's base seemed to give a collective shrug of the shoulders that it didn't matter, maybe thinking enviously that they only wished they had tax lawyers able to work the same magic for them. For much of the campaign it seemed he had been given carte blanche to say or do whatever he wanted with absolutely no ill effect. And he took full advantage of that.

He turned conventional arguments about money in politics upside down. He boasted about how much money he'd spent 'buying' politicians – not my word, his – to encourage them to make the right decisions about planning and the like – and he was not discriminating with his largesse – Republicans or Democrats, they all received cheques from Donald J. Trump towards their campaigns for the city council, or the state legislature, or Congress, or the Senate. Anywhere, in fact, where a light sprinkling of Trump cash might add the necessary fairy dust to planning decisions so that they fell in the right direction for his company.

And he had another unique argument to make to the American public. He said that because he was a self-funding billionaire, he wouldn't have to go cap in hand to anyone, asking them to contribute towards the cost of his campaign. And because of that he would not be a captive of lobbyists or special interest groups. Only he would keep the wicked influence peddlers at bay. And the Trump supporters loved that argument – but it did seem to suggest a rather substantial rewriting of the notion that anyone could be president; the logic of the Trump argument is that only billionaires need apply. And after the election when it came to appointing his cabinet there were only two types of people that the president chose – billionaires and generals. You needed either a lot of bread or a lot of braid.

And just as aghast as the Republican Party at its choice of candidate was the Democratic Party establishment at the prospect of a 74-year-old, badly dressed, grumpy old curmudgeon from Vermont called Senator Bernie Sanders being their torch-bearer. In this capitalist country he called for revolution. He talked openly about being a socialist. He didn't speak so much as bellow. He promised to take money from the rich bankers and give it to the poor. It resulted in young people (mainly) in their millions in this most capitalist economy screaming for him and his offer of a political revolution.

A man so far out of the mainstream that no one paid him any attention when he announced his decision to run. But, like a latterday Pied Piper, each time he looked over his shoulder he found hundreds of thousands more people were falling in behind him. Seduced by his seditious whistle and revolutionary tune, angry America was showing its distaste for the conventional. Month after month he grew in stature – and his campaign grew in wealth – not through cosy deals with a handful of billionaires, but from vast numbers of ordinary people handing over a few dollars here, a few dollars there, that kept him and his ever more professional campaign afloat.

And with monotonous regularity the media class and the political establishment would predict the imminent demise of these two septuagenarians, but each month they just grew more vigorous and strong. What both men had from their supporters was unwavering enthusiasm. Crazy, wild enthusiasm. Because these were men who were going to rip everything up, and start all over again.

And what was striking was the overlap in the support they were drawing. The blue-collar workers – predominantly – who'd seen their industries decline and disappear saw, both in this rabble-rouser from the right and this populist from the left, an answer. Both men promised they would renegotiate the trade deals that had led to jobs being shipped out of the country; both men wanted to make it much more difficult for companies to move their operations to countries overseas with a cheaper labour force and alluring tax breaks. Both men decried the power of Wall Street and the money men. Forget globalisation and free trade – these were economic national-ists, protectionists, who would put American workers first.

In some of the traditional northern, rust-belt Democratic states, many of the people who, during the primary process, were rock solid behind Bernie Sanders, went straight to Donald Trump in the general election. They were unable to bring themselves to vote for the 'established' Democratic candidate, Hillary Clinton. In Michigan, Wisconsin and Pennsylvania – if she had polled just a hundred thousand more votes combined, she would have become the president. Not Donald Trump. These are small margins.

Politics borrows heavily from the language of war, so it's all about enemies and battle lines being drawn, of attack, of smoke clearing from the field of battle. So it's no wonder that in the struggle for the Democratic nomination things got a little heated. But here, too, it went beyond that. Many of the Bernie Sanders supporters loathed Hillary Clinton with a passion. They saw her as the tool of the establishment, a wholly owned subsidiary of Wall Street and the hedge-fund guys. And on the first day of the Democratic Party Convention in Philadelphia the mood was uneasy.

Disaffected Bernie supporters booed every time Hillary Clinton's name was mentioned. Any time anything to do with national security was mentioned they chanted 'No more war'. One earnest young man I spoke to sitting in the California delegation told me he was not going to support her, come what may. 'She's a war-hawk, a liar and a bad person,' he told me. But wasn't she better than Donald Trump, I asked him. 'It doesn't matter. She's only slightly better.' A Hillary supporter sitting next to him couldn't keep quiet any longer, accusing the Sanders supporters of being morons and behaving like a cult. Some Sanders supporters said they would rather vote for Trump than give their backing to Hillary Clinton.

And where the Trump and Sanders supporters could agree was that something had gone seriously awry with the America they had grown up believing in.

One reason so many Americans tolerate inequality is their belief that it's not here to stay; it's not a permanent condition. Yes, you might start out disadvantaged and without much money. But through hard work and playing by the rules, you'll get ahead. You might even become a Donald Trump billionaire (although his path was of course made easier by a $1 million gift from his father as he was setting out). He, of course, was born into privilege, or, to use the fabulous American phrase borrowed from the game of baseball, 'He was born on third base and thinks he hit a triple.' Actually the *New Yorker* magazine put it especially neatly: 'Donald Trump was born on third base and thinks he invented baseball. Trump's father Fred made himself, building an empire from nothing. Donald Trump took what his father had already created and made it bigger, flashier, and, sometimes, more bankrupt.'

But no matter. With the mechanisms of social mobility functioning, opportunity would be open to everyone. Work hard and you will do better than your parents. And then your kids will have a chance of doing even better than you. And their children, your grandchildren, better still. Sociologists call this 'transgenerational mobility'. It's better known as 'the American dream'.

Both the USA and much of modern-day Europe have their foundations in that astonishing period of intellectual creativity, scientific discovery and philosophical ferment, the Enlightenment. The great thinkers of the day in Scotland, France and Germany (less so in England, where for the universities of Oxford and Cambridge to challenge the authority of the monarchy and the church was a more risky undertaking) would freely discuss the role of the state, the rights of the individual, the separation of powers.

We love to talk of turning points. This was such a moment. The absolute rule of monarchy had to be supplanted; the church must be disentangled from the state. The French Revolution would take place just 13 years after the 1776 Declaration of Independence and the beginning of American nationhood. On 4 July that year the United States became a new nation in the new world.

The Enlightenment would be the intellectual underpinning of the French Revolution (if not the Terror) and for the Founding Fathers framing the original seven articles of the US Constitution. The US Declaration of Independence proclaims that 'all men are created equal', with the right to 'Life, Liberty and the pursuit of Happiness'. Very similar to the tripartite motto of the French Republic, which even today is etched onto all public buildings and schools in France – *Liberté, Egalité, Fraternité.*

But look at the first ten amendments to the US Constitution – often referred to as the Bill of Rights – and they are about offering specific protections to the individual and placing restrictions on the powers of government. Where Europe preached collectivism, the United States was striking out for the individual. Where Europe spoke of equality, America became the land of opportunity. Where Europe to a greater or lesser extent championed the ideas of democratic socialism, Americans looked to ideals of liberalism and the fundamental rights of the individual against the state. Where Britain built a welfare state, America left it up to individuals and families to make their own insurance arrangements.

The phrase 'the American Dream' was coined in 1931, in James Truslow Adams's book *The Epic of America*. He defined it as 'that dream of a land in which life should be better and richer and fuller for every man, with opportunity for each according to his ability or achievement'. Its antecedents, though, go right back to the formation of the Republic.

It is a fundamental difference between European and American thinking. Donald Trump doesn't mention philosophers much in his speeches (well, to be strictly accurate, he doesn't mention them at all), but the ideas that are fundamental to America's idea of itself – home of opportunity, land of the free, a place where anyone can rise from poverty to the highest office – are the benchmarks against which he measured 2016 America, and how it was failing to meet those goals and aspirations.

But are these two insurgents of left and right correct? Is the critique fair?

Since the turn of the millennium more than 80 per cent of America's metropolitan areas have seen household income decline. The research by the respected – and non-partisan – Pew Research Center found that in just 39 out of 229 urban areas had median household income risen. And in the US three-quarters of the population live in urban areas.

This means the middle class was in retreat – in 2016 it formed less than half the population for the first time in 40 years. With its numbers in decline, the forces of technological change seemed to be driving an ever bigger wedge between the winners and losers of an increasingly fractured America. And then there was the convulsion brought about by the financial collapse of 2008. It is hard to overstate the extent to which it disrupted lives, affected confidence and made Americans question. The sub-prime mortgage crisis resulted in millions of families losing their homes, as the banks foreclosed on loans that should have never been made in the first place. More Americans were dislocated by this crisis than during the great Dust Bowl famine of the 1930s.

In this vast, diverse country wherever I travelled with my film crew we found people with strikingly similar stories to tell. Though the industries may have differed, the impact of globalisation was the same. Not far out of Cleveland, where the Republicans held their 2016 convention, is Youngstown, Ohio. A few decades ago the skies were lit up by the city's blast furnaces. The iron ore would come ashore from Lake Erie before being turned into steel and put on those great, long trains snaking along America's transcontinental rail lines to feed the nation's manufacturing industries. Now America cannot compete with the cheap foreign imports, so the steel mills lie empty; rusty chains keep people out, though not many want to get in. Those who can leave these impoverished towns, and those who can't are left behind, angry.

In the Appalachian Mountains is a town called Blue Ridge. It's just on the northern edge of Georgia, very close to the state line with Tennessee, and used to be a textiles town – clothes and carpets were its stock in trade. We went to film at the only factory left still making denim jeans. It employs just 18 people. Until 2002, it was the home of the most quintessential US product – Levi's. But they have long since gone to factories in India. That summer Levi's also closed factories in San Francisco, California, in Powell, Tennessee, and in the Texan cities of Brownsville, El Paso and San Benito. Embarrassingly, it was discovered that 3 per cent of the jeans that they were selling under the 'Made in America' label were in fact made in China. Blue Ridge is now trying to re-invent itself as a tourist centre. If friendliness alone would win business, then this delightful spot would do well.

In Chicago we went to the Nabisco factory – home to another favourite American brand, the Oreo biscuit – where production has ceased with the decision to ship production to Mexico. The company decided that rather than investing $130 million in modernising the Chicago plant, it was more cost effective to move the entire operation to the other side of the border. The workers are furious. They feel they have done nothing wrong, have met all the productivity targets, yet still been thrown onto the scrapheap. And you can find any number of other case studies.

In total the number of manufacturing jobs that have gone from America since 2000 is estimated to be five million. In angry America the blame is put fairly and squarely on cheap Chinese imports and trade deals that have disadvantaged the American blue-collar worker – the North Atlantic Free Trade Agreement is vilified for the effect it has had on US jobs. No wonder that two massive trade deals that were in the pipeline at the end of the Obama presidency – with Asia and Europe – were consigned to the scrapheap the moment Trump won the election.

In 1960, 24 per cent of Americans were employed in manufacturing; today it's around 6 per cent. But to put the blame exclusively on China and trade deals is to ignore profound technological change. A huge number of those jobs have not gone to cheap labour abroad – they've gone to non-passport-carrying robots. Yes, five million manufacturing jobs may have disappeared between 2000 and 2010. According to a study carried out by the Center for

Business and Economic Research at Ball State University, 85 per cent of those job losses can be explained by technological change in manufacturing processes. Robotics might just be the next stage of an industrial revolution that goes back to the spinning jenny and the steam engine – a way of producing more with fewer people. This automation has rendered many low-skill jobs redundant, and as advances in robotics and 3D printing develop it is hard to see that turning round any time soon.

But what has seemed like an inexorable decline may be turning round. Since March 2010, when the number of manufacturing jobs in the America hit a low of 11.45 million, nearly a million new factory positions have been created, most of them in the Southern states, particularly North Carolina, South Carolina and Tennessee.

But empirical data didn't win an argument in the fractious, roiling atmosphere of 2016. A politician turning up and telling the former steel worker in Youngstown, or the unemployed textile worker in Blue Ridge, or the person in Chicago who's just seen his or her job go to Mexico, that really GDP growth is better than many of the other advanced industrial economies is going to cut little ice. What has been striking is the gap between what you read on the financial pages of the smart newspapers and what is the perception of ordinary people who feel that they will never get a job, or if they have a job, will never see a pay increase.

The facts are plentiful, and can be weaponised to suit either side. So if you were a supporter of the Obama administration you'd deploy the following arguments. By the time Obama left office, the private sector had added jobs for 81 consecutive months – some 15 million new jobs in all. President

Obama is quick to point out that this is the longest period of sustained job growth on record. Unemployment, which peaked at 10 per cent in 2008, had more than halved. The budget deficit had fallen by roughly $1 trillion during his two terms. And overall US economic growth had significantly outpaced that of every other advanced nation.

A survey by the Boston Consulting Group in 2016 found that, of the manufacturing companies in the US which responded, 31 per cent said they were going to add production capacity to their factories in America. A separate survey found fewer American companies were going offshore for back-office functions, and many were repatriating jobs. General Electric announced plans to invest a billion dollars in an appliance plant in Louisville, Kentucky, bringing back 4,000 jobs that had been in China and Mexico. So it was not all one-way traffic. And this at a time when the Chinese economy was slowing and struggling.

One of the themes President Obama returned to again and again in his speeches was that, despite all the problems, there had never been a better time to be born in America. When asked why people weren't more appreciative, the president blamed his political opponents. 'If you have a political party – in this case, the Republicans – that denies any progress and is constantly channelling to their base, which is sizable – say, 40 per cent of the population – that things are terrible all the time, then people will start absorbing that.'

But from one of the greatest communicators ever to inhabit the White House, that was disingenuous. His critics would counter by pointing out that a big chunk of the labour force had dropped out of the job market altogether and, for the average American family, its income was $4,000 less than it was when Bill Clinton left office in 2000. Economic inequality has become more accentuated – half the recent rise that there had been in income growth went to the highest 1 per cent of earners. Also, it's not just Republicans who don't recognise the president's Panglossian view. This was Bill Clinton on the campaign trail with his wife: 'Millions and millions and millions and millions of people look at that pretty picture of America he [Barack Obama] painted and they cannot find themselves in it to save their lives ... People are upset, frankly; they're anxiety-ridden, they're disoriented, because they don't see themselves in that picture.'

But given where the US economy was when President Obama took office at the height of the banking crisis, the performance of the US economy in the eight years of his two terms was a minor miracle.

But politics at the best of times doesn't do nuance very well, and in 2016 it did it terribly. If you want to connect with the voters, don't give them shades of grey. They want jet black and brilliant white.

And what they saw was an America where social mobility had ground to a halt; where to do well and see your living standards improve you had to be part of the 1 per cent. Where unemployment, which once was seen as cyclical, had become structural. If you haven't got the right educational qualifications then there's no point waiting for an economic upturn: the jobs have gone abroad and are not coming back. Disillusionment was rife. And that is why so much ire was aimed at the 1 per cent by an angry America. It wasn't that people resented that there was a top tier doing very well indeed. The fuel for the antagonism was the belief that, in this post-industrial society, there was no mechanism for the ordinary Joe to join them. The elite members club had closed the waiting list to future applicants. Social mobility was being replaced by a calcified structure that owed more to 19th-century hidebound England, with 'The rich man in his castle, The poor man at his gate, He made them high and lowly, And ordered their estate.' That is not the 'All Things Bright and Beautiful' of the American dream.

Which brings us to the solutions. Well, the answers being offered by both Donald Trump on the populist right and Bernie Sanders on the populist left were practically identical. If you were to play the old game that used to be in comics and magazines of 'spot the difference', you might struggle. This is Senator Sanders: 'Corporate America said, "Why do I want to pay somebody in Michigan a living wage when I can pay slave wages in Mexico or China? We're going to shut down, we're going to move abroad." We're going to bring those products back into this country,' he said at one of his rallies. 'They're going to start having to, if I'm president, invest in this country.'

And this is Donald Trump: 'I am going to turn our bad trade agreements into great trade agreements ... I am going to bring back our jobs to Ohio, and Pennsylvania, and New York, and Michigan and to all of America – and I am not going to let companies move to other countries, firing their employees along the way, without consequence.'

But how easy is this to achieve? In an age where capital is mobile, how do you stop companies moving from one state to another, or from one country to another? And are you really going to start a trade war with China – and everyone else for that matter, with all the consequences that might bring for the global economy? The last time

America went down that route it didn't work out so well. The Smoot–Hawley Tariff Act of 1930 only intensified the Great Depression. The old joke is that if you put 10 economists in a room you will come out with 11 different opinions, but on this piece of protectionism there is consensus – it was a disaster. As Ben Bernanke, the former chief of the Federal Reserve, put it: 'Economists still agree that Smoot–Hawley and the ensuing tariff wars were highly counterproductive and contributed to the depth and length of the global Depression.' The estimate is that it cost the United States half its exports.

The desire to bring manufacturing jobs back to the US – or never let them go away in the first place – was not new. There was a famous meeting between Barack Obama and the chiefs of Silicon Valley, including the legendary Apple CEO, Steve Jobs. Each of the tech entrepreneurs was asked to come up with a question they would like to ask Barack Obama over dinner.

When it was Steve Jobs's turn, the president interrupted him. Barack Obama said, 'I have a question for you.' It was February 2011, and the iPhone was the hottest thing around – though not as sizzling as it would become. The president wanted to know what it would take to make iPhones in the United States. When you're Steve Jobs, you don't worry about diplomatic niceties. He never had done. And wasn't about to start now. According to those who were there he simply replied, 'Those jobs aren't coming back.' And then he went on to explain it wasn't just that labour was cheaper in China, it was better in other ways.

The flexibility, the expertise, the scale of overseas factories were something that the US couldn't come close to matching.

A story is told of a redesign to the phone that was made at the last minute. Eight thousand factory workers who lived in dormitories next to the factory in China were woken up and given tea and biscuits before working a 12-hour shift to produce this revamped phone that California had demanded. There was no way that would have or could have happened in the US.

He also explained to the president that if production of the iPhone were to return to the US the cost would be so much higher that it would be out of reach to most Americans. And so working-class Americans would have found themselves shut out of the market. And sales would have dropped around the world. Surely a phenomenon that would be repeated. 'Made in America' may be a rousing slogan, but the family on modest means going into the out-of-town Walmart just before the school term starts – do they want to buy one $50 pair of trousers made in the US, or for the same $50 get five pairs that may have been made in China, Vietnam, the Philippines or Mexico? Consumers have seen a sustained period where the absolute and relative price of a whole basket of goods has fallen. Do they want to go back?

One other thing that happened in the Apple example was that because the headquarters of the company was in California, a number of other companies set up there: web designers, app creators, tech companies, all essentially feeding off the revolution that the iPhone and the iPad heralded – and Google, and Uber and Snapchat, etc., etc. So that now when people talk of innovation, start-ups and the like, they think of Palo Alto. A massive American success story – but without the manufacturing jobs.

Who knows whether textiles will come back to Blue Ridge, blast furnaces will light up the Ohio skies and biscuits will start to roll off the Illinois production line again? But that is what many millions of disenchanted Americans believed would happen if you just let a proper businessman take charge of running the world's biggest economy, and get rid of all those useless, corrupt, self-serving politicians.

This is not the way the Republican Party saw it. Its leaders in Congress were passionate advocates of free trade. Indeed, after Barack Obama won his second term, fretful leaders of the Grand Old Party (GOP), as the Republican Party is known, commissioned research on a path to victory for 2016. There was recognition that the party was too male, pale and stale. In other words it was a party made up of angry, old white men. The best brains were summoned and a report was produced called the Growth and Opportunity Project.

The recommendations were clear. The party needed to win the support of more women, more young people and more immigrants. And the recommendations were equally focused – particularly when it came to Hispanic voters. This fast-growing demographic in the US – partly because of the numbers who've come into America and partly because of their much higher birth rate – needed to be wooed, not booed. This is what the report's authors said:

> If Hispanic Americans hear that the GOP doesn't want them in the United States, they won't pay attention to our next sentence. It doesn't matter what we say about education, jobs or the economy; if Hispanics think that we do not want them here, they will close their ears to our policies. In essence, Hispanic voters tell us our

Party's position on immigration has become a litmus test, measuring whether we are meeting them with a welcome mat or a closed door.

In 2016 it was as though Donald Trump took a cursory glance at the report and threw it on the bonfire. Forget the pathway the GOP leadership had marked out; he took one of his building-site wrecking balls and smashed every idea in it to pieces. It wasn't just a closed door that Donald Trump was proposing, but a wall, 2,000 miles long, to create a physical barrier between the US and Mexico. Calling Mexicans thieves and rapists, his approach to Muslims was little different. After the Islamic State-inspired attack in San Bernardino, he called for a complete ban on Muslims entering the United States. This policy prescription bogged President Trump down in treacle in the first months of his administration as the constitutionality of his 'travel ban' was repeatedly challenged in the courts.

It wasn't just that he wanted to go back to fighting the election the way Republicans had always fought, he was seeking to rewrite the rule book entirely. He wanted to bring in disaffected Democratic working-class voters, and wanted to pull in those who hadn't voted in previous elections and lived in that grey zone on the margins of society. And, along with a rewrite of the rule book, he wanted also to redraw the political map. He promised that he would win in places that had hitherto been regarded as totally unwinnable. In the primary campaign he saw his strategy working. Not only did he win the nomination, his 13.4 million votes in the primaries exceeded by a million the most any Republican candidate had won in history. He was going to take no lectures now from the elders of the party on how the campaign should be fought. And though everyone said it was impossible and that he was living in a fantasy land, he succeeded in rewriting the rule book and winning in unimaginable places.

In a flash he became the trusted tribune for those who felt themselves marginalised and ignored by conventional politics. In February 2016, at the very start of the long, exhausting, complicated primary process, I interviewed his son, Donald Jr, at a massive out-of-town evangelical church in Midwest Iowa, and he offered an insight that really stood out. He said, 'My dad is just like any other blue-collar worker in America – he's just got a better bank balance.' Yes indeed.

But he's right. Donald Trump, for all his gilded upbringing, spoke the language of ordinary Americans, a language that the rest of the Republican field, for all its focus groups and polling and data analysis, struggled to articulate. Trump could instinctively reach for and find the pulse of 2016 middle America in a way that no other politician or pollster came close to replicating.

In the course of the campaign I saw Trump hold rallies in Iowa, New Hampshire, South Carolina, Georgia, Texas and California – and many other states in between. Everywhere it was the same. He would identify the ills of modern America thus: 'We no longer win any more, our politicians have let us down, they've made lousy trade deals that have cost our jobs. They've let in millions of illegal immigrants who have to be kicked out. America is no longer respected around the world. Our enemies are laughing at us.' And then the prescription: 'We're going to start winning again when I am president. Trust me, I will make wonderful deals, and we're going to win so much you will get bored of winning.' Those words would be played back to the president when his attempt to repeal and replace Obama's health reforms ended in a catastrophic and humiliating defeat in Congress. The self-proclaimed winner had lost and, to use a Trump word, 'bigly'. All this despite a historically high Republican majority in the House of Representatives. In his first comments afterwards he blamed the Democrats for his defeat. As a Tottenham Hotspur supporter, that is akin to me blaming our defeat against Arsenal on them scoring more goals. It's sort of what they are meant to do.

But the language he spoke during the campaign was the language of the street, or the building sites around New York City, where he'd spent so much of his formative years. 'Presidential' was not a word that attached itself to Donald Trump very easily during the campaign. Nor was 'lawyerly'. He sprayed words out without any care, often resulting in his deputies having to clear up the linguistic mess, having to clarify that when the president said A, what he really meant was B. But in campaigning mode this didn't matter, and the language would get rougher still.

The anger that was so evident among many of his supporters would come to be expressed in often incendiary ways. There were charges that he was inciting violence, repeatedly talking about wanting to punch protestors and see them taken out on stretchers. One demonstrator, as he was being led away by police, was punched by a Trump supporter. Trump would offer to pay the supporter's legal fees if he was charged. If Hispanic protestors made their voices heard, the crowd would chant, 'Build the wall, build the wall.' At which point Mr Trump would pitch in with 'And who's going to pay?' And the crowd would yell back in unison, 'Mex-i-co.' There was a Christmas panto element to all of this.

After the election, things didn't get much better. Far from America coming together, the violent imagery of the campaign seemed to be taken up by some Trump supporters to create civil unrest. Immigrants were told to go home. Jewish cemeteries were desecrated, community centres sent bomb threats. Graffiti with 'whites only' appeared on build-ings. The far right, whom Donald Trump had done little to discourage during the campaign, saw this as their moment to strike.

Throughout the campaign he repeatedly demeaned his opponents – his main rival, Ted Cruz, became 'lyin' Ted'. Senator Marco Rubio was 'little Marco'. And Jeb Bush was 'low-energy Jeb'. Everything about Trump is pugilistic. He sneers, he mocks, he demeans. And if ever given the choice between calming a crowd or winding them up, he always chose the latter course. And the crowds yelled for more. He once joked that he would be able to walk down Fifth Avenue and kill someone and it wouldn't affect his support. Those who queued for hours to see him wouldn't hear a word said against him. And they stayed loyal whatever the latest fracas, whatever the latest storm.

But this left many other Republicans feeling decidedly queasy. The convention is a time when the party gathers to unite, but not Cleveland 2016. Jeb Bush and Marco Rubio chose to stay away; Ted Cruz came but was booed off stage when he refused to endorse Trump. The two previous living Republican presidents chose to give it a miss; the two Repub-lican candidates who'd last run for president found they had other pressing matters in their diaries.

But this was all playground joshing compared to the barrage of vitriol he had stored up for his Democratic Party opponent, Hillary Clinton. She soon was given the moniker 'crooked Hillary'. She was a liar and a disgrace, and on several occasions he called her 'the devil'. She was the worst secretary of state there had ever been. And the new piece of crowd participation was for his supporters to chant 'Lock her up, lock her up' at the mere mention of her name. It was raw.

He trumped all of that when he was in Wilmington, North Carolina, and was wandering from his script and riffing on the threat posed by Hillary Clinton. Of course one of the most consequential things that a president will ever do in office is make recommendations for who should sit on the Supreme Court, the nine-person body, charged with interpreting the laws of the land and how they sit with America's written constitution. Justices are appointed for life. And one of the greatest fears of Republicans was that Hillary Clinton would appoint justices who would seek to rewrite the Second Amendment, the almost sacred law that allows all US citizens the right to bear arms. This is what he said: 'Hillary wants to abolish, essentially abolish the Second Amendment, by the way, and if she gets to pick her judges, nothing you can do, folks. But the Second Amendment, people, maybe there is, I don't know.' It sounded like a call for supporters of the gun lobby to take the law into their own hands, and – potentially – assassinate the Democratic candidate. It horrified Democrats; more importantly it set alarm bells ringing among a good many Republicans too.

If the cable TV channels were concerned they hid it well. The reality was they were loving it. Couldn't get enough of

Donald Trump. He was box office. Imagine you are in the television control room of one of these networks and on a bank of screens in front of you is a series of different empty podiums about to be filled by one or other of the candidates. And any second you are going to have a choice. Do I cue one of the conventional politicians, who will go through their over-rehearsed speech, which they recite by heart in a dull monotone? Or do I go to Donald Trump, where there is a real sense of jeopardy – who will he attack, who will he turn his fire on, how will he react to a protestor? For the directors and producers there was no dilemma. Trump won every time. And the audiences lapped it up.

After the first Republican TV debate, which was hosted by Fox, it was the turn of CNN. The venue was the Ronald Reagan Presidential Library in California in the autumn of 2015. To call it a library is a misnomer. If you're thinking the Bodleian in Oxford, you're not even close. The Reagan Library is in Simi Valley about 40 miles northwest of downtown Los Angeles. And it is a vast sprawling estate, with beautifully manicured lawns and contains Reagan memorabilia from the quite small – his letters – to the really quite, well, substantial: the actual Air Force One plane he used when he was president. The debate had been scheduled for three hours. Three hours. Now that is a long time and a lot of politics and politicians. Can you *ever* imagine three solid hours of prime-time being given over to a political debate in the UK? And this was not even the eve of voting – this was the start of the Republican primary, well over a year *before* the presidential election. It's not my habit to feel sorry for politicians, but I did that night. This was an entirely commercial decision. It was entirely down to Donald Trump being in the race, and it pulled in 15.5 million viewers. The advertising revenues were enormous as CNN banked millions from it.

The distinction between reality TV and politics had never seemed so small. Donald Trump was an instinctive genius at knowing how to work the crowd; how to work the audience. He would start to talk about reforming Washington politics and the crowd would begin chanting, 'Drain the swamp, drain the swamp.' When he was appointing his running mate, Mike Pence, it was a process that played out over days. It could have been a prolonged episode of *The Apprentice*, which Trump had hosted for so many years, as we waited on tenterhooks to see who would be hired. After the election, when Trump was deciding who should be his secretary of state, he tweeted about 'meeting the finalists'. And each of the hopefuls would be marched before the cameras in a humiliating beauty-contest-type parade. Mercifully they weren't wearing swimsuits or sashes, and telling us how much they liked horseback riding and helping small children.

The networks, with their wall-to-wall coverage of the Trump campaign to the exclusion of all others, propelled him to the Republican nomination, and arguably to the presidency. And it meant he spent a fraction of what his rivals spent on TV advertising. He didn't need to match their spending. In the BBC (or ITV or Sky for that matter), memos would have gone out at the outset reminding us of our duty of impartiality, but there were no such inhibitions in the United States. All the channels were airing the Trump Show. And the audience watched with bated breath to see what drama would unfold next.

And did he, at the end of this, send boxes of chocolates and bunches of roses to the TV executives, and shower them with appreciative love? No. It was the complete opposite. As the election got tighter, he blamed the media for every problem he had. We were liars, dishonest and untrustworthy. At his rallies, he would single us out for opprobrium. He would ask his audience to turn to us – and he would accuse the media of being part of a conspiracy against him. And in angry America, the audience needed no further encouragement. We would be booed and abused – and worse. By the end of the campaign, police were being posted to patrol the press areas to stop us being attacked by his supporters. Some news organisations were banned altogether from attending his rallies if they were deemed to have been disobliging to Mr Trump, a practice he took with him into the White House where, after a particularly turbulent period, his press secretary sought to prevent some news organisations from attending what is called a 'gaggle' (i.e. for a smaller group than for a full briefing). The *New York Times*, CNN and even the BBC were barred. But it was a move that brought very strong protests, and that way of operating was quickly abandoned. In the eyes of the candidate and his supporters we were as much a part of the swamp as any of the other establishment pillars – and needed to be drained.

But it wasn't only the cable channels who were actors in this contest. The cast-list for the US presidential election in its final weeks grew increasingly bizarre. There were walk-on roles for the Russians, the so-called 'alt-right' and the FBI – and all seemingly designed to get Donald Trump across the line. The successful hack by the Russians of Democratic Party computers and the private emails of Hillary Clinton's chief of staff, John Podesta, provided an endless drip, drip of damaging stories about the Democratic candidate.

There was the long-running embarrassment of Hillary Clinton's own email arrangements – the private server she used when she was secretary of state was a terrible error of judgement that cost her dearly, though after an exhaustive investigation the FBI announced that no further action would be taken. However, 11 days out from polling day, the director of the agency James Comey wrote to Congressional leaders to announce that he was re-opening the investigation. It was a devastating blow. The FBI is not meant to give a running commentary on its investigations, but bizarrely in this case it did. And then a week later, almost on the eve of polling, announced that it had found nothing new, and the investigation was again closed. But it ensured another news cycle would be dominated by the issue of Hillary Clinton's emails. Whole books I am sure will be devoted to exploring the role of the FBI, and whether its intervention tilted the election in Donald Trump's favour.

One of the truly astonishing moments in the first few months of President Trump's administration came with the appearance of the FBI director before the House Intelligence Committee. It was dumfounding for two reasons in particular. For a start, Mr Comey confirmed for the first time that there was a formal investigation going on into the Trump campaign's links with the Russian government, and that it had been going on for months before the election. The rumours about Russian links to the Trump campaign had never gone away; ditto the extent to which Moscow affected the outcome of the election. Clearly the FBI felt there was enough smoke of a suspicious nature that it needed to investigate the source of the fire. But the second even more astonishing thing about this was that no Democrat ventured to ask the blindingly obvious, staring-you-in-the-face question: why, Mr Comey, did you think it was necessary, indeed vital, two weeks before voting to make Congress aware that the FBI had reopened its investigation into Hillary Clinton's emails, but not mention that you had launched an investigation into Donald Trump and his campaign's links to Vladimir Putin's government? As I say, whole books, theses and conspiracy theories will be devoted to this.

Comey would later say that it left him feeling 'mildly nauseous' to think that he might have affected the outcome of the election (only mildly?). Comey would explain that he simply had bad and terrible choices. His rationale for revealing the renewed investigation into Hillary Clinton 11 days before polling, but nothing about Trump and the Russia inquiry, has an internal logic. Having told Congress that the initial Clinton email investigation had been concluded, he said he felt honour bound to update lawmakers on the change. Because nothing had been said before about Trump to Congress, there was no need to mention it at all.

But if you think this intervention might have earned Comey kudos with the new president, you would be very much mistaken. President Trump wanted the criminal investigation into his relationship with the Russians halted, and he was seething about it. Out of the blue, one Tuesday evening in May 2017, came bombshell news. The president had fired his FBI director. In scenes that were part Tom Clancy and part Keystone Cops, the administration went into meltdown. With journalists desperate to find out what on earth was going on, the president's spokesman, Sean Spicer, hid in the bushes in the White House grounds to avoid the press. No really. Eventually we were told the FBI director had been dismissed because there was a need for new management, that he had lost the confidence of his staff, and he had mishandled the Hillary Clinton email investigation (in other words, he should have brought charges against her).

Except the president would quickly contradict that carefully constructed version of events. In an interview with NBC he would say 'it was the Russian thing' that led to his dismissal. Not only that, the next day – and with a plot line too absurd for any screenwriter to consider – the president would meet the Russian foreign minister, Sergey Lavrov, in the Oval Office. In that meeting the president, according to the *New York Times*, is said to have told his Russian guest, 'I just fired the head of the FBI. He was crazy, a real nut job ... I faced great pressure because of Russia. That's taken off.'

Asonishingly (and we'll come to 'why' in a second), the White House did not contradict this version of events. Instead, it added to it saying, 'The president has always emphasised the importance of making deals with Russia ... by grandstanding and politicising the investigation into Russia's actions, James Comey created unnecessary pressure on our ability to engage and negotiate with Russia.'

What makes this astonishing is that the White House statement seemed to make clear that the country's top law-enforcement official had to be fired because of his criminal investigation into the Trump campaign's links to Russia. But, as Democrats and some Republicans were quick to point out – any way you cut it – that is obstruction of justice. And obstruction of justice is one of the 'high crimes and misdemeanours' as laid down in the US Constitution that can lead to a president's impeachment. The waters around the president were becoming more treacherous by the hour.

When newspaper reports emerged suggesting that Comey might have kept records that would challenge Donald Trump's version(s) of events, the president tweeted: 'James Comey better hope there are no "tapes" of our conversations before he starts leaking to the press.' The echoes of President Richard Nixon and Watergate were unmistakable. The White House would not confirm whether or not it was taping conversations.

When asked about this at a later hearing, James Comey brought laughter to a highly charged committee when he said, 'Lordy, I hope there are tapes.' But six weeks after setting a million hares running, the president would finally admit via Twitter – how else? – that 'I did not make, and do not have, any such recording.'

In light of all this, the Deputy Attorney General Rod Rosenstein stepped in (and it was Rosenstein's email about Comey and his management at the FBI a few days earlier that was used as the pretext for firing him). Without giving advance warning to the White House, he announced the appointment of a special counsel (it used to be called the special prosecutor) to take over this investigation. Robert Mueller, a fiercely independent former FBI director, would take on the role. It is something Democrats had long been calling for, and something the White House had said was totally unnecessary. Far from Comey's sacking relieving the pressure on the president, the stakes had suddenly become way higher. The special counsel has extensive powers and resources to conduct an investigation, and to follow it wherever it may lead. And sure enough, reports quickly emerged that Mueller's investigation had moved from the simple question of whether there was collusion between the Trump campaign and Russia to investigating the President himself, and whether he had sought to obstruct justice by allegedly asking Comey to 'drop' a criminal investigation into the former National Security Advisor, Michael Flynn. (Flynn had lied to the vice president, Mike Pence, over his contacts with the Russian ambassador.) Also coming under the scope of the investigation was whether the reasons for firing Comey amounted to an attempt to obstruct justice. The headline 'President Under Criminal Investigation' would come just a little over 100 days into this presidency. In the Bill Clinton era, the special prosecutor, Kenneth Starr, was initially appointed to look at a property deal called Whitewater, but then his investigation morphed into what the president had said during the Lewinsky scandal, and whether he had perjured himself. That investigation would lead to Bill Clinton's impeachment in the House, though it failed to get through the Senate. President Trump put out a conciliatory statement on the night the appointment of Mueller was announced, but, clearly, after a bad night's sleep his mood had darkened considerably, and he tweeted furiously that he was the subject of a witch-hunt.

At a speech to the Coast Guard Academy that day, he would tell the graduating officers that 'No politician in history, and I can say this with great surety, has been treated worse or more unfairly.' Someone sent me a picture of Nelson Mandela in his prison cell, with the caption 'hmmm'.

But Donald Trump's diehard supporters wouldn't hear a word said against him, just as they had refused to countenance criticism during the campaign – and they have a powerful voice.

And the alt-right, or far right, or racist right, or nationalist right, or anti-establishment right (you choose the title you want to give it) – previously on the margins of US politics – was becoming a much more influential voice. The chief executive of Breitbart News, Steve Bannon, ran the most successful of these alt-right websites – it was simultaneously fervent and fanatical in its support of Donald Trump. After the election Mr Bannon was rewarded with the post as Donald Trump's chief strategist in the White House, marking a dramatic move from scourge of the establishment to a place in its most decorous inner sanctum. Throughout the election Breitbart produced an endless diet of stories (with varying degrees of veracity) that were designed to lift Donald Trump's insurgent campaign and to denigrate Hillary Clinton. And if they were racist, sexist, homophobic and anti-Semitic along the way, well then so be it. One Conservative critic of Donald Trump, who just happened to be a Jew, was headlined as a 'Jewish Renegade'. There were stories about how birth control makes women ugly. There was the headline exhorting people to fly the Confederate flag as a symbol of America's 'glorious heritage'. Another stated, 'The West Versus Islam is the New Cold War. Here's how we win,' while 'Political Correctness Protects Muslim Rape Culture' likewise showed hostility towards Muslims

My lightbulb moment of just how divided America had become came a couple of weeks before polling day. On a rare visit to Washington I had met a woman who worked in a beautician's there, and the subject came round to the impending election. She told me she couldn't decide how to vote because she liked Donald Trump and Hillary Clinton. Sorry. Say that again. You like Hillary *and* Donald? That's just not possible. You can like one and hate the other. You can dislike them both but one marginally less than the other. You can hate them both equally and decide you're not going to vote. But no one in America liked *both* of them.

It was an opinion I just hadn't heard expressed anywhere at any time during the 15 months of the campaign. It was astonishing, and just brought home to me how deep the fissures were.

One of the things most difficult to convey as the BBC's correspondent covering the election was the extent to which Hillary Clinton was loathed and detested by so many Americans. In a conventional political cycle she was the best qualified candidate by a good distance (among all the Republican and Democratic hopefuls), she has devoted her life to public service, she was a loyal servant to President Obama as secretary of state, she was a patriotic American who wanted to do the best for her country. Yes, she was a lousy campaigner and speech maker; yes, she had made a terrible error over her use of a private email server. Could she have been more open and transparent in her dealings with the press? Of course she could. The death of the US ambassador in Benghazi was awful, but was Hillary Clinton really culpable; had she truly been negligent? Could she have really prevented the attack by extremists on the embassy compound?

It was easy to understand why Hillary Clinton was not everyone's cup of tea. She was in many ways a terrible candidate, with a manifesto that was so achingly liberal that no wonder it alienated many 'old-fashioned' Democrats. But the number of people I saw at Trump rallies who completely detested her with such a visceral hatred was slightly beyond comprehension. And it should be said there were many liberal, highly educated people I knew who had a similarly hostile view of her. Many blamed her for her husband's infidelities, and accused her of being an 'enabler' of his indiscretions, whatever that meant. People wanted her locked up for her handling of secure information from when she was secretary of state.

And there was a good dollop of misogyny in it too. She didn't have the stamina. Was bossy, manipulative, too conniving and ambitious – because of course none of the men who had run for president over the previous 240 years were ...

What was certainly true was that Hillary Clinton was the wrong candidate at the wrong time given the anger felt towards politics and politicians by so many Americans. Although of course the central paradox is that, for all her unpopularity, she polled three million more votes than Donald Trump – but by the rules of America's electoral college, they were in the wrong places. Winning big in California and New York does you no good when the middle of America has taken against you.

Modern-day America, for all its complexities, geographical variation, its patchwork of cultures and backgrounds and ethnicities, feels – at least where politics is concerned – like two tribes who don't understand or talk to each other. They live in different worlds. The Trump base will support the gun lobby, they will be blue collar, they will make a lot of noise about supporting military veterans. They will watch Fox News, whose best-known anchors are openly hostile to the Democratic Party, and they will listen to talk-radio hosts who express their right-wing prejudices with gusto and aggression. And these are the people who have been the big losers from globalisation.

What's crucial to understand is that in America what you listen to and watch will confirm your prejudices, not challenge them. It is life in the echo chamber. And it is the same on the other side. Liberal America will get its news from CNN and MSNBC – television channels that Republicans think are just as left-wing as Democrats think Fox is to the right. And they will read the *New York Times* and the *Washington Post*. You look at the Hillary Clinton crowd and it will be more diverse with many more Latinos and African Americans than you'd find at a Trump rally. They will be better educated, more concerned with America's position in the world, equal pay, LGBT rights, maternity pay, racism in the police and environmental issues.

The yawning chasm between the two parties – and in particular their supporters – has never been more evident. And nowhere is the bile and lack of comprehension of one another more evident than on the internet and social media. The lack of tolerance is astonishing and some would say worrying. Many have expressed the worry that the hatred on show is heralding a descent into nihilism for US democracy. Politics has always been a contact sport, but in this unpredictable election year it was more *Mad Max* than *The West Wing*.

And there was something very recognisable about the anger so widespread in America that would find an echo in Britain – and who was on hand to take advantage of it? Why, of course, Donald J. Trump. Now, one of the things you quickly realise as you follow him around is that there is no difference between Donald Trump the individual, Donald Trump the businessman and Donald Trump the politician. It is one brand. Who else in the midst of a US election campaign would take time out to inspect the refurbishment of two of his golf courses in Scotland? No one. All your efforts would be – normally – spent on convincing the American electorate that your only focus is on governing, and that your business activities are inconsequential next to that, and were being run by someone else. But when what you are selling is a brand – and go into the pro shop at either Turnberry or Trump International Golf Links in Aberdeen, and every single item in the shop is branded with the Trump name – the front man has to be there.

For a would-be president to travel to Europe ahead of the November election is commonplace. Mitt Romney memorably came to London in 2012 and openly questioned whether London was ready to host the Olympics – to the immense consternation of his Downing Street hosts; four years earlier Barack Obama went to the Brandenburg Gate in Berlin and drew audiences in their hundreds of thousands, as Europeans sought to embrace a new and coming era.

Add to that Trump at Turnberry and Aberdeen in 2016. But this wasn't to meet Britain's political leaders; it was to inspect his two golfing properties. And the timing was exquisite or exquisitely awful depending on your viewpoint. It was Friday, 24 June, Day 1 of Brexit.

As the BBC's North America Editor I was sent to cover his trip. On the lunchtime of polling day I was in New York at a conference interviewing José Manuel Barroso, the former European Commission president, about the vote. As I went on stage the betting markets had it as an 82 per cent probability that Britain would remain within the European Union, odds that would go up to 90 per cent as I made my way to the airport to catch the overnight United Airlines flight to Glasgow.

When we left the gate and were ordered to put our phones into 'flight safe' mode, Britain was firmly in the EU, David Cameron was prime minister with four years left of his term of office, and the pound was rock solid against the dollar. By the time we landed and I turned my phone back on, none of those things was true. Who'd seen any of that coming? Well, one person had.

Donald Trump stood on the ninth tee at Turnberry, with the famous lighthouse in the background. The sea was flat calm, the sun was shining and he looked pleased with the world. No anger today. From tee to green the ninth is 143 yards – on a still, calm day like that, probably an easy nine iron or maybe a pitching wedge. From tee to the United States is a slightly more challenging 3,000 miles – and with a very big lateral water hazard in the way called the Atlantic Ocean. No free drops or mulligans from there ...

But never mind that, the distance in Donald Trump's mind had never seemed closer, because the political upheaval that he was promising in the US had arrived overnight in the UK. As any golfer knows, it's never about muscle – the key is rhythm and timing. And what exquisite timing it was that Mr Trump had pitched up in the UK to cut the ribbon on his refurbished links course that day.

There were some striking parallels. Just look at the forces that were driving Brexit: they were mass immigration (and a sense it was out of control), insecure borders, interfering bureaucracy, depressed wages and sovereignty. Exactly the same concerns that Mr Trump has made his own in the US. He thought it was anything but a calamity that Britain had left, and told me in the news conference – with a good deal of sangfroid – that, yes, Britain's departure could lead to the break-up of the EU.

Beneath the white cap with 'Make America Great Again' on it, there was very little scowling from Mr Trump, and a huge amount of beaming. Was he having fun? He was having the time of his life. On about half a dozen occasions he said, 'Right, final question' – only then to go on to invite a fresh volley of enquiries. Some reporters had so many bites of the cherry they must have been chewing on the stone. It was a news conference he hoped would never end.

The thing about golf is that it is a maddening and frustrating game, but hit one perfect seven iron that comes off the centre of the club, soars into the air and lands stone dead within three feet of the pin – and you forget about all the missed putts, the sliced drives, the heavy divots and the ball that takes four thwacks to get out of the bunker. In Donald Trump's head that day every shot was finding the sweet spot.

Not so Barack Obama. He had played a round of golf with David Cameron a couple of months earlier when the president was in London. Barack Obama loves the game. But his efforts to influence the outcome of the Brexit debate had turned out to be as wayward as a badly hooked drive. He had certainly used muscle to try to influence the outcome of the referendum – and the British people didn't much care for his intervention.

And Hillary Clinton of course was also firmly in the 'Remain' camp. She had been unequivocal about the importance of Britain staying in. But once again the person who had read the mood of the people was Donald Trump – a point, you won't be surprised to hear, the presumptive Republican nominee (as he was still then) was happy to remind us of, more than once. Politics in the UK rarely impinges on the US, which is much more inwardly focused. For the first time in decades something that had happened on the British side of the Atlantic was making waves all along the eastern seaboard of the USA and across this vast country.

Politics doesn't always need to be a zero-sum game, but invariably is. And on 24 June Donald Trump was up and the political establishment was down.

Donald Trump looked around him: at his gleaming hotel, at his golf course without a blade of grass out place and his equally expensively manicured children standing deferentially in the background, and said to the news conference: if I can fix Turnberry, think what I can do for America. A reporter had the temerity to ask whether they weren't slightly different things. 'You'd be amazed how similar it is. It's called a place that has to be fixed,' replied Trump, as we sat and listened, perched on the edge of a cliff.

CHAPTER 2

Race

There was a phrase-cum-question that gained currency after Barack Obama's historic victory in 2008. 'What's your excuse?' It came from within the African American community as a sort of chiding reproach to young people who were blaming racism and prejudice, and every wrong done to them going back to slavery, through to the Jim Crow laws that enforced segregation in the Southern states, through to the failure of the civil rights struggle, for their lack of a job, for their poor prospects, for their dropping out of college, for their criminal record. The thinking being that if an African American child could rise from humble origins, brought up by a single mum in Hawaii, to Harvard and then Chicago and on to the highest office in the land – with all the same obstacles to navigate as everyone else – then what's stopping you?

'Yes, we can' might have been a slogan to millions of Americans invoking possibility and a brighter future. To America's black community it seemed like an injunction. Get on with it. Don't blame anyone but yourself. If he can, you can. Following the arc of history started by Rosa Parks refusing to give up her seat on a segregated bus, and then Martin Luther King's march, that mood was captured in the brilliant slogan 'Rosa sat, so that Martin could walk, so that Barack could run, so that you could fly.'

And in Obama's first term in the White House little attention was paid to issues of race. As America's first ever 'African American president', one part of his legacy was already secure. Whatever else he did or didn't do, whatever magnificent policy successes or crushing reverses he faced, whatever scandals rocked his administration, the top line in the history books would be the same: Barack Obama came to power as America's first black president.

So, understandably, President Obama was keen to define himself by everything other than that as he set out to honour the central policy objectives of his 2008 campaign. Domestically it was about putting the economy on an even keel after the banking crisis, but also driving through Obamacare. Internationally it was about bringing the troops home from Afghanistan and Iraq. And, to borrow another of the memorable lines from that rhetoric-rich campaign, there would be no more blue states, there would be no more red states – there would only be the United States. Barack Obama wanted to be a president for all the people, not perceived as the wholly owned subsidiary of the black lobby.

There was no doubting the spectacular symbolism of a black man arriving to take up occupancy of the White House. This fabulous neo-classical mansion on 1600 Pennsylvania Avenue, which had been built in part by slaves, was now home to an African American president. But it was fatuous to think that his arrival would, with the wave of a magic wand, consign 200 years of contested history and pain to the rubbish bin. Many in the black population would go on experiencing the covert and overt racism, the slights, the brushes with authority that were a feature of their lives BO (before Obama) and continued AO (after Obama).

But then came the explosion in the president's second term – and given what unfolded, explosion is not a hyperbolic word – in Ferguson, Missouri. Ferguson, where? When you think of the great centres of black population, you think of New York, Chicago, Detroit, Los Angeles, New Orleans. But who'd ever heard of Ferguson, a slightly nondescript town just outside St Louis? It is a touch down at heel, but not ever so poor. It is an anonymous, anywheresville of a town – the usual strip malls filled with nail parlours, nickel and dime stores, barber shops and diners. And that's what made the events in Ferguson so remarkable and, simultaneously, unremarkable. If it could happen there, then surely it could happen anywhere.

It is worth dwelling a little bit on what happened that day and what unfolded in the days and months that followed in Ferguson, because it is so instructive about what it says about race, the criminal justice system and policing in America today. In the UK, if you speak to any chief constable, they will tell you that the key to good policing is 'consent'. You are of the community, for the community. In Ferguson it felt anything but that.

It is 9 August 2014, and a white police officer, Darren Wilson, is called to a robbery and assault at Ferguson Market and Liquor, a convenience store on 9101 West Florissant Avenue, next to the highway. The store-owner is jostled and pushed. The two young men walk out with a box of cigarillos. The shopkeeper dials 911 and gives a description of one of the suspects. It fits 18-year-old Michael Brown – later confirmed by CCTV footage. He was a black kid who hadn't been in trouble before and had just graduated from high school and was due to go to college. He was also a very large young man, both tall and wide. And he was armed with nothing more dangerous than perhaps a big mouth and quite a lot of attitude. What happened next became the subject of intense controversy.

In Officer Wilson's account, when he attempted to question Brown a struggle ensued, with Wilson inside his police cruiser and Brown outside. Brown tried to get hold of the officer's sidearm. That led to the weapon being discharged, slightly wounding Brown, who then fled the scene. Wilson gave chase and got out of his vehicle, ordering Brown to freeze. But Brown turned and charged towards Officer Wilson. In self-protection the officer fired his gun five more times, ultimately fatally wounding the unarmed 18-year-old, who died a few feet in front of him.

The rival version of events is that the 28-year-old white officer was the aggressor. That he had been disrespectful, shouting and swearing at Brown, and that in the fatal confrontation, when Brown turned to face Wilson, it was not to charge him – but to surrender. Yet despite that, Wilson discharged his weapon five more times. According to one eyewitness, 'He was running for his life and just got shot and turned around and didn't try to reach for anything. He put his hands in the air being compliant and he still got shot down like a dog.'

This is all horrific enough – but what happened next was in some ways even worse. It was a slow motion car crash that revealed a mindset and set of assumptions about policing and the criminal justice system that were – quite simply – hard to believe. This was now much bigger than a contested account of a white officer who shot and killed an unarmed black teenager. This was about a largely white police force that had become so militarised that it looked like something out of *RoboCop*. About a legal apparatus that was anything but colour blind in its administration of justice.

After his death, the body lay on the ground for seemingly ages; information from the police over what happened was scant. A makeshift memorial where he died was established, and people came to lay flowers. A police dog handler allowed his canine to urinate on it.

And then there was the organised police response. In the nights after the killing, as unrest grew – not only about the shooting but the insensitive official reaction to it – the police came out onto the streets with all this heavy-duty kit that America had never seen on its streets before. The end of the combat mission in Iraq meant that the army came back with tons of equipment that was surplus to requirements. There was also a tight squeeze on Department of Defense budgets. So what they did was sell a lot of the military equipment that had been used to keep order in Iraq to local police forces in the US.

That in turn led to the equipment – and tactics – that had been used to keep order against the organised militias of Fallujah and Sadr City being deployed on the increasingly angry and alienated protestors on the streets of Ferguson. It was quite a spectacle. Tanks, grenade launchers and Humvees were on the streets. There was smoke, stun grenades, flashes and bangs in this Midwestern town night after night. It was made for cable television. It was a godsend for the networks. Not that far to travel, fantastic pictures, easy to broadcast with good internet connections. What was not to like?

Well, everything as it turned out. In the midst of a sweaty Washington summer when the politicians were on their sun loungers and dozing on verandahs, a hue and cry was gathering force. It would lead eventually to a bar on the federal government selling such equipment to the police, and a ban on the law enforcement agencies using it. The president said: 'We've seen how militarised gear can sometimes give people the feeling like there's an occupying force – as opposed to a force that's part of the community that's protecting them and serving them,' adding that such gear 'can alienate and intimidate residents and make them feel scared.'

Indeed. But the episode had only served to strain relations between police and local community still further.

All this unfolded in the days after the shooting, and was really about how the police interacted with the community it purported to serve.

What happened next was the keenly awaited decision of the grand jury on whether Officer Wilson would face any charges in connection with the killing of Michael Brown. In late November it came. No action would be taken against the police officer. He had acted lawfully in self-defence.

That sparked another night of rioting, where I wandered the streets of Ferguson with gas mask and BBC-issued riot gear. We needed all of it – legitimate protestors were joined by some hell-bent on causing trouble. Gang members who saw this as an opportunity to fight with police pitched in; political extremists who wanted to hitch their wagon to a cause were there too. And there were a good many local, disaffected, alienated young people with legitimate grievances to air. The thickest line of police was outside the city of Ferguson Police Department and Municipal Court. As we filmed there, one thing became immediately apparent. Every face, and I mean literally every face, behind the blue helmets and visors was white. And virtually every face lined up against the police – some wearing balaclavas and bandanas – was black.

Mayhem soon erupted. Shops were looted, police cars set on fire, running battles took place and, just two days before Thanksgiving when Americans gather to celebrate all that they have, tear gas hung heavy in the air, sirens wailed and police loud hailers mounted on armoured personnel carriers ordered the crowds to disperse – appeals that fell on deaf ears. There was not much thankfulness that night in Ferguson.

The subsequent Department of Justice inquiry found that Ferguson's police department and court system 'reflect and exacerbate existing racial bias'. The 105-page study added that 'discriminatory intent' among city officials – several of whom were found to have sent racist emails – was partly responsible.

In Washington, the then US Attorney General Eric Holder blamed Ferguson police for creating a 'toxic environment, defined by mistrust and resentment' that had been ignited 'like a powder keg' by the white officer shooting dead an unarmed black 18-year-old. 'It is time for Ferguson's leaders to take immediate, wholesale and structural corrective action,' said Holder. 'Let me be clear: the United States Department of Justice reserves all its rights and abilities to force compliance and implement basic change. Nothing is off the table.'

The investigators concluded: 'Over time, Ferguson's police and municipal court practices have sown deep mistrust between parts of the community and the police department, undermining law enforcement legitimacy among African Americans in particular.' They also unearthed evidence of wider corruption among white court officials.

The point is, and the question was raised: how different was what was happening in Ferguson to what was going on in any number of small police forces across the great land mass of the United States? An answer of sorts came in a whole pile of other cases that came to the fore in this period.

There was the case of Trayvon Martin in Sanford, Florida – killed by a white security guard, George Zimmerman. There was Eric Garner in New York, put in a deadly choke hold as he was pinned to the ground by a number of New York cops – his offence was that he had been selling contraband cigarettes on the street. In the video recorded of his death, you hear him gasping, 'I can't breathe.' It became a protestor's chant that would become a slogan to be emblazoned on T-shirts – and it didn't matter whether you were a kid on the street or a mega-rich NBA basketball player – 'I Can't Breathe' became the angry cry of the black community feeling that it was suffering collective suffocation from the indifference of the authorities. But the killings went on.

Tamir Rice in Cleveland was an 11-year-old who had been playing in a park with a toy gun. Someone called the police to say there was a young person with a firearm. That was enough for the patrolmen who were first on the scene. They pulled up beside the youngster and literally within seconds they had shot him dead – it was shoot first, ask questions later. The City of Cleveland paid the Rice family $6 million in a civil suit but admitted no wrongdoing. A grand jury declined to indict the two officers. Another case that sparked protests, burning and looting was that of Freddie Gray in Baltimore. He was arrested and put in a police van. He was handled so violently that his spinal cord had been literally severed by the time he arrived at the police station. In this notorious case, six police officers were initially charged – but no one was found guilty. The list went on and on. And what was remarkable was how many of these deaths were captured on smartphones.

One woman, Diamond Reynolds, even live-streamed the killing of her boyfriend as she sat beside him in a car in Minnesota. Philando Castile was shot five times through the car window as he sat in the passenger seat with his safety belt on. And you could watch on Facebook as the life drained away from him. The woman's four-year-old daughter was sitting in the back of the car. The cops had wanted to see his ID – as he reached to get it from his wallet, an officer opened fire. This was the second killing of a black man in 24 hours in Minnesota.

Then there was the man in Charleston, South Carolina, called Walter Scott. He was stopped because the rear brake light on his car wasn't working. Seeing the police bearing down on him he started to run. Not the smartest thing to do, but he had been stopped for a faulty brake light, not an armed robbery. The white police officer who had pulled him over shot him multiple times in the back before he fell and died. It was all caught with crystal clarity on the smartphone of a passer-by. If ever there seemed to be an open and shut case of disproportionate force being used, this was it. But the policeman, Michael Slager, argued in court that he was acting in self-defence because he thought his life was in danger from the fleeing, unarmed man. At the trial, the panel of jurors – one black and eleven white – was unable to reach a verdict.

Then, not to be confused with the killing of Walter Scott in Charleston, South Carolina, there was the shooting in the back of Keith Scott in Charlotte, North Carolina. A different episode, but having uncanny parallels with all the others. His death in September 2016 sparked days of protests with an angry community demanding to see the police 'dashcam' video of the event. The crowds chanted 'Release the tape' and 'We want the tape'. There was violence and looting. The mayor sought to impose a midnight-to-dawn curfew in the city. The district attorney in this case, after a two-month long investigation, decided there was no justification to bring charges against the officer involved in the shooting.

The protests were still going on when, with impeccable timing, 400 miles north in the nation's capital, the black community was coming together to celebrate the opening of the spectacular National Museum of African American History and Culture. The president was there, along with his predecessor, George W. Bush; leading figures of the civil rights movement rubbed shoulders with luminaries from the worlds of sport, music and entertainment. And this museum, like the story of the black person's advance in America, was a long time in the making. The museum had first been conceived of a hundred years ago, but it wasn't until 2003 that its construction was given approval by Congress. Now, 13 years and $540 million later, its doors were finally opened, with the tolling of a bell from a black Virginian church that had been built by slaves.

In his address to mark its opening, the president didn't shy away from the history of protest and unrest and dissatisfaction across the country, saying:

> African American history is not somehow separate from our larger American story, it's not the underside of the American story. It is central to the American story, that our glory derives not just from our most obvious triumphs, but how we've wrested triumph from tragedy ... This is the place to understand how protests and love of country don't merely coexist, but inform each other. How men can probably win the gold for their country, but still insist on raising a black-gloved fist. How we can wear an 'I Can't Breathe' T-shirt, and still grieve for fallen police officers. Here, the America where the razor-sharp uniform of the chairman of the Joint Chiefs of Staff belongs alongside the cape of the Godfather of Soul.

It is the nineteenth Smithsonian museum, and has pride of place on the Mall in Washington, just a short distance from the Washington Monument. And it is unlike anything else you will see in Washington both in terms of its physical appearance and the atmosphere inside. The Smithsonian museums are the crown jewels of Washington – covering everything from air and space, through to natural history, to art and sculpture, to the history of the Native American. But travel along the Mall and what is striking is the architectural uniformity – all the buildings are white and marble, and to be honest, when you go inside them, that is overwhelmingly the skin colour you will see too.

Not the African American museum. Designed by the Tanzanian-born British architect David Adjaye, the eight-storey building is brown. Well, not exactly brown, but it has the most delicate bronze lattice work cladding the exterior – apparently an homage by the architect to the intricate ironwork crafted by enslaved African Americans in Louisiana and elsewhere. Other African influences are found throughout the museum's design. The building stands out proudly, unashamedly different from anything else you will see in the city.

And the experience inside is just as unique. For a start, if you are white, you will be very much in the minority. On the day I went I would guess that 80 per cent of those queuing to get in were African American – of all generations, from all backgrounds, from all over the United States. Three of the eight storeys are underground, and the descent below ground is to enter a darkened world, as though being in the bowels of a slave ship – which is where the museum's journey begins. The terrible story of the literally millions of Africans rounded up and shipped off in the most appalling, fetid conditions to the East Coast of America to work on the lucrative plantations, helping their white owners amass vast wealth in the process.

This all happening as the United States of America was coming into life in the late 18th century. And it is hard not to be struck by the amazing contradictions of the lofty idealism of the Founding Fathers and the reality of their lives. These icons of liberty were framing a constitution whose central declaration would be that 'all men are created equal, that they are endowed by their Creator with certain unalienable Rights, that among these are Life, Liberty and the pursuit of

Happiness.' Yet so many of these thoughtful, idealistic men depended on slaves to keep their homes and farms running. Thomas Jefferson over his lifetime kept hundreds of slaves at his Monticello estate in Virginia. Or go to George Washington's home at Mount Vernon (I don't want to sound like a tour guide, but both are fantastic and illuminating days out if you are visiting Washington). There you will see the Orangerie and behind it the place where the slaves worked day and night to keep the fires burning, to keep the exotic plants from succumbing to a chill East Coast winter.

Twelve and a half million people left the ports of Africa and came to America in leg irons, to be bought and sold like cattle. The ships would arrive in places like Charleston on the East Coast, and the brokers would advertise the auction of the cargo, specifying numbers of women, men, children of various ages, and what sort of condition these negroes were in. To read the accounts of how they were inspected prior to purchase still has the power to shock and shame.

The museum charts the battles in which the slaves were conscripted to fight in the Revolutionary Wars – the British Loyalists saying, 'Fight with us and we'll give you your freedom.' It was an offer that the Patriots then had to reciprocate – although after the war on the American side it was an offer that was reneged on.

You learn about the abolitionist movement and the legislation to ban the slave trade in the United States in 1808. But you equally realise that is just the trade. Slavery itself is not abolished until after the bloody American Civil War between the Southern Confederate States, who fought to maintain slavery and wanted to secede from the Union states of the North, who fought for its abolition.

In 1864 the Senate passed the 13th Amendment to the Constitution; ratified at the end of 1865, this states that 'Neither slavery nor involuntary servitude, except as a punishment for crime whereof the party shall have been duly convicted, shall exist within the United States, or any place subject to their jurisdiction.'

Without getting overly bogged down in constitutional politics, the next two amendments to the constitution are equally important – and enlightened. The 14th Amendment grants citizenship to 'all persons born or naturalized in the United States', which includes former slaves who had just been freed after the Civil War. It also contains a provision that 'no state shall … deny to any person within its jurisdiction the equal protection of the laws'. And finally the 15th Amendment, which grants African American men the right to vote by declaring that the 'right of citizens of the United States to vote shall not be denied or abridged by the United States or by any state on account of race, color, or previous condition of servitude'.

If you were to freeze-frame history at that moment in time, it would look as though these amendments in the wake of the Civil War – or the Reconstruction Amendments as they became known – had delivered everything that the liberated slaves wanted. The battle for emancipation, citizenship, the right to vote and equality before the law looked won. The passing of these amendments brought greater political organisation and awareness within the black community. The report of the Coloured Convention in Montgomery, Alabama, stated: 'We claim exactly the same rights, privileges and immunities as are enjoyed by white men – we ask nothing more and will be content with nothing less. The law no longer knows white nor black, but simply men, and consequently we are entitled to ride in public conveyances, hold office, sit on juries and do everything we have in the past been preventing from doing solely on the ground of colour.'

But the sweeping political change heralded by these constitutional amendments did not translate into reality. Or they did, but for a very brief time. The chains and padlocks may have gone, but the treatment of the black person as an inferior being and a second-class citizen had not. After over 200 years of slavery, America was now entering the era of segregation. And this, in its various cruel manifestations, would go on for nearly another 100 years. The activists who had gathered in Montgomery did get their way for a while. They were able to ride on public conveyances like a white man – even *with* a white man – stay in the same hotels, wander in the same parks. But the legal challenges would come and everything would soon change.

In 1883, the Supreme Court ruled the statute unconstitutional. The argument that the justices put forward was that it was none of the government's business what private companies, such as streetcar vendors and entertainment facilities, did. Their judgment coincided with the interracial governments falling in the South and the federal government deciding it had other things to worry about than black civil rights. With white-controlled governments back in power, the situation of blacks, still largely congregated in the South, gradually deteriorated. Two unshackled steps forward, one back.

And the Southern states were quick to seize on this. Between 1887 and 1892, Alabama, Arkansas, Florida, Georgia, Louisiana, Mississippi, Maryland, North Carolina, Kentucky, Tennessee and Virginia all passed measures to deny equal access to African Americans in public accommodation and transport. These laws forced blacks to sit in the back of the bus, in separate carriages on trains and in the balcony at theatres. This is now known as the era of the Jim Crow laws. A slightly misleading description as he wasn't a legislator but a white minstrel who performed with his face blacked up. But the phrase stuck. What the Jim Crow laws did was transform racist customs into legal statute.

So in Georgia the law was wonderfully unambiguous: 'All persons licenced to conduct a restaurant, shall serve either white people exclusively or colored people exclusively and shall not sell to the two races within the same room or serve the two races anywhere under the same licence.' In Maryland this was the statute as it related to the railway: 'All railroad companies and corporations ... are hereby required to provide separate cars or coaches for the travel and transportation of the white and colored passengers.' In Missouri when it came to schools this was the law: 'Separate schools shall be established for the education of children of African descent; and it shall be unlawful for any colored child to attend any white school, or any white child to attend a colored school.'

Separating the races became absolute in the South. A white child would be born at a different hospital to a black one, go to a different school and college, work in a different job, retire to a different old people's home and be buried in a different cemetery. The separation was more complete than it was under slavery when white man and slave lived cheek by jowl on the plantations. Then there was no need for such laws. The slave had no rights. But in the post-slavery world there would no longer be tolerance of the flexibility in the racial interactions that had previously existed. The constitutional cloak of respectability that the lawmakers came up with was this: segregation was fine so long as the accommodation on the railroad or anywhere else for that matter was 'separate but equal'. Which of course was never enforced, and it wasn't equal. And the situation would only get worse.

In 1896, the federal government gave racial segregation its blessing. The constitutional rationale for keeping the races legally apart came in the case of Plessy vs Ferguson. In this the Supreme Court ruled that a Louisiana law providing for 'equal but separate' accommodation for 'whites' and 'coloureds' did not violate the Equal Protection Clause of the 14th Amendment. The argument was unashamedly white supremacist. The majority of the court took the view that civil rights laws could not challenge the laws of nature and racial destiny. 'If one race be inferior to the other socially the Constitution of the United States cannot put them on the same plane.' Whites were superior to blacks. Fact. This was all derived from the popular pseudo science of the time that fair-skinned people had a higher IQ and a higher degree of civilisation than darker-skinned groups. The Supreme Court was way ahead of Hitler, who would come along decades later with his Nietzschean theories of the *Übermensch* and *Untermensch*.

Voting rights were untouched by statute. They didn't need to be. The ever diligent white polling clerks would devise new ways to ensure that black people didn't vote; couldn't vote. In some polling areas there would be a literacy test – you couldn't vote unless you could read. Other areas used poll taxes to disenfranchise African Americans. And at some polling stations unless you could guess the number of jelly-beans in the jar then, really sorry, unfortunately you won't be able to vote today.

And if those tactics didn't work, there was a more muscular way of dissuading the black man from going to vote. For that there was the Ku Klux Klan. With their menacing white costumes and grotesque hats, which covered their faces, they were a terrifying force in discouraging blacks from exercising their democratic rights. All this condoned to a greater or lesser extent by the complicity of the completely white forces of law and order. Black churches were burned out and there were the lynchings where black men would be left hanging from lamp-posts and trees, their necks distended by the hangman's noose. It was a brutal reminder of white supremacy at the end of the 19th century and for much of the 20th. This was a white population terrified that if they didn't assert their power and control over the black man they would lose it.

What is astonishing is just how late into the 20th century segregation went on. The landmark case, which ruled segregation in schools to be illegal, didn't come until after the Second World War. The judgment in Brown vs Board of Education came from the Supreme Court in 1954, in a unanimous decision. The judgment stated that 'separate educational facilities are inherently unequal'. No longer would states be able to sanction racial segregation. But in their 14-page judgment the justices had nothing to say about how segregation should be ended, nor in what timeframe. Yes, this was a hard won victory for the civil rights movement, but in reality it changed little. It would be a brave black child who would run the gauntlet of hostility and turn up for classes at still almost 100 per cent white schools.

In Arkansas nine black students enrolled at Little Rock High School in 1957 in the wake of the Supreme Court ruling. State Governor Orval Faubus was having none of it, though. He banned the teenagers from attending class. It eventually took the intervention of President Eisenhower to overturn this. But such was the hostility shown towards these nine youngsters by the other white pupils and their families that they had to be escorted into school. They went in under the protection of armed soldiers from the 101st Airborne Division of the United States Army, which on the face of it sounds like using a sledgehammer to crack a nut. Here were these heroic paratroopers from the D-Day landings, now on a mission to deliver nine children to their classrooms.

In the North there was not the same *de jure* segregation, but *de facto* it wasn't so very different. Economics settled that. The fact was that the black population was the least educated, in the lowest paid jobs and most socially disadvantaged. So, no, there were no racist segregation laws, but black and white lived distinct lives with very little social, cultural overlap.

And just as nearly 200 years earlier the Founding Fathers had declared that 'all men are created equal' while surrounded by their slaves, so the United States in the early 1960s was berating the Soviet Union for not being a 'free society' when millions of its own citizens were still facing the most deeply ingrained, legally sanctioned racial discrimination. The hypocrisy was crystal clear – but not quite so clear that it could be overturned without a battle. The civil rights struggle was long and painful as campaigners faced violence, intimidation and a pile of Southern states determined to resist change.

It wouldn't be until the Civil Rights Act of 1964, passed by Lyndon B. Johnson, that – finally – segregation in public places would come to an end. No longer would parks, courthouses, theatres, sports stadiums or hotels decide who they would let in on the basis of skin colour; employment discrimination based on race would be outlawed too. This legislation would be followed a year later by the Voting Rights Act, which forbade literacy tests and other discriminatory practices to stop black people from voting. Then in 1968 the Fair Housing Act banned discrimination in the sale, rental and financing of property. The hero of the civil rights movement, Martin Luther King Jr, would declare the changes wrought by these pieces of legislation to be nothing short of a 'second emancipation'.

The genius of the design of the African American museum is that you start in a low-ceilinged, dimly lit basement where you learn about slavery, then you move up a level to where the roof space is a bit more generous and it is a little brighter to discover that it would only be replaced by segregation. The next level takes you to the civil rights struggle of the 1950s and 60s, and after that you are suddenly above ground in a giant, spacious atrium, with brilliant daylight flooding in. Enlightenment! Deliverance!

What gives the museum its power, however, is that this is history that still has a pulse. It may be faint but the battles of the last 300 years still resonate with a black population that has to fight on a daily basis against casual and not so casual racism. This is history that has not gasped its last breath. The battles against segregation, voter suppression, institutional racism and discrimination go on. They may be more insidious and subliminal than they were in the Jim Crow era – but ask any black person in America today about their experiences, and they will have a story to tell.

There are the everyday things that happen. It may sound trivial, but at the 2016 Oscars when not one person of colour was nominated for anything, it seemed a remarkable omission, and was felt as another slight to the wider community.

Just look at the 2016 election, and some of what went on. North Carolina is a prime example, though not the only one. From 1965, following the passing of the Voting Rights Act, North Carolina could only change its statewide voting laws if they had been approved by a federal judge or the Department of Justice and 'did not abridge the right to vote on account of race'. But then, in 2013, a ruling by the Supreme Court held that federal oversight of elections was an unconstitutional intrusion on state autonomy. In effect, a majority of the court decided that the 1965 law was obsolete. It had done its job. Voter participation was the same in the African American community as it was in the white population. Individual states were now free to go their own way.

So North Carolina with its Republican legislature went about reframing its voter laws. Nothing crude like literacy tests, or guessing how many jelly beans there were in the jar before you were handed your polling card. It was far more subtle than that, though it could have resulted in a similar outcome. The measures would be framed with the seemingly laudable goal of cutting down on voter fraud.

Who could possibly be against that? So everyone coming to vote would be required to show ID – either a passport or a driving licence. The Republican state legislators also wanted to cut the number of days during which early voting could take place (a feature of US elections that is very different from the UK), eliminate same-day registration for voters and restrict provisional ballots for those who sought to vote in a different precinct from where they were registered.

Here's the thing, though. Just before introducing these measures, the legislature had asked its research team to dig deep into the racial breakdown of voter behaviour. And look at what their research threw up. They discovered that a very high percentage of African Americans prefer to vote early (60 per cent in 2008; 64 per cent in 2012). They are also the poorest in the state, more likely to suffer from ill health and unlikely to be able to drive themselves to the polling stations – if they are to vote they needed the early voting option, and needed other people to drive them there. The black community also moves about more than white residents, which means they are more likely to want to vote in a different precinct than the one where they may be registered. And one final thing the legislature's research team turned up – many African Americans are not drivers, and therefore have no driving licence; and they certainly won't have a passport. No ID equals no vote.

The measures were adopted by North Carolina's legislature but then challenged by civil rights groups. The case was heard by the federal appeals court in Richmond, Virginia. And their verdict was damning. The court ruled that the law had been framed to curtail severely the number of black voters eligible to participate in the election. Judge Diana Motz wrote: 'Because of race the legislature enacted one of the largest restrictions of the franchise in modern North Carolina history.' The measures, she said, had been designed to 'target African American voters with almost surgical precision'.

It should be added that, in the course of the hearing, no evidence was ever provided that there was *any* problem whatsoever with voter fraud. Oh, and it is probably worth mentioning *en passant* that in North Carolina in 2008 and 2012, the black vote was something like 95 per cent in favour of the Democratic Party. It may be that it wasn't about race, it was just about good, old-fashioned political gerrymandering. But my guess is that if you have grown up in an African American community, and know the painful history of how the white man has tried down the ages to deny you the most fundamental right of a citizen in a democracy, then you're not much interested in what the motivation might be, because the effect is the same: to stop black people from voting – again. 'This ruling means that thousands of voters who would have been disenfranchised will now be able to participate in the presidential election,' said Dale Ho, director of the American Civil Liberties Union Voting Rights Project. The Republican legislature said that it respected the court's decision but it was disappointed.

And lest you think that what I am describing is a one-off, egregious example from a backwater, redneck state (which North Carolina most certainly is not), there are plenty of other cases too. In Texas, just months before polling day in the 2016 presidential election, proposals to introduce stricter voter ID laws were struck down by a federal appeals court on the basis that they would be discriminatory to blacks and Hispanics.

It was a similar story in Wisconsin. There too the legislators sought to introduce tougher laws in order to crack down on voter fraud, and once again federal judges intervened to overturn the legislation. The judge, James Peterson, said in his hundred-plus pages of summing up that the state legislature's efforts to enact strict voter ID laws were an overreaction: 'The Wisconsin experience demonstrates that a preoccupation with mostly phantom election fraud leads to real incidents of disenfranchisement, which undermine rather than enhance confidence in elections, particularly in minority communities,' he wrote. 'To put it bluntly, Wisconsin's strict version of voter ID law is a cure worse than the disease.'

As a state Wisconsin is also interesting for other reasons. It is primarily known as the cheese capital of the United States – and go to either of the political conventions and you can tell the state delegation because they are wearing frankly ludicrous hats that look like wedges of cheese. That, I should quickly add, is not why it is famous. Not for the gritty industrial city of Milwaukee, home to the Harley-Davidson motorcycle museum, the Green Bay Packers football team, a lot of beer production. No. What makes Milwaukee famous (with all due respect to Rod Stewart) is the astonishing rate at which it locks up black men in prison. About one in eight of all adult black males have spent time inside. According to a University of Wisconsin–Milwaukee study, nearly 13 per cent of the adult male black population is in prison. In Britain, by contrast, there are roughly 85,000 prisoners, which equates to 0.13 per cent of the population. In other words in Wisconsin the incarceration rate is 100 times higher. So is there something particularly nefarious about the young black man in Wisconsin or is it the legal system?

To put these figures in some kind of context, the average percentage of black men in prison nationwide in the US is about half that. The nearest to Wisconsin is Oklahoma, which has locked up roughly 10 per cent of the adult male black population. But what is odd is that Wisconsin is not particularly keen overall in throwing people in prison. For white men it is not much different than the national average – about 1.2 per cent. There are no very satisfactory answers to explain this disparity. Well, obviously there is one. It's simply a question of race.

Back in 2002 the Justice Policy Institute wrote a report called 'Cell Blocks Versus Classroom', which analysed statistics for the number of African American men in college and the Department of Justice figures on the number of inmates in prison. It gave the headline grabbing, cor-blimey-would-you-believe-it figure that there were more African American men between the ages of 18 and 25 in prison than there were in higher education. That figure is outdated, but it didn't stop Barack Obama using it five years later when he was running for the presidency, saying, 'We have more to do when more young black men languish in prison than attend colleges and universities across America.'

Interestingly, the roots of this lay not with the Republicans, but with the two terms of Bill Clinton – and in particular his attempts to prove that he could be tougher on crime than the Republicans. His 1994 Violent Crime Control and Law Enforcement Act contained the famous 'three strikes' policy. It meant anyone who was convicted of a serious violent crime and who had two or more prior convictions, including drug crimes, would be locked up for life. It heralded a massive programme of prison building to cope with the extra demand for cells. The overwhelming majority of those convicted were black. President Clinton some years later would tell a civil rights group that 'I signed a bill that made the problem worse and I want to admit it.' He conceded that minor criminals were locked up 'way too long'. Of the 208,000 people held in federal (as opposed to state) prisons, 48 per cent are there for drug offences and over 70 per cent of them are either black or Hispanic.

It is a policy that Barack Obama, in the dying days of his presidency, tried to unwind. He became the first sitting president to visit a federal jail – in Oklahoma – and while there he made the argument that the criminal justice system needed to distinguish between young people who had made mistakes, and those who were truly dangerous. At the end of his second term he sought to make amends for past mistakes by using his right of presidential pardon in a way never seen before. On his final day in office 330 prisoners who were inside for drugs offences were freed. It was a tiny fraction of the black prison population, but a message to his successor that further action was needed. And in Washington's dysfunctional and polarised politics, this is something on which there is cross-party agreement: that penal reform is long overdue.

And of course in modern-day America segregation is now a distant memory. But economic segregation is alive. If you visit Washington DC it has the appearance of a well-integrated city. But where I live in the Northwest quadrant of the city, the population is predominantly white and affluent. Go to

Southeast Washington and the area around Anacostia, and it is overwhelmingly black and poor. And if you speak to someone who lives in Northwest DC, ask him or her how often they go to the Southeast neighbourhoods. It just doesn't happen. I was filming there with my crew recently at a food bank. Afterwards we waited on the street for about 10 minutes trying to get a taxi back to the office. None came past; and the people who ran the community centre told us that none would. Through a mixture of fear and lack of business, taxi drivers stay away from this area. And this, I should add, is not some far-flung deserted suburb – this is a couple of miles from the White House and the Capitol Building.

But this type of segregation is totally inconsequential compared with what happened in a small city called Flint, Michigan. Flint is a city that is located 70 miles north of Detroit. If Detroit is Motown – the motor city – then Flint is its smaller cousin. It too grew up as a motor city – General Motors had its biggest car plant there. It is a city of around a hundred thousand people, where four out of ten residents live below the poverty line. Median income is half that of the rest of Michigan. Oh. And one other important statistic: this is a city where more than half the population is African American.

The city has been in decline since GM started scaling back production. And with a decline in income so the local authorities struggled to make ends meet – to meet their commitments towards schooling and public health, and all the other basic civil amenities that it is the responsibility of public services to provide. What happened next is something you might expect to read about in a Third World country or in a dictatorship, not in the richest country in the world.

The allocated fund that was for the city's water supply had an $11 million shortfall. So the city switched its water supplier. While a new pipeline was under construction that would draw water from Lake Huron, the city turned to the Flint River as its water source. The trouble was the water supply was contaminated and polluted beyond belief – and everybody knew it was. No other community was drawing water from the Flint River. But, hey, they had to save money – so you switch to a supplier who will give you water at a much lower cost.

According to a class-action lawsuit, the state's Department of Environmental Quality was not treating the Flint River water with an anti-corrosive agent, which was a straight violation of federal law. According to a study by scientists at Virginia Tech the water from the Flint River that was coming out of people's taps was 19 times more corrosive than water from Lake Huron. Because the water had not been treated with that agent, lead from aging mains pipes started leaching into the Flint water supply – and going directly into family homes. People started developing skin complaints. A mother of four was one of the first to raise the alarm, when she noticed that her children were losing their hair in great clumps. People were suddenly going to their doctors with skin complaints and respiratory problems, who had never had problems before.

During this period between 6,000 and 12,000 children were exposed to drinking water with dangerously high levels of lead, and who knows what range of serious health problems they may encounter in the future as a result. These could include impaired cognition, behavioural disorders, hearing problems and delayed puberty. In pregnant women, lead is associated with reduced foetal growth. The water change is also a possible cause of an outbreak of legionnaires' disease in the county, which killed ten people and affected many more.

But the authorities were slow to act, and seemed far more interested in covering their tracks over the calamitous decisions that were made. The switchover to water from the Flint happened in April 2014. In August the authorities knew something was wrong and advised people in certain areas of the city to boil their water. The city council wanted to reconnect to the supply from Lake Huron, but they were overruled by the state. By October 2014, General Motors announced it would stop using the Flint tap water because – get this – it was corroding engine parts. But despite all the studies, like the one from Virginia Tech, all the medical evidence, the complaints and the sickness of the population, the fact that you could see with the naked eye that the water was polluted, it wouldn't be until January 2016 that a state of emergency was declared by the governor of Michigan. Now the whole city was told not to drink the water coming out of the taps under any circumstances, nor use it for bathing. For month after month the only source of water was from bottles. It is scarcely believable.

In June 2017, a number of senior officials were charged with involuntary manslaughter for their part in the Flint lead-poisoning scandal. But the most uncomfortable question was this: could this or would this have happened in a city that was predominantly white and wealthy? The Michigan Civil Rights Commission's official report into the scandal didn't seem to have much doubt about the answer: the decisions that were made were down to 'historical, structural and systemic racism combined with implicit bias'. A judge in March 2017 ordered that the state of Michigan should pay the city of Flint $87 million to remove and replace 18,000 unsafe water pipes, and to pay the legal fees of those who brought the class-action lawsuit.

It is perhaps no wonder that one of the fastest growing political movements in recent years in America has been Black Lives Matter. A campaigning organisation born out of the killings of young black men by the police, it soon found a voice on all manner of other social issues and, because this is a social media age, is perhaps best known as #blacklivesmatter – a hashtag that has given a rallying point for those who feel that racism in American society is as endemic as ever it was. Black kids are disproportionately educated in poverty-soaked sink schools; they are far more likely to be homeless, unemployed and to have a criminal record. They will have worse health and die younger. The bald figures are stark and leave little room for ambiguity. Black Lives Matter is seen as the civil rights movement 2.0. And just like the movement of the 1950s and 60s, it is sparking opposition from those – mainly white and on the right – who either don't believe that racism is still a problem or don't care. They have tried to push an All Lives Matter agenda, or Blue Lives Matter – the latter being a defence of the police.

And ominously in the summer of 2016 it looked like some on the far right and among militant black groups wanted to spark a race war. In July 2016, a black army veteran who had served in Afghanistan set an ambush for police in Dallas. Micah Xavier Johnson targeted white police officers, killing five and injuring seven others. Two civilians were also shot and injured. It was the deadliest single attack on the forces of law and order since 9/11. Johnson told negotiators during attempts to get him to surrender that he was upset about recent police shootings, that he wanted to kill white people – especially white officers. Ten days later a similar incident unfolded in Baton Rouge, Louisiana. A trap was laid, police were lured out and within minutes three police officers were killed. The shooter was an African American military veteran from Missouri. Under a pseudonym, Gavin Long, he posted videos on social media saying, 'Zero have been successful just over simple protesting ... You gotta fight back.' This killing took place on the day the Republican Convention was getting underway in Cleveland, when a lot of Donald Trump's supporters – and Mr Trump himself – were in confrontational mood. There were a few weeks in 2016 when it really did seem that America was on the brink of something extremely ugly.

At the end of the Obama presidency, I went back to Charleston – the city where a jury was unable to reach a verdict after a policeman had shot an unarmed black man in the back several times, and where Dylann Roof had killed those black worshippers at a Bible study class. A week after the church shootings, Barack Obama came to Charleston and, in an unforgettable moment, sang 'Amazing Grace' at the memorial service for the pastor who had been gunned down. It stunned the largely black audience packed inside the sports hall as their president, quietly at first, launched himself into the gospel hymn, bringing all the other worshippers to their feet. This was *their* black president, binding himself to *their* community. Some would also quietly add the word 'finally'.

If he was colour blind at the start of his presidency, he wasn't any more. But as I returned to this elegant, historic city at the end of 2016, the view of some civil rights leaders was that after eight years of the first African American president the lot of the black man and woman hadn't really changed. In this port city which, perhaps more than any other city in the United States, is stained by the slave trade, there was a feeling articulated by one particular pastor, Elder James Johnson, that the president wasn't really one of them. His ancestors weren't slaves, he hadn't had to fight every step of the way, like the generations of the pastor's family had had to fight. And he didn't have the rage coursing round his veins, like so many whose forefathers had suffered the indignities or racism, generation after generation.

And it's true: with a white mother, growing up in Kansas and Hawaii (his Kenyan father had abandoned him), he had not had the classic upbringing. The novelist and essayist Ta-Nehisi Coates came to know the president well. He wrote a fascinating piece, based on a series of interviews he conducted with the outgoing president. He wrote in the *Atlantic* magazine in January 2017:

> The kinds of traumas that marked African Americans of his generation – beatings at the hands of racist police, being herded into poor schools, grinding out a life in a tenement building – were mostly abstract for him. Moreover, the kind of spatial restriction that most black people feel at an early age – having rocks thrown at you for being on the wrong side of the tracks, for instance – was largely absent from his life. In its place, Obama was gifted with a well-stamped passport and admittance to elite private schools – all of which spoke of other identities, other lives and other worlds where the color line was neither determinative nor especially relevant. Obama could have grown into a raceless cosmopolitan.

Surely he would have lived in a world of problems, but problems not embodied by him. Instead, he decided to enter this world.

He then quotes the president telling him that when he was growing up he thought it was cool to be black. It was not 'something to run away from but something to embrace. Why that is, I think, is complicated. Part of it is I think that my mother thought black folks were cool, and if your mother loves you and is praising you – and says you look good, are smart – as you are, then you don't kind of think in terms of *How can I avoid this?* You feel pretty good about it.'

This was a man who had embraced blackness when he could have easily chosen a different path. He may not have achieved everything that he set out to as president, and there is no doubt there were policy shortcomings, and groups left disappointed. But with Michelle at his side, was there ever an eight-year period in the White House so free of scandal and embarrassment, even if some of the problems with race that he inherited were still there when he left? The most dystopian vision of conflict between black and white at the end of his presidency did not come to pass, but America, for all its long journey from slavery through segregation, through the civil rights struggle to the present day, is still a very long way away from being a post-racial society that people had allowed themselves to believe in, in those heady days after Barack Obama had won the White House.

Chapter 3

Patriotism

When I arrived in Washington, the first major sporting event I went to was the basketball match between the Washington Wizards and the New Orleans Pelicans at the Verizon Center in downtown DC. It's all cheerleaders, crowd entertainment, T-shirts being fired into the audience, kiss-cam – where a roving camera alights on a couple and they kiss for the crowd. Fans are brought onto the court and try to score a basket from the centre-line. And then there is the food. It is remarkable how many hot dogs and pretzels some fans can put away in the course of one match. A truth about *all* American sport is that watching and eating go hand in hand. Forget the dodgy, limp, sweaty pasty at half-time at a chilly British football ground, if you can face the queues – in the US you eat from start to finish.

Yes, US sport does great hoop-la, but more important than that it does patriotism too. Go to any public event in the US, and the business in hand will not get underway until the national anthem has been sung. And this is not some tedious piece of ritual. It is relished; the choir or soloist sings it with gusto and passion. And it helps that it is such a stirring, musically challenging piece. And when the singer or singers hit the highest notes and reach the finale, 'O'er the land of the free and the home of the brave,' the crowd is usually roaring its approval. Like historic paintings that hang in national galleries that tell important stories of a country's history, so 'The Star-Spangled Banner' is a tale of America prevailing.

Written in 1814 when the country was at war with the British, it tells the story of the bombardment of Fort McHenry in Baltimore Harbor by the Royal Navy. Francis Scott Key, a 35-year-old lawyer and a bit of a poet on the side, witnessed the battle, and he wrote about how, despite the fearsome battle of the night, the US banner with its broad stripes and bright stars was still flying in the early light of dawn. In a few lines it tells a compelling story.

The story of a new nation born in a new world, unhindered by the old, repressive European order, free from the religious and political persecution that the colonists took enormous risks to escape when they set sail and travelled west across the Atlantic. It would be a land of freedom and opportunity. A place that would fashion its own constitution, with a central radical idea: that the government can only rule with the consent of the people. A new nation that would fight off its former British colonial masters as they sought to re-impose their rule.

Now I know I could probably be shipped off to the Tower of London for saying so, but the British national anthem is a dreadful dirge by comparison. A terrible droning tune with rather dull lyrics to match. I love the Queen, I think she has been magnificent – and I really hope that she continues 'long to reign over us' – but it is hardly the stuff of passion and inspiration. Can anyone really say it gives them goosebumps? Give me 'The Star-Spangled Banner', the bloodthirsty 'Marseillaise' or the jauntiness of the Italian and Brazilian anthems any time.

There is something else as well, that British people occasionally sneer at, but which seems to me totally misplaced. There's just a teeny bit of an air of condescension when I have heard *bien pensant* Brits discuss American patriotism and national pride, as though it is somehow immature or bragging or juvenile even.

I think many British people have a problem with patriotism. With all its history and baggage, and having experienced the pain of decolonisation, Britain suffers from an identity crisis, and there is a sense of guilt about the flag.

The same cannot be said of the United States. The Stars and Stripes flies from all public buildings – and a good many homes as well. It's estimated that half of all households in the US own a Stars and Stripes flag. In Britain to fly the national flag (whether it's the Union Jack or the Cross of St George) from your home is often seen as a sign that you are a supporter of a far-right grouping, or else an eccentric old colonel who has a wind-up gramophone and thinks the empire is still alive. How did that ever happen?

In the US the flag is something you salute each morning at school as you recite the pledge of allegiance. And *the* national holiday of America is the 4th of July weekend, when the nation celebrates its independence and its birth. An occasion for fireworks, barbecues and mass flag waving. And a lot of other national holidays celebrate either great moments in the nation's story or people whose contribution to the success of the United States has been so notable that it warrants a public holiday.

Americans also grow up profoundly aware of the key moments of history that have shaped and moulded their country's national identity. I arrived in the US to start my posting just before the 200th anniversary of the Battle of New Orleans, a piece of military history that I have to confess I had little awareness of when I arrived in the US. That was when British troops tried to take control of the city and the state of Louisiana, and to separate it from the rest of the US. But the US forces were waiting. In two separate assaults, the 7,500 British soldiers were unable to penetrate their defences, and the American troops under the leadership of General Andrew Jackson, many of them expert marksmen from Kentucky and Tennessee, decimated the British lines. In half an hour, the British had retreated, the general leading the assault was dead and nearly 2,000 of his men were killed, wounded or missing. US losses were only 8 killed and 13 wounded. Interesting we don't learn much about that in school!

Americans tend to be aware of their history, and for all the anger and anxiety, there is still intense patriotism. A huge number of Americans still believe they live in the greatest country on earth. A General Social Survey found that 84 per cent of people agree with the statement 'I would rather be a citizen of America than of any other country in the world.' Yes, the American dream may have a few dents in it, and the mechanics that allow social mobility might need a bit of oiling, but the American people still believe in their flag, and what it stands for.

But in 2017 America, while practically everyone would describe themselves as being a patriotic American, what that means depends on where you locate yourself across the political spectrum.

Love of country and pride in its values can be variously described as national pride (good) through to nationalism (not so good) until it reaches jingoism/xenophobia (bad). But in the US there is a whole school of intellectual thought that considers the peculiarly US nature of this question. It is what is called 'American exceptionalism'. Put crudely it can be summed up in the words of philosopher and songwriter Tina Turner: 'Simply the best, better than all the rest'. Well, some see American exceptionalism as that. But it is a more serious idea. The view is that because of the unique circumstances under which the USA was founded – the New World, forged out of the revolutionary wars with the British – America also had a mission. Abraham Lincoln in his extraordinary and concise Gettysburg Address said that Americans had a duty to see that 'government of the people, by the people, for the people shall not perish from the earth'. In other words America had a responsibility not only to ensure that its revolution should succeed at home – and Lincoln's remarks in Pennsylvania in 1863 came after the decisive battle of the brutal Civil War which had pitted American against American, Southern states against Northern ones, when the young republic could have been torn apart – but that those values of liberty, individualism and republicanism should prevail overseas too. The idea of American exceptionalism in the corporate-speak of today would be viewed as akin to a national 'mission statement'.

There is another thing about the town of Gettysburg that tells you something about how important the nation's story is to its sense of self-identity. Gettysburg in Pennsylvania is a relatively small town, but there were more casualties there than in any other Civil War battle – in the three days of fighting around 25,000 were killed. This would be the decisive battle for the Confederates, who wanted to secede from the rest of the US, as they tried to push north. But General Robert E. Lee's forces were stopped in their tracks by George C. Meade's Union army.

The thousands of acres of battlefield surrounding the town – the ridges, the woods, the open fields – have been magnificently preserved, with field guns, defences and barricades still in place. My wife and I went there on my birthday and it really did feel as though history had come to life. It was an awful spring day, with the rain pouring down incessantly. But in the museum, and driving around the well laid-out areas where key battles unfolded, thousands of Americans of all ages were taking it in, as they do every day. Of course the island story of Britain is far longer, and the Americans can't compete with the castles and ruins of the UK – but I can't think of anywhere in Britain that is so brilliantly laid out and organised, and over such a vast area.

When he became president, Barack Obama took a much wider view of American exceptionalism than perhaps the history books allowed. He did not so much cast doubt on it, but expressed certainty that a lot of other countries 'like the Brits and the Greeks think their countries are pretty special too'. Yes, we're exceptional, he seemed to be saying, but – hey – a lot of other countries think they're damned good too. On the right those words were seen as almost heretical; they seemed to be a denial that America was exceptional; that America was just another country – warts and all – that you would find anywhere else on the planet.

His opponents were circling. Rudolph W. Giuliani, the former mayor of New York City, told a group of Republican donors, 'I know this is a horrible thing to say, but I do not believe the president loves America ... He wasn't brought up the way you were brought up and I was brought up, through love of the country.' That critique, with just a light tinge of racism running through it, was typical. Marco Rubio, the Florida senator who ran for the Republican nomination, said that Obama had 'demonstrated a disregard for our moral purpose that at times flirted with disdain'.

All the other Republican candidates in the run-up to the 2016 election joined in. He was too quick to criticise the country for shortcomings at home and abroad; he was too cautious to use America's military might overseas when it was entirely justified; and far too timid in extolling the overall contention that America is an unmatched force for good.

Instead, something that the first African American president has sought to do is redefine patriotism. From early on in his political career he has spoken about American exceptionalism through the prism of his own exceptional life and upbringing. His father had grown up herding goats in British colonial Kenya. His wife carried 'blood of slaves and slave owners', as he remarked during his first presidential campaign. He has relatives scattered to the four winds, on different continents, practising different religions in different cultures.

On that night of victory in Grant Park, Chicago, in 2008, he said his life was proof of American exceptionalism: 'If there is anyone out there who still doubts that America is a place where all things are possible, who still wonders if the dream of our founders is alive in our time, who still questions the power of our democracy, tonight is your answer.'

But his American exceptionalism was very different from that of another president who – like Obama – came to power at a period of great uncertainty and a difficult time economically. In 1989 Ronald Reagan delivered his famous City on a Hill speech – the title drawn from the idea, going back to America's puritan roots, of that 'City Upon a Hill' in New England which would serve as a model community that the rest of the world could follow. In Reagan's hands America itself was the city on a hill, also of near perfection. This was his farewell speech to the nation at the end of his two tumultuous terms of office. Events like the divisive Vietnam War were used to show American greatness. The speech started with the story of a Vietnamese boat person rescued by an American sailor – someone adrift, yearning for freedom, falling into the warm embrace of a US serviceman.

> I've spoken of the shining city all my political life ... And how stands the city on this winter night? ... After two hundred years, two centuries, she still stands strong and true to the granite ridge, and her glow has held no matter what the storm. And she's still a magnet, still a beacon for all who must have freedom, for all the pilgrims from all the lost places who are hurtling through the darkness, toward home.

Barack Obama's definitive iteration of what it meant to be a patriot would come when he went to the Edmund Pettus Bridge in Selma, Alabama, to mark the 50th anniversary of America's 'bloody Sunday' when civil rights protestors were brutally beaten by state troopers for having the temerity to march for the right to vote. It was a day full of powerful imagery. The young firebrands of the civil rights movement were now old and bent double, some in their wheelchairs, as they made the symbolic journey across the bridge, holding hands. It was a speech that enormous effort was put into and went through umpteen drafts. Obama wanted to paint a picture of a proud America, but not a romantic, soft-focused, Vaseline-round-the-lens picture. An America that celebrated the diversity of the nation. An America whose story isn't written only by the winners.

What could be more American than what happened in this place? What could more profoundly vindicate the idea of America than plain and humble people – the unsung, the downtrodden, the dreamers not of high station, not born to wealth or privilege, not of one religious tradition but many, coming together to shape their country's course. That's what America is. Not stock photos or airbrushed history, or feeble attempts to define some of us as more American than others. We respect the past, but we don't pine for the past. We don't fear the future; we grab for it. America is not some fragile thing.

The same poll which found that 84 per cent of Americans wouldn't want to be from any other country, also found that 64 per cent of US adults agreed with the statement that 'There are some things about America today that make me feel ashamed,' while 70 per cent of US adults agreed 'The world would be a better place if Americans acknowledged

America's shortcomings.' Maybe Obama's new, redefined patriotism wasn't so out of kilter with public opinion.

America – historically speaking – is still a young nation, proud of what has been achieved, aware of the fight and sacrifices that have been made by others. When my son was at university in Massachusetts it coincided with the news that a military operation led by US Navy Seals had killed Osama bin Laden in a daring night mission to Abbottabad in Pakistan. The students poured out of their dormitories and onto the streets chanting 'U-S-A, U-S-A!' At a number of political rallies that chant will often just start spontaneously, apropos of nothing in particular. Interestingly, it was quite often used as a rejoinder to protest.

At Trump rallies spontaneous outbursts of 'U-S-A!' were a regular occurrence. But even during the Democratic Convention it was the cry that went up when Bernie Sanders supporters or anti-war protestors were seeking to disrupt events. At sporting events too – even when it's not the national side playing – up will go the cry.

We have no British equivalent. I reported on the fantastic 2012 London Olympics, and was in the stadium that fabulous Saturday when Jessica Ennis, Mo Farah and Greg Rutherford brought home three gold medals – and somehow shouting 'Come on Great Britain!' seemed a bit awkward. Few people did. We screamed for the athletes, but not really for the nation. Football matches are a lot easier when it's just England you are shouting for – or Eng-er-land, Eng-er-land, Eng-er-land, to be precise. The chant works so much better when the nation is given an extra syllable. But I don't think I have ever heard us chanting 'U-K, U-K, U-K!'

Football also brings out something very interesting about English (yes, I use the word advisedly) patriotism. Just before any international tournament, the press and the fans are full of brio and bravado. There's nothing our brave young men with the three lions on their chest can't do. We mock and belittle our opponents. I was in Bloemfontein in South Africa in 2010 when England were about to thrash Germany in the World Cup, and the fans sang endless songs about the Second World War, and what happened to the Germans then. Tasteful? Not ever so.

Then reality hits. We underachieve spectacularly. In Bloemfontein that day it wasn't even close (regardless of the one egregious refereeing decision over the Frank Lampard goal that wasn't given). And then, having had our collective chests puffed out far too far pre-match, we go into a kind of post-tournament inferiority-complex fug. Morose, self-recriminating – why are we so useless, why are we so awful as a nation? And then, none the wiser, as a new tournament approaches we immediately resort to our braying worst. In America patriotism is on show pretty constantly.

The chants of U-S-A may be quite trivial – just the simple overt manifestation of self-belief. But there is one other area where you see American national pride on a day-to-day basis, and it is fabulous. And that is the way the public treats its military veterans. This is another thing that changed in America in the wake of 9/11, when thousands of young men took themselves off to the recruiting office, wanting to sign up for military service to avenge what had happened to their country. I use the word 'public' rather than 'nation' – because how veterans have been treated in federally run hospitals is the source of much controversy. In the absence of a National

Health Service, veterans have their own hospital network run by the Veterans Association, which has been mired in scandal. So let us stick to how the public treats – and reveres – its former servicemen and women.

Go to an airport in the US (as I spend far too much of my life doing) and there will be a first-class lounge – and there'll be a veterans lounge. When the airline gate-staff go through the boarding procedure, military in uniform will be invited to board first alongside those in business class. It is a commonplace for a person in uniform to be thanked for their service by total strangers. My favourite day was when I was at Reagan National Airport in Washington one Saturday morning and veterans of conflicts going back to the Second World War were being flown into the nation's capital for a day of celebration and commemoration. And at the gates there were musicians playing Glenn Miller and the tunes of the big-band era to greet these old boys in their wheelchairs off the plane. At basketball matches, at the football, at the baseball, the tannoy will ask the servicemen and women in the crowd to stand and receive the acclamation of the rest of the fans in the stadium. Is this schmaltzy or cheesey? Possibly. But is it cynical? Not at all.

Contrast this with the UK and the hospital in Margate where a serviceman in uniform, who had seen duty in Iraq and Afghanistan, was moved to a back room for fear of upsetting patients from minority groups who were also seeking medical attention. His family was told, 'We've lots of cultures coming in.' Twice he was moved because he was in uniform. The hospital would later apologise for any embarrassment caused.

Yes, it's different in the US but it wasn't always like this. During the Vietnam era when the nation was so bitterly divided and anti-war protest was at its height, those coming back from the horrors of Southeast Asia found themselves vilified by their fellow citizens, spat at, shunned, isolated – as though they had some kind of culpability for the decisions made by the politicians who had put them there in the first place. But it seems the country has moved on. Iraq and Afghanistan are hardly seen as towering achievements of foreign policy in the US – but the men and women who fought and died there are seen as heroes – in the land of the free and the home of the brave.

One of the most spectacular things I did during the 2016 election year was to ride in Rolling Thunder. It takes place on the Sunday before Memorial Day, a public holiday to remember those who died while serving in the US armed forces. Rolling Thunder is a little more niche. It was set up originally to honour those who were taken as prisoners of war in Vietnam, or who were reported Missing in Action. It is an occasion when – literally – hundreds of thousands of Harley-Davidson riders converge on Washington DC from all over the United States to take part in what has become a quasi-pilgrimage. It is hard to describe what it looks like to see so many motorcyclists gathered in one place.

On their leather vests are the badges that read like a history of US military engagement over the past 50 years – Vietnam airborne division, Desert Storm artillery, Operation Iraqi Freedom, Afghanistan, and the list goes on. One veteran tells me he worked with the British SAS at the time of the Falklands War in 1982. Then the tannoy system crackles into life.

'Ladies and Gentlemen, please may we have silence for the presentation of Colours and the singing of the national anthem.' Crash helmets are taken off, engines are cut, heads are bowed to the ground and right hands are held firmly across the chest. It is all done with absolute decorum.

Then we are told there will be prayers. A preacher takes over the microphone. I am not listening that intently, probably focused instead on the technical difficulties of filming this with my cameraman on another bike, as I ride mine. I am dimly aware of 'we are gathered here today' and 'in the name of our Lord, Jesus Christ'. But then my ears really do prick up – 'And if you wish harm upon this country then you are a son of a bitch, and may you burn in hell.' I wonder whether that's from the King James edition (new or old) or the New American Standard Bible. I'm not a biblical scholar, but I suspect neither.

And then, with that spiritual nourishment filling our souls, we are off. Between half a million and a million motorcycle engines fire up, and over several hours man (it is mostly men) and machine funnel their way out of the car park.

You cross the memorial bridge next to the Arlington military cemetery, and go round the Lincoln Memorial, the national monument, up to the Capitol and then back round to the Wall, the famous Vietnam memorial where the names of the nearly 60,000 who died in the Vietnam War are etched in stone in the two-acre plot in Constitution Gardens.

It is hard to mix solemnity with the thunderous noise of so many V-twin engines roaring. But it was unbelievable. Vast crowds line the streets – seriously huge numbers – to wave at the bikers, a large percentage of them Vietnam veterans. They are thanked; people are shouting their love and appreciation. I am riding with them to do a report on the news that evening, as Donald Trump is to be the keynote speaker at the rally afterwards. But under a crash helmet it is hard to tell who is who, and I can't tell you how many people on the sides of the road are shouting out their blessings to me. It is fabulously moving. Americans may not be proud of what was achieved in either Vietnam, Iraq or Afghanistan – but they lionise the men and women who went to serve there.

I was in northern Afghanistan in November 2001, when the Northern Alliance, backed by the US and other allied forces, were pushing the Taliban back from their last remaining strongholds in the north. We arrived in Taloqan the day it fell, and then watched the slow process as US air power and Northern Alliance mujahideen on the ground fought to retake Kunduz, the last remaining centre of population – and whose capitulation would open up the vital supply route from Kabul to Mazar-e-Shareef, and then north up to Uzbekistan.

I was with a colleague who had earlier been reporting from Pakistan, where after Friday prayers it was routine for the crowds to gather in main squares and scream 'Death to America, Death to America!' There would be the ritual burning of US flags. Sometimes the crowds would disperse peacefully, sometimes the Pakistani police, wielding batons, would gently assist them on their journey home. What, we wondered, would have happened if a US embassy van had driven into the square with a loudhailer saying, 'Get your green cards here.' Maybe the van would have been torched along with all the green-card applications and the diplomatic staff inside. Or maybe the van would have been mobbed with people fighting now to get their hands on a green-card application form.

*

Each year there is the green-card lottery. There are 50,000 winners. Applications tend to average 10–15 million per annum. For all the problems that America may be suffering, it is still a dream, *the* dream, for millions of people around the world. Because once you have a green card, you are on a path to citizenship.

Indeed, there are people I know living in the US whose heavily pregnant relatives make a point of coming to visit as late on in their pregnancy as they can on a tourist or visitor visa, to ensure that the baby is born on American soil. That way the baby qualifies for a US passport. Data on it is, needless to say, not very accurate, but the Center for Immigration Studies in Washington DC estimates that up to 36,000 babies a year are born to foreign tourists who want their offspring to qualify for a US passport. Some have called it birth tourism; the more pejorative term is 'anchor babies' – because of the (mistaken) belief that if a baby is born in the US it will allow the child's parents and siblings to settle and anchor themselves in the US. But it is another indicator of how much people from around the world want to make their lives in the United States. Of course, a big part of this is straightforward economics. America is the richest country in the world – who wouldn't want a piece of that?

But it is more than that. There is still the idea of America and the ideal of America. It is an ideal to live in a country where there is freedom of expression, where there are free and fair elections, where there is the rule of law and equality of the sexes, where you have a right to practise your religion free from the fear of persecution and where there are strictly prescribed limits to the power of the state.

Washington, where I live – admittedly not typical of the rest of the US in terms of wealth or education – is a giant melting pot. People there have come from all over. The woman who worked in the nail parlour that my wife went to was from Mongolia. Ulan Bator to be precise. My producer is from Bulgaria. Our cleaner is from Salvador. My cameraman is Australian. The office finance manager is from West Africa. A lot of the taxi drivers are Ethiopian, Afghanis or from the Middle East. There's a massage place down the street where all the staff are Chinese.

Well, they are and they aren't. Because once they have got their citizenship, they are Americans, contributing not only their tax dollars to the IRS but also – hopefully – culturally enriching the neighbourhoods where they live. And if you are ever in a long taxi ride, it's always interesting to ask the driver what brought them to America and how they qualified to get a visa. For some it is the green-card lottery, but many others are there because they have managed to escape lives of unspeakable danger, persecution and hardship. America, they say, is the land of second chances. Many of these people feel they have been lucky to be given a second chance. And the most patriotic Americans that you will find are invariably the ones who've recently come to the US, having fled oppression in their country of birth.

We tend to love most those things we have chosen, and so many Americans, whether first, second or third generation, have chosen to be Americans. It wasn't some casual accident of birth where you can trace your ancestry back to William the Conqueror. America is the most complex of patchwork quilts, with only a small percentage of indigenous Americans able to trace their ancestry right the way back.

The Islamic cultural centre in Washington DC is on Massachusetts Avenue, where nearly all the grand embassies are found, and at lunchtime it's where a lot of the city's taxis are parked. Many of the drivers are from Pakistan and Somalia and congregate there for lunchtime prayers. I went there to speak to some of them after Donald Trump had made his comments about banning all Muslims from entering the US. There was horror at his comments. They told me they were loyal Americans who saluted the flag, paid their taxes and served their communities.

And no one is prouder of being an American than Khizr Khan. He is from Pakistan, studied law in Lahore and moved to practise in the United Arab Emirates. But then he came to America with his wife Ghazala in 1980. He would finish his studies at the Harvard Law School, then move to Maryland before eventually settling in the delightful university town of Charlottesville, Virginia. He would always carry a copy of the constitution in the breast pocket of his jacket, and had a whole pile of them at home which he would give to visitors. They had three children.

Their middle son, Humayun, joined the US Army, rising to the rank of captain when the 2003 invasion of Iraq took place. A year after that he was blown up and killed by an IED packed inside a car. He had ordered his men to retreat and take cover while he went to inspect a taxi that had aroused suspicion. As he got close, the 200 pounds of explosives packed inside it detonated. He was blown to pieces. He was posthumously awarded the Bronze Star for his gallantry and a Purple Heart. He was buried in the Arlington National Cemetery alongside so many of his comrades from the Iraq conflict. Except instead of a cross on his headstone, there is a star and a crescent moon, denoting his faith as a Muslim.

If ever there was an example of a true American patriot, surely this was it: the immigrant family, who become American, who pledge their allegiance to the flag, and then their son makes the ultimate sacrifice. But Humayun Khan's story became politicised when his parents took to the stage at the Democratic National Convention in Philadelphia in the summer of 2016 to berate Donald Trump for his views on Muslims in particular and minorities in general. The convention is an astonishing four-day production. There is no British equivalent. The autumn party conferences don't begin to come close. And it is made up of the starriest political speakers – the Clintons, the Obamas, the grandees of the Democratic Party and the up and coming stars. It is also littered with Hollywood A-listers and rock superstars, past and present. In the final two days Alicia Keys sang, Meryl Streep howled (she came on stage and let out this rather strange banshee-style wail), Carole King rocked the elderly, Katy Perry the young. But the headline, scene-stealing superstar of the convention was 66-year-old Mr Khan.

Speaking about Mr Trump's views on minorities, Mr Khan said: 'Donald Trump, you're asking Americans to trust you with their future. Let me ask you, have you ever read the United States Constitution? [at which point he produced from his breast pocket his own slightly dog-eared copy] ... I will gladly lend you my copy. In this document, look for the words, look for the words, liberty and equal protection (under) law ... Have you ever been to Arlington Cemetery?' he continued. 'Go look at the graves of brave patriots who died defending the United States of America. You will see all faiths, genders and ethnicities. You have sacrificed nothing and no one.'

The atmosphere in the convention centre was now electric. People had stopped what they were doing and put down their smartphones as they slowly realised they were witnessing something remarkable. I had been sitting cross-legged on the floor behind the New Jersey delegation, trying to avoid being thrown out by one of the fire marshals for blocking the aisle, but you could sense the change in mood sweeping across the convention centre. Mr Khan's wife stood by his side, an outwardly calm and supportive figure who said nothing. The ovation at the end was deafening as millions of hairs on the backs of thousands of necks stood to attention to salute the sacrifice of a true American patriot.

But, inevitably, in the atmosphere of 2016 his action brought a very swift reaction from Mr Trump. In her convention speech there was a zinger of a line from Hillary Clinton when she said, 'A man you can bait with a tweet is not a man we can trust with nuclear weapons.' If the speech from Mr Khan was designed to bait Mr Trump, goodness did he bite.

In Ghazala Khan he didn't see a woman consumed by grief at the loss of a son; he saw a Muslim. In his first comments he wondered aloud why she hadn't spoken. Was it Sharia law that forced her to be quiet; was she banned from speaking? 'His wife, if you look at his wife, she was standing there. She had nothing to say. She probably – maybe she wasn't allowed to have anything to say. You tell me.' In her own account afterwards, she said she had come on stage and seen a giant photo of her son behind her, and was too overwhelmed with emotion to trust herself to open her mouth. Trump was then asked in the same interview what sacrifices he had made.

'I've worked very, very hard' was one comment; 'I've raised millions of dollars for the vets' was another; 'and built great structures' the final sacrifice that he spoke of.

The Twittersphere lit up. The medium that Trump had used so brilliantly was now turned witheringly against him. Under the hashtag #TrumpSacrifices, users wrote sarcastically that the candidate had, among other things, been subjected to such hardships as having to fly on commercial aircraft, playing golf on a public course and staying at a three-star hotel.

Mr Khan meanwhile was not retreating, particularly after Mr Trump insisted on describing Mr Khan's words as a 'vicious attack' which the property mogul had the right to respond to. One of the more unintended hilarious comments came in a written statement from Mr Trump which was meant to be an attempt at damage limitation, in which he said: 'While I feel deeply for the loss of his son, Mr Khan, who has never met me, has no right to stand in front of millions of people and claim I have never read the constitution.' Well, the whole point of the First Amendment is that you have freedom of speech – that is precisely the right you have. It rather elegantly reinforced Mr Khan's point that Mr Trump didn't seem overly familiar with the constitution.

For days afterwards Mr Khan politely, doggedly gave interviews setting out his belief on what constitutes being a good American. And as befitted a legal scholar his view was not some misty-eyed romantic view, it was drawn from the constitution that he was still carrying with him – and which bizarrely had suddenly become a bestseller on Amazon after its unexpected appearance from Mr Khan's pocket at the convention.

When I interviewed him and his wife at the beginning of August four days after his convention speech, he told me that he had meant to take the copy out of his pocket before he left for the Wells Fargo Arena, where the convention was taking place, as he had been told that security would be so tight he wouldn't be able to carry anything with him. But he had forgotten about it.

After our BBC interview I walked with them to their car, parked just up the road from our bureau. I can only say it was extraordinary. This elderly couple, who four days earlier were totally anonymous, were stopped by everyone – and I mean everyone, all of them total strangers – to be told that they were being prayed for, to be thanked for saying what needed to be said, to be wished courage and strength. To be congratulated. A young African American hugged them both and said in a hushed voice, 'Thank you for your son's service and sacrifice.' It was overwhelming. I went back inside the office somewhat choked up by what I had witnessed. I would have been oh so proud to have been an American that hot August morning, because it spoke to the dream, the ideal of America, that is found in the Emma Lazarus poem carved onto a bronze plaque on the side of the Statue of Liberty at the entrance to New York:

> Not like the brazen giant of Greek fame,
> With conquering limbs astride from land to land;
> Here at our sea-washed, sunset gates shall stand
> A mighty woman with a torch, whose flame
> Is the imprisoned lightning, and her name
> Mother of Exiles. From her beacon-hand
> Glows world-wide welcome, her mild eyes command
> The air-bridged harbor that twin cities frame.
> 'Keep ancient lands, your storied pomp!' cries she

With silent lips. 'Give me your tired, your poor,
Your huddled masses yearning to breathe free,
The wretched refuse of your teeming shore.
Send these, the homeless, tempest-tost to me,
I lift my lamp beside the golden door!'

The golden door indeed. America may feel like a less welcoming place in 2016 compared to when the previous waves of migrants were washing up at Ellis Island at the end of the 19th and early 20th century to have their applications processed. The Irish escaping famine, Italians wanting a better life, the Jews fleeing the pogroms of Eastern Europe, and any number of other communities who wanted to build a new life in the New World.

But as in the America of today, the 1920s saw a very different mood towards an open door. The Immigration Act of 1924 signed into law by President Calvin Coolidge would put severe caps on the number of people allowed into the country. The aim was clear: to reduce severely the number of people flooding in from Southern Europe, and of Jews from Eastern Europe. It severely restricted the number of Africans and halted all migrants from Arab and Asian countries. There is an interesting account of it from the Office of the Historian at the State Department. 'In all of its parts, the most basic purpose of the 1924 Immigration Act was to preserve the ideal of US homogeneity.' And it should be added that Congressional resistance to the measure was negligible.

And if you want an echo from history, look at the arguments being made against taking Jewish refugees escaping the horrors of Nazi Germany. How could one be certain that the people fleeing weren't spies or Nazi infiltrators? They could be threats to national security. These are the same arguments that Donald Trump advanced for his travel ban from Middle Eastern and African nations most plagued by terrorism. But it brought some fairly inglorious moments. In June 1939, the German ocean liner *St Louis* tried to dock in Miami. The nearly thousand passengers aboard were Jews. But the vessel was turned away. More than a quarter of those on board would die in the German concentration camps.

In 2016 there were competing visions of what it was to be a patriot, and how America should view its position internationally. In the Donald Trump world view, patriotism meant Americanism, not Globalism, and a very determined move to put a check on America's international obligations. America should no longer prop up NATO, unless the other members of the alliance were prepared to pay much more into Europe's collective defence. Japan and South Korea must pony up a lot more if they wanted protection and the maintenance of American forces in South Asia – and if those countries wanted to arm themselves with their own nuclear weapons, well that was fine too. In effect he was ripping up decades of US policy of backing nuclear non-proliferation. A position he, to some extent, walked back from once in the White House, particularly as it seemed North Korea was getting closer to developing an intercontinental ballistic missile, capable of reaching America's West Coast. In President Trump's developing world view, the provocations of Pyongyang were much more than a little local difficulty for the Korean peninsula. He also expressed admiration for Russia's leader Vladimir Putin; getting himself into a mighty tangle over what sort of relationship he had with the former KGB chief.

Indeed, soon after coming to office, when interviewed about his admiration for the Russian leader, he seemed to argue that whatever the excesses of President Putin, America was no better. It was an interview that horrified senior Republicans, as the new president was seemingly advancing a doctrine of American unexceptionalism. A parade of senior senators were quick to point out that the US did not imprison and poison opponents.

Donald Trump, in his key foreign policy speech before the election, made great play of the fact that everything about his approach would put America first. 'My foreign policy will always put the interests of the American people, and American security, above all else. That will be the foundation of every decision that I will make. America First will be the major and overriding theme of my administration.'

The phrase 'America First' may sound innocuous enough. Indeed, it would be somewhat strange for any politician seeking elected office to stand on the platform of, say, 'America Last'. But America First has a provenance, and does not reflect the most glorious moment in American history. It was the name of the organisation which campaigned for America to stay out of the Second World War, even if Britain was on the brink of defeat. It was isolationist, broadly anti-Semitic and defeatist – it wanted the US to cosy up to Adolf Hitler and do deals with him.

Charles Lindbergh was an all-American hero. A man who shot to fame in 1927 as a 25-year-old who made the longest ever solo flight, taking off from Long Island, New York, and landing at Le Bourget, Paris. In the 1930s he would become the principal spokesman and the top-of-the-bill draw at the organisation's rallies.

He would make an infamous speech in Des Moines, Iowa, in which he initially attacked President Roosevelt for 'manufacturing' incidents to draw the US into the war, but then claimed: 'The British and the Jewish races for reasons which are not American wish to involve us in the war.' And then went into classic Zionist conspiracy-theory territory when talking about the Jews: 'Their greatest danger to this country lies in their large influence and ownership and influence in our motion pictures, our press, our radio and our government.'

Interesting that Donald Trump would choose to align himself to an historical movement that is widely seen as an appeaser of Nazism, isolationist and firmly anti-Semitic. When those charges were laid at Donald Trump's feet he emphatically denied being in any way anti-Semitic. But those who had never reconciled themselves to a black president (of whom there were still many), who want America to retreat into itself, who are sick of the US having to act as the world's policeman, who want to ban all Muslims from entering, they would have been more interested in what Donald Trump said, rather than what he would subsequently deny.

It elicited from Vice President Joe Biden a forceful counter-blast. Yes, he deployed the standard attack lines about Donald Trump: he was temperamentally unsuited to be commander in chief, and no presidential candidate had been so ill-informed about the challenges that America faced. But he said something else. He said a lot of what Donald Trump said was un-American.

The word un-American is another blast from the past. Seeking to define who is a patriot and who isn't has been a constant feature of the US political landscape. But it took on epic and grotesque proportions in 1938 when the House

Un-American Activities Committee was established. Although it was set up just before the Second World War, HUAC really came to the fore in the suspicious post-war, Cold War environment when relations between the USA and the Soviet Union were frosty and dangerous.

The committee was chaired by a Wisconsin senator, Joseph McCarthy, and it was a period when paranoia about commies, fellow travellers, reds-under-the-beds and anarchists was rife. Witnesses before the committee were treated harshly. If they wouldn't give lists of names of like-minded people they were accused of being 'reds'. If you were active in a trade union, you were likely to be vilified. Any number of Hollywood producers and writers were hauled to Washington to be questioned about their political views. A climate of fear and intolerance prevailed. Thousands of people were brought before the committee and accused of either being a communist or a communist sympathiser.

This was drift-net fishing, with no care taken over who was caught, and whose lives were destroyed in the process. Evidence was scant, natural justice dispensed with by a committee whose instincts were demagogic and authoritarian. And McCarthy would soon have an 'ism' added to the end of his name. McCarthyism today is synonymous with the making of wild, unsubstantiated accusations to attack the character or patriotism of those who are your political opponents. Was it accidental that Joe Biden would call Mr Trump un-American?

Barack Obama had tried to define patriotism in one way; Donald Trump was re-fashioning it. But although Donald Trump was proclaiming America First, he is no ideological purist. He sees his flexibility of beliefs, and how quickly he can change his mind, as a positive strength. This was spectacularly evident when it came to his dealings with Syria. He had berated his predecessor for getting involved in the Syrian conflict. It was nothing to do with US interests. Stay out of it. Steer clear. But on 4 April, the Syrian leader, Bashar al-Assad, ordered his air force to drop chemical weapons on a town held by rebels. The scenes from Khan Sheikhoun were deeply distressing. In a moment, the president changed his mind. On 5 April in the Rose Garden of the White House, the president condemned the attack. On the 6th I had flown down to Donald Trump's exclusive country club, Mar-a-Lago, in Florida ahead of the president's eagerly anticipated meeting with the Chinese leader. By the time we had landed, it had become clear from my sources that not only was US military action being considered, it was going to happen very quickly indeed. On that night's *News at Ten* I stuck my neck out and said I wouldn't be surprised if people woke up the next morning to hear that US strikes had taken place. They had and they did. That evening, Mr Trump was having dinner with President Xi Jinping when he was informed that the Tomahawk cruise missile strike was underway. He would later recount the drama of this episode in an interview with Fox. 'We had finished dinner, we were now having dessert and we had the most beautiful piece of chocolate cake you have ever seen. President Xi was enjoying it … so what happens is I said, "We have just launched 59 missiles, heading to Iraq."'

Close, but no cigar. Seems the chocolate cake was more memorable than the final destination of the Tomahawks. But what this episode demonstrates is that yes, 'America First' may be the ideological leitmotif, but with Donald Trump everything is up for grabs.

American displays of economic patriotism also demonstrate fundamental differences to the UK. This was brought home to me during the United Nations General Assembly in New York in 2015. This is the annual get-together of global leaders, when the world's ruling class converges on the city, and when traffic comes to a halt as motorcade after motorcade takes over the streets, with flags fluttering on car bonnets, blacked-out windows in black SUVs – and police escorts everywhere. The president and his massive entourage had traditionally stayed at the Waldorf Astoria on Park Avenue in the heart of New York (now closed indefinitely for refurbishment).

In fact not just Obama. Every president going back to the 31st president of the United States, Herbert Hoover at the end of the 1920s, had stayed there when in New York. When President Roosevelt used to visit, he would arrive via a secret train station underneath the hotel, which is now no longer operational.

This change of address was not born of unhappiness with the quality of the bed turndown service at this venerable institution or the chocolates put on the pillow, but the fact that the Hilton Hotel group had sold this most famous piece of New York real estate to the Chinese. The official line from senior officials was that the decision had been taken 'due to costs and space needs of the US government as well as security concerns'. Those security concerns were a potential cyber threat. So the White House decided it would up sticks and move to the New York Palace hotel instead. Flash five-star New York hotels don't qualify as essential infrastructure, but much else does.

So although America professes itself to be an absolute believer in free trade, there is much of America that is out of bounds to foreign investors for reasons of national security.

You can understand that America might not want to sell its ports to foreign owners. But the following saga is solely about their management. A company called DP World wanted to take over the management of some of the nation's busiest ports – in Miami, New York, Newark and Baltimore. DP World is a state-owned Dubai company, headed by the Gulf emirate's ruler, Sheikh Mohammed bin Rashid Al Maktoum. And relations between the United Arab Emirates and the United States could not be warmer. President Bush wanted to give the deal his blessing. But in a rare bipartisan move, Congress did everything to scupper the deal on grounds that the ports were vital economic infrastructure whose sale could jeopardise the state.

Really? Foreign companies have long dominated the business of loading and unloading container ships. There aren't that many American companies doing this. There are failures of security at America's ports from time to time, but is that down to the nationality of the port manager? The collapse of the deal in 2006 was the second time in a year that a major foreign acquisition had aroused protests about the economic security of the United States. Forget closing deals with foreigners, the only auction that was taking place was between Republicans and Democrats – over who could appear to be more patriotic by being the greatest protector of American security.

In Britain the government would come to an agreement with Chinese investors to put up 30 per cent of the finance for an £18 billion nuclear power station that would be built by a French company. Could a Hinkley Point-type investment have ever happened in the United States? Not a cat's chance.

In Washington these decisions were viewed with utter bewilderment.

When Britain became the first major Western power to back the Asian Infrastructure Investment Bank that was set up by the Chinese as a sort of Asian rival to the World Bank, bewilderment gave way to downright anger. Given that public scoldings by the US administration are normally reserved for enemies, not your closest ally, it was extraordinary that a White House official should be quoted as saying that it is 'worried about a trend of constant accommodation' of China by the UK.

The official White House line was slightly more emollient: 'This is the UK's sovereign decision. We hope and expect that the UK will use its voice to push for adoption of high standards.' When I would later ask a senior aide to the president about this spat, I was given one of the best lines I have ever heard. 'Oh that,' he shrugged, 'it was nothing much, just a bit of stray voltage.' Like being tasered ...

Or take concern over telecoms. Travel along a street in a British city where there are roadworks underway (I know, quite a lot to choose from), and there's a fair chance you will see a sign saying, 'Huawei apologises for any inconvenience caused.' The Chinese-owned telecoms behemoth, with its anonymous-looking headquarters on the outskirts of Banbury in Oxfordshire, is busy laying cables and, with its extensive infrastructure, is well on its way to becoming the world's biggest telecoms company. It's been operating in the UK for about a decade.

That's not the case in America. In 2012 the government claimed that Huawei could be a risk to national security. The worry was that it could build 'back doors' into their equipment in the US that could compromise government information and the intellectual property of private companies. Huawei say this is nonsense and insist the only loser in this is the US consumer. Guo Ping, the company's chief executive officer, said, 'The American friends need to pay a higher price to purchase less competitive services. If the US needs Huawei to do something, we will be happy to do it, and if the US do not welcome it then we can wait.'

It's a good thing the Chinese are known for their patience – because in the current climate of American patriotism, it's hard to see which member of the Senate will be leading the calls to open the telecoms market to the Chinese. But where is the line between being protective and being protectionist?

Keeping key foreign companies out of America is one thing; attracting the best and most talented foreigners is something different. America's wealth has been built by those who came to live in the US. Consider this: 40 per cent of America's 'Fortune 500' companies were founded by immigrants who came to settle in the United States. Look at the massive success of the tech companies in Palo Alto in California and the crucial role played by software engineers and entrepreneurs from around the world. The secret of American success has been its recognition of the importance of importing talent. American companies are like English Premier League teams – they want the best, brightest most promising players from around the world. They don't care where they come from so long as their presence helps them win. Except that America today seems to want to show immigrants the door, not open it to them.

CHAPTER 4

Government

This is the parable of the pavement and the street. And the setting for this story is January 2016. Washington has just been blanketed in snow. And I'm not talking about one or two inches. We are talking three feet. It has invited headlines like 'the snowpocalypse' and 'snowmageddon', and the city authorities have declared a state of emergency. All public transport has been shut down, and people are told not to go out under any circumstances. The streets are empty and deserted. All the shops are shut.

In the days leading up to the storm – a storm which the weather forecasters have charted and followed with spectacular accuracy, and inexhaustible fascination and enthusiasm – supermarkets which normally bulge with plenty, almost obscenely at times, in the world's richest nation, take on the appearance of a Soviet department store after a particularly busy Saturday.

There is nothing to be had. The shelves are stripped bare. People have filled trollies to overflowing – there is no fresh fruit or bread. The meat counter has been stripped to the bone, so to speak. We shopped as though the end of the world was nigh.

And then we waited. The temperature started to drop on Friday and by lunchtime there was the odd flurry, and then as the day wore on the snow got heavier. And heavier. And it snowed relentlessly until late on Saturday night, by which time we were up to our thighs in snow. And on Sunday morning what is the sound we all woke to? Scraping.

Soon we were all out with our shovels and picks, brooms and salt, digging out and clearing the sidewalk, sorry, pavement. It is what you do. There is no waiting for the council to come along; everyone has an individual responsibility. So I am responsible for clearing the length of pavement where my house begins and ends. This is a legal responsibility, I should add. If anyone slips and breaks something outside my house, I am the one who gets sued, not the council. If your neighbour is elderly or disabled, you dig out their path too. By late Sunday morning, despite record-breaking snowfall, you can walk unhindered along the length of our street. The hospitals' emergency rooms are not overflowing with elderly people who have slipped and broken ankles and wrists and hips, because the paths have been cleared. Or people have heeded the warnings, and not ventured out.

And once the pavements were snow-free people set about digging out each other's cars that had been left on the street. In fairness not that many had. Some of us had received emails from the local underground car park on Wisconsin Avenue – which were then circulated to everyone else – that for $1 we could park our cars for the weekend in their commercial car park because of the storm.

On the Saturday night the family who live five doors down invited everyone on the block to an impromptu dinner. There was a log fire, a ton of food – and an extraordinary sense of goodwill. This was community and American self-reliance at its best. Where my house is in London, no one would dream of digging out the pavements. That is what we pay our taxes to the local council for. Not in the US.

My only other foreign correspondent job was as the BBC's Paris correspondent (I only do the hardship postings …), and we lived in the most bourgeois arrondissement of Paris, the snooty 16th. It is elegant, affluent and recherché. But walking along the elegant boulevards do your eyes look up to the beautiful Haussmann *belle époque* buildings? No, they are fixed firmly to the ground, because you have to navigate your way round the dog poop which is *partout*. People in France love their little frou-frou dogs, but you can't expect Parisians to bend over and pick up. There are special council vehicles that drive up and down the pavements with rotating brushes, whose job it is to clear the sidewalks of litter and what the dogs (and in fairness their owners) have left behind. And each day the gutters would be flushed out to clear away the litter. I always laughed when I saw signs on lampposts, put up by the council, saying, '*J'aime mon quartier, je ramasse.*' It has a picture of a man walking a dog, with a little bag in his hand. In other words, I like where I live. I pick up. The sign should have more honestly read '*J'aime mon quartier mais je ne ramasse pas*' – or I like where I live, but I DON'T pick up.

Since I have been living in Washington I have not seen a single council employee coming along the road where we live – or any other road for that matter – to sweep or wash the pavements. And I have never lived anywhere where there is so little litter. There are no discarded crisp wrappers, people don't walk down the street drinking tins of beer, there are rubbish bins (I stopped myself from writing 'trash cans' ...) and – weirdly – people use them to dispose of their trash.

And our neighbours are fantastic. They are friendly, helpful and organised. As America started to grapple with the unpleasantness of the Zika virus, one contacted everyone about collectively getting our gardens sprayed to eliminate the risk. Washington is built on a swamp (who thought that was a good idea?) and mosquitoes are a big problem in the steamy hot summers that you have to endure here. Maybe the president will develop a policy to drain the actual swamp ...

This is exactly what is right with America. Why have the council do things that you are perfectly capable of doing yourself? It speaks of self-reliance, of duty, of responsibility, of community, of respect.

And then you come to the roads, which tells you much of what is wrong with America. After the snow fell it was days before the road was 'ploughed', and because so much snow fell, and the winters are so cold, it was weeks and weeks before they were completely clear. And of course what was left once everything had gone was a potholed mess. Because no one likes to pay taxes, there is precious little budget for repairing the roads.

When we lived in Paris I met Aaron. He is a very close friend and is a fantastically hard-working American who has spent most of his career in the pharmaceuticals industry. In some ways he embodies the American dream. He grew up in modest surroundings in Niagara in upstate New York, where a lot of the people he knew ended up in gangs and in trouble with the police. He worked hard and is now the CEO of a big privately owned company with its US headquarters in New Jersey, and he lives in the trendy district called Hoboken. It is a commuter town for New York, just a ten-minute ferry ride across the Hudson into Midtown Manhattan. After a particularly good year for his company, and being a bit of a petrol head, he bought himself something he had always wanted. A fabulous Ferrari.

So it was inevitable that when I went to see him we would go out for a spin. Except forget vertiginous acceleration and massive g-force going into the bends – on the streets around Hoboken you wouldn't dare move out of first gear. That would do untold damage to a low-slung supercar along these cratered and potholed roads.

It is hard to exaggerate the dilapidated state of so much American infrastructure. Roads are crumbling, bridges are regularly closed for emergency maintenance, airports are in a terrible state. Just for a minute let's go back to the comparison I made earlier between France and the US. France has the most superb road network you could possibly imagine, and the TGVs move effortlessly (obviously with the exception of when their staff are on strike, and that is not a rarity) on the high-speed rail lines that criss-cross the country and connect the key centres of commerce. But it comes with a tax bill that no American would ever countenance.

Take the example of the Anderson Memorial Bridge that crosses the Charles River in Boston, Massachusetts. It was built in 1912, and construction took precisely 11 months. In mid 2016 it was about to close for repairs because it was so structurally unsound – and the estimate for how long the repairs will take? Five years, and many millions of dollars.

The bridge is next to the office of Lawrence Summers, the former US Treasury secretary. Summers served in the Clinton administration, so is no Tea Party liberal who believes that government spending should be slashed. But he describes a situation where the contractor, the environment agencies, the different advocacy groups, the state transportation department all believe they have a vested interest in how the bridge refurbishment should be handled. Each has a good case, but the combination of them all sticking their oar in just means interminable delay, a massive escalation of costs – and fury among the people in Boston who will have to wait so long to have their bridge repaired. 'I'm a progressive,' he declares, 'but it seems plausible to wonder if government can build a nation abroad, fight social decay, run schools, mandate the design of cars, run health insurance exchanges or set proper sexual harassment policies on college campuses, if it cannot even fix a 232-foot bridge competently.' Doubts about government efficacity are pervasive.

That is from someone who believes in government, has worked in government and advocates government solutions. You don't need to stray far from him to find altogether more caustic views.

For over 50 years the Pew Research Center has been polling public attitudes towards government. When the polling started in 1958, about 75 per cent of Americans trusted the federal government to do the right thing always or most of the time. If you look at the numbers today – they are down to 19 per cent. That is a profound deterioration.

The decline dates back to America's involvement in Vietnam. That carried on into the 1970s as the US military engagement in Southeast Asia became a quagmire, and America was rocked by the Watergate scandal and a deteriorating economy. Confidence picks up in the 1980s and stays that way for a sustained period as America goes through a long stretch of economic growth. It really takes a leap after the attacks on 9/11 – probably a patriotic response to the shocking events that convulsed the nation – but declines pretty steeply after that. And confidence continues to slide through the rest of the Bush era into the Obama administration

How this translates politically is that Democrat-leaning voters tend, overall, to take a slightly more favourable view of government – and that remains pretty constant irrespective of whether it's a Democrat or Republican in the White House. Republicans are more predisposed to think favourably of Washington if their guy is running the country, but are overall more suspicious of government.

There are other striking differences in attitude – both Republicans and Democrats think that it is the government's job to create a basic safety net for the elderly, but when it comes to helping young families out of poverty, Republican support winnows considerably.

And what you get from government depends heavily on where you live. If you live in Britain, you are not going to be moving home because of a much more beneficial tax regime in one part of the country compared to another. Income tax is the same throughout the UK, and although the Scottish government has tax-varying powers, they have not been used. And what local councils can raise in terms of local taxation is strictly prescribed by central government. In the US, taxes can vary considerably from one state to another.

One of my colleagues at work grew up in Valdez, Alaska. It is an isolated place that has long, brutal winters with precious little daylight. In summer it is a little piece of paradise on earth. Her parents, who grew up in Georgia – over 4,000 miles away – were teachers. They moved there not just because it was beautiful, but because you pay no local income tax. None. And there are six other states like that in the US – Florida, Nevada, South Dakota, Texas, Washington and Wyoming. Those states would argue that this is the way to become a beacon for growth. You're better at creating jobs and keeping a core of motivated, well-educated young people from upping sticks and moving to another state. The argument against, though, is that the governor is still going to have to balance a budget, and to do that you're going to have to increase the burden of indirect taxation, which will hit the poor disproportionately harder. In other words it is a regressive system of taxation.

The governor of Louisiana, Bobby Jindal – who had a brief tilt at winning the Republican nomination for the presidency before flaring out – wants to scrap income tax in his state. 'We need to do more to stay competitive,' he says. 'States with no income taxes are outperforming other states in terms of economic growth and population growth.'

But of course there are consequences. If you have a no-taxing, low-spending state you will end up with more money in your pocket to spend how you wish, but you might not have the facilities. Going back to my mate Aaron – you might have one of the fastest cars in the world, but you won't have the roads you can drive it on.

You have the richest country in the world with an infrastructure that is now looking decidedly Third World. The Center on Budget and Policy Priorities warned at the beginning of 2016 that state and local spending on infrastructure – that's schools and wastewater treatment plants, as well as highways and bridges – was at a 30-year low. Total capital spending as a share of state GDP had fallen in all but five states. A 2013 report by the American Society of Civil Engineers provided a shopping list of what needed doing to modernise the infrastructure of America, and came up with a bill of more than $3.4 trillion. That's serious money.

This all stems from fundamental differences over what Americans see as the role of the state. The best quote on this still comes from Ronald Reagan, who said, 'The most terrifying words in the English language are: "I am from the government and I am here to help."'

Americans fundamentally mistrust what government is, what it does, and how it spends your tax dollar. The very name of Washington – this beautifully laid-out, elegant city, where no building stands taller than the Capitol, where the Mall, which reaches from Congress down to the Washington Monument, is lined with the most stunning collection of museums that you will find anywhere in the world, where the property at 1600 Pennsylvania Avenue is among the most famous in the world – is for an awful lot of Americans a swear word. Washington for them is what is wrong with America. As I said earlier, it is literally built on a swamp. For a lot of Americans it is *the* swamp. A city of corrupt, self-serving politicians and lobbyists who long ago lost the ability to distinguish between what was the national interest and what was in *their* interests. A city that knows nothing of the concerns of ordinary Americans and the lives they lead.

To understand the point, delete the word Washington and insert the word Brussels. The feelings of antipathy that so many Britons feel towards the machinery of the European

Union is what many Americans think about their own federal government: unaccountable, bloated, corrupt, incompetent, self-serving. The views you hear expressed as you travel round the US are strikingly consistent.

But hating the government, its machinery and its elected representatives, who seem to love creating logjams more than they do passing legislation, is not the whole story. Attitudes are complex. Ask people if they want less government and they will reply, 'Hell, yes.' But ask them what they think government should do and they will come up with quite a shopping list.

Clearly the first duty of government is to keep its citizens safe – so it's agreed that America needs to have armed forces and an intelligence agency that will prevent acts of terror from taking place. Because the country is at the mercy of so much extreme weather, people support the need for Washington to be able to respond quickly to natural disasters. They want the government to ensure food safety and medicines; they accept it's the federal government's job to manage immigration, and to maintain infrastructure and to protect the environment.

Oh, and they accept it's the government's job to strengthen the economy, provide education, ensure retirement income, maintain safety standards at work, have some kind of healthcare system for the most needy and do something to alleviate poverty. The polling data shows these are all areas in which a majority of Americans think the government should have a 'major role'. So while Americans might like the rhetoric of small government, they nevertheless want the tentacles of the state to reach far and wide.

The comparative data is interesting too because of what it reveals about the 'value gap' between the US and Western

Europe. The Pew Research Center asked this question: which is more important, freedom to pursue life's goals without state interference OR state guarantees ensuring nobody is in need? The responses were sharply contrasting: 58 per cent of Americans think it is more important for the state to just let people get on with their lives; in Britain, Germany, France and Spain, it's just over a third. Only a third of Americans think it's important for the state to guarantee that no one is in need, compared to roughly two-thirds in the Western European countries.

There is also an interesting existential question buried in this Aladdin's cave of data. Is success in life determined by forces outside our control? In Western Europe far more people think that to be the case than in the US. In other words, if you live in America it is up to you to shape your own destiny, not the state.

These views find voice in one of the burgeoning political movements in the US, the Libertarians, whose manifesto can be broadly summed up in four words – maximum freedom, minimum government. There has always been a strong streak of libertarianism in US politics, but the movement was given a mighty fillip – particularly among young people – when Edward Snowden shared his treasure trove of stolen state surveillance goodies with the world. What is astonishing, in some ways, is that people were astonished. After all, 'spy agency spies' is not much of a headline – it's like 'bus driver drives bus' – but the scale of what the National Security Agency seemed to be doing caught many Americans by surprise. It seemed that technological developments meant it had become the easiest thing in the world to spy on just about everyone and anyone – and there seemed to be no limits to what the state could do or would do. And checks and balances were scant in the extreme.

For Libertarians, who had been on the margins of US politics with rather dusty, dry debates about the role of the nation state, their moment had come. Privacy was under assault by a state harvesting personal information without regard, and it was time to fight back. Combine that with a sense of weariness among Americans about the protracted foreign commitments in Afghanistan and Iraq, and this fringe political concern was becoming much more mainstream.

The party would cut back the money spent on national security, and would repeal drug laws so that it was a matter of personal responsibility – likewise the wearing of seat belts or crash helmets. The state wouldn't tell you what to do.

America doesn't lack for shootings, but one of the more bizarre was the killing by the FBI at the beginning of 2016 of LaVoy Finicum in a remote part of Oregon on the West Coast, after a protracted protest that seemed to belong to a different age. He and his band of men, the Citizens for Constitutional Freedom – they also called themselves leaders of the Oregon Freedom Revolution – had taken over a federal wildlife reserve in a wilderness called Malheur. To the authorities, they were nothing more than an armed militia who had to accept the rule of law. To their supporters, they were heroic figures from a bygone Wild West era, seeking to ride their horses and drive their cattle wherever they saw fit, refusing to accept that the federal government could put limits on their right to roam. It was the small guys standing up to an over-mighty state. And it also played to that most romantic of American narratives – the lonesome cowboys travelling the vast plains and prairies in America's great outdoors. If the land they wanted for their cattle was wilderness, how could 'the state' tell them otherwise?

This was rugged, gun-toting libertarianism which came to a deadly end, as the patience of the authorities ran out with this slightly eccentric but well-armed band. The shootout conferred virtual martyrdom to the leader of the gang among his supporters. Today there are exceptionally few Americans living their lives on the back of a horse, lassoing stray animals, spurs on their heels and cowboy hat on their heads, lighting a campfire under the stars and playing a lament on a mouth organ – but it is an essential part of American identity. Just as in France they romanticise the small farmer, working the land, the bucolic Jean de Florette figure living off the *terroir*.

In America the ideas around libertarianism are going through a resurgence in a country where the political centre of gravity is in a very different place than in the UK – and it is instructive to realise how many Americans view Britain as an over-centralised, stifling bureaucratic quagmire.

I chaired a conference recently where one of the speakers was a professor in drone technology. Most of what she said went straight over my head (sorry, that was irresistible). She was from Duke University, and was discussing the application of drone technology and doing a bit of futurology – how long before we had drone flights landing at Heathrow Airport and the like. She was bemoaning the restrictive regulatory environment in the US that has hindered the development of the market. And then she said something that I understood, but which startled me. 'It comes to something,' she opined, 'when even a socialist country like Britain has better regulations than the US.'

Sorry, I wanted to say. Are you kidding me? Britain a socialist country? I should add that David Cameron was prime minister at the time, and the howls of protest emanating from Britain then were about the austerity programme as the government sought to tackle the deficit. But the BBC-fitted microchip kicked in, and the neutrality of the chair just about held firm. I said nothing.

But that is how many in the United States view the UK. A quasi-socialist country where people are overtaxed and overburdened by regulation, where too many people wait for the state to do things that should be the responsibility of the individual. Walking our dog one day I met a woman who has a company in the US with a smaller office in Marylebone in London. And she couldn't stop herself from berating me about how much more difficult it was to get things done in Britain compared to the US. Too much red tape, difficult to find good workers, exorbitant office costs etc., etc. (In fact for red tape it's hard to beat the US when it comes to the rules concerning your dog: where you can take it, when and where they can go off the lead – you can't take your dog on Amtrak trains or buses, unless they are 'service dogs'. In the UK everyone is familiar with the wonderful guide dogs, which of course you have in the US too – but the service dog is something else. You go to your doctor, you get a letter saying your pooch is an 'emotional support' animal, it gets given a red coat as a service dog and, hey presto, you can take it into restaurants with you and on trains and buses – please excuse that small vent.)

And in these over-simplifications there are elements of truth. In Britain something bad happens and the cry goes up, 'What is the government going to do about it?' In the

United States it is much more likely to be 'What has this got to do with the government?'

There is also a tendency in the UK for people to equate government spending with outcomes, which are two totally different things. One of the huge differences between the US and the UK is the importance of non-state actors in America. For example, in Britain it became a huge thing for the coalition government in 2010 to be able to announce that it was spending 0.7 per cent of gross national income on foreign aid. This was the target set by the United Nations for donor countries all the way back in 1970, and it was something that had been an aspiration of many governments – one of those aspirations you have, but know that you are never going to achieve.

However, for a mix of reasons this now became a priority. For a Conservative Party that wanted to broaden the base of its support, this was a way of showing its more 'caring' credentials. It would be a popular measure internationally, and would please the Liberal Democrat half of the coalition. Years later the government would pass legislation committing the UK to maintaining that notional 0.7 per cent target. The UK's International Development secretary at the time, Justine Greening, said, 'Britain is the first major economy to meet the UN's target on aid spending and I am proud that parliament has now passed this bill, which cements Britain's global leadership in creating a world that is healthier, more stable and increasingly prosperous.'

Now leave to one side the question of the randomness of 0.7 per cent as a target (why not 0.6 per cent or 0.8 per cent?), and even the more important question of the difference between spending and spending wisely. In 2014 there was surely the madness that in the space of two months the UK rushed through £1 billion into foreign aid projects – only because had it not done so it would have fallen short of the 0.7 per cent target, worthy though that goal might be. It seemed more important to hit the totemic target than it did to know where the money was being allocated. There were a lot of people in the UK government and working for NGOs who wanted to paint Britain as a beacon, and the US as laggards. So, for example, Oxfam points out that Americans spend more on sweets, lawn care and soft drinks than the US government spends on 'poverty-reducing foreign assistance'. That is one of those statistics that is simultaneously arresting and meaningless. They also say that in a league table of industrialised nations, America comes 19th in terms of relative spending on aid.

And that is equally meaningless. Yes, America as a federal government spends less on aid than the UK, but going back to where this chapter started, Americans don't just look to government-led solutions – whether it be in clearing the pavement outside your house of snow or helping those most in need in the Third World. This gets to the heart of the difference in attitudes between how the role of government is seen on both sides of the Atlantic

Philanthropy plays a completely different role in American society than it does possibly anywhere else in the world. And it has a history going right the way back to before the founding of the nation, when voluntary organisations came to the fore to improve the 'common wealth' – or the public good of citizens. States like Pennsylvania, Virginia and Massachusetts styled themselves as 'commonwealths'. Hospitals, schools and public libraries were founded by benefactors worried about the number of widows and orphans who had no means to look after themselves following the revolutionary wars. As the industrial revolution took hold and people lived in appalling conditions, the philanthropists saw that they had a gap to fill where industry and government fell short. Education, sanitation and housing would now be the priority.

If you're in London and you love art you will go to the National Gallery, the National Portrait Gallery, Tate Modern or Tate Britain – all bodies that are heavily dependent on the Department of Culture, Media and Sport for their funding. If you're in New York you will go to the Guggenheim, the Whitney, the Frick; in Philadelphia you will go to the Barnes. In LA you will go to the spectacular Getty.

And the names rattle down the ages of the foundations whose work has been vital for the development of the arts, for education and for international understanding. And yes, foreign aid too. Rockefeller, Getty, Carnegie, Ford, Kellogg, Lilly, Howard Hughes: all of them hugely wealthy individuals, but all of them leaving a lasting legacy as a result of their philanthropy. And that work carries on today.

I have heard many people in Europe argue that something as vital as foreign aid – and whether a child in Africa gets fed – shouldn't depend on the whim and largesse of a few plutocrats. But does it matter who the provider is? Isn't the only thing that matters is that the child does get food in its stomach? Also why is government – or indeed a multinational body – thought to be better at delivering aid than the private sector? The United Nations is a wonderful body, but even its greatest admirers would not be able to say with a straight face that it is the most streamlined organisation in the world in its delivery of service. And governments are not only subject to budgetary pressures that might make them chop and change their funding, they are subject to political pressures on what causes to support and why. In the world of politics aid too often gets caught up in trade and all manner of other confusing variables.

Not that long ago I interviewed the Microsoft founder, Bill Gates, on the foundation he runs with his wife, Melinda. Thanks to the fortune that he has made, and to his persuasive powers of bringing other similarly wealthy individuals on board, it is now the largest private foundation in the world. It has an endowment of something like $45 billion. That is serious money. Its reach, its ambition, its laser-like focus on delivering and measuring are nothing short of extraordinary. Just listening to him describe how they are setting about the goal of eradicating polio from the planet is both inspiring and, you quickly realise, achievable. The only discombobulating thing is to hear him describe how they go about their work. There is nothing woolly or 'do-goody' about it. He has brought the practices of running a successful corporation into the field of foreign aid – it is all targets, deliverables and measurables – in fact some from a traditional aid background might find his MBA business-school language jarring, but who cares what he sounds like? Judge him and people like him by what they get done.

However, don't come away with the impression that the US government plays no role in this – charitable giving and the voluntary sector are much more highly developed than they are in Europe, so what the state does is give generous tax breaks to encourage giving. Go to any fundraiser in the US (and there are an awful lot of fundraisers for any number of worthy causes) and after you've written out your cheque, or handed over your credit card number, you will get a certificate in the post that is for you to include with your tax return to the IRS. That way you get relief on the charitable donations you have made over the course of a year.

But it is right that there is debate over what is a core activity for the state, and what is best done either by relying on benefactors, or by the individual taking responsibility for his or her own needs. So, for example, take the Olympic Games. When London bid for the 2012 Games the first key steps were to get financial backing for the bid from the government and from the London mayor's office. And remember how integral figures like Prime Minister Tony Blair, the Culture Secretary Tessa Jowell and the London mayor, Ken Livingstone, were to that bid. Now go onto the US Olympic Committee website, and you will read this on the front page: 'The United States Olympic Committee is a 501(c)(3) not-for-profit corporation supported by American individuals and corporate sponsors. Unlike most other nations, the USOC does not receive direct government funding for Olympic programs (except for select Paralympic military programs).'

That debate over what is the role of the state is played out in spades over the issue of healthcare. On the Republican right they look at the National Health Service in the UK not as a source of envy, but as what happens when the state becomes too mighty. Socialised medicine (as they refer to the British system) is anathema to many Americans. And when there was a junior doctors' strike in the UK, people were aghast that front-line health workers would down stethoscopes and walk out. In the US you might get held up because a bridge has fallen down or there's been a serious outage at an air-traffic control centre (coming back from Cuba, I had to spend an extra 24 hours in Tampa, Florida, because of that), or there's been a points failure on the railways – but you are rarely inconvenienced by workers going on strike.

With that in mind, you can understand why Obamacare, or the Affordable Care Act, has been so fiercely resisted in the US. Some of it has been opposed on very legitimate practical grounds – for many people who had existing cover before Obamacare was introduced, their costs have gone up and their cover has worsened – and it is immensely complicated bureaucratically. There is also no doubt that the best American healthcare is way, way better than you might get in the UK – the hospitals have some of the best and most innovative surgeons, the equipment is second to none, and there is much wider availability of drugs than would be allowed in the NHS.

Interestingly, when you talk to people about their jobs and career choices, you find that one of the primary considerations will be what the health insurance arrangements are. An American working for a British multinational who had been very senior in the company was anxious to avoid being forced to take early retirement. When a British colleague pointed out that he must have a tidy sum of money stashed away, he said he needed to work for the health insurance. A Florida urologist who had been in private practice for nearly all his career suddenly changed track and went to work in a Veterans Association hospital. His British relatives, bewildered at this change of career, asked him what had prompted this change. Because, he explained, if you work for a federal health provider for five years, you will get free healthcare for the rest of your life. If your policy doesn't cover you for some expensive treatment, you can be bank-rupted very quickly. Even very wealthy people. These are not concerns that people have in the UK.

But there are millions still without insurance, and for them healthcare is second class. Many seeking routine care will clog Emergency Rooms with trivial complaints because they don't have the insurance to go to a GP. And it goes without saying that the poorer and less educated you are the more likely it is that you will die young.

Some of the opposition to Obamacare, though, has been rooted in ideological concerns. Look at the anti-government/libertarian websites, and there you will find any number of extraordinary reasons given why socialised medicine is bad. These examples are taken from the Foundation for Economic Education – not, I would guess, the most middle-of-the-road organisation that you will find.

Here's one: 'If you ask the government to force others (through taxes) to help you in your particular [medical] situation, you cannot expect others not to ask government to force you to help them.' Or this: 'Since the programme [an NHS-style system] would be designed to help millions of others, competition for supplies and services, in addition to raising costs, might make it difficult to obtain any at all.' And then my favourite: 'The temptation to get something for nothing would prove irresistible for many people.' And then the kicker: 'Socialized medicine would be another long step to total socialism.' I like that it is not just socialism, but *total* socialism.

The logic is fascinating. It is all based on the idea that there is no social contract between the citizen and the state, that there is no such thing as society, just individuals whose sole job is to look after themselves. And that if anything is ever organised collectively for 'the common wealth' it will be worse than doing things for yourself. It is the minimalist view of what the state does. Under this logic, presumably, we would only pay taxes towards schools if we had children. And the other fundamental argument is that if the state takes charge of something like health provision, then the bureaucratic leviathan that will go with it will drive costs upwards and care down. The case though for universal healthcare to be included in what Americans view as 'core activities' of the state is an argument that is not won, and is likely to rumble on for many more decades to come. Not least because to move to something like that is going to mean facing down the American Medical Association, which remains implacably opposed to the introduction of socialised medicine – just as the British Medical Association did before the NHS was created in 1948.

But here's the thing. No country on earth spends nearly as much per capita on healthcare as the United States – but the US has worse outcomes when it comes to obesity, child mortality and other chronic conditions. A report in 2013 by the Commonwealth Fund found that health spending in the US relative to GDP is about 50 per cent higher than any of the other advanced economies. And it found that US spending on government-sponsored healthcare was also significantly higher per capita than in the other countries, 'despite being the only country in the study without universal health coverage'.

Whatever other things you might accuse Donald Trump of, ideological rigidity is not one of them. As befitting someone who has dished out money to Republicans and Democrats alike, and dissed Republicans and Democrats alike, he is not overly weighed down by philosophical baggage. And over health provision, there were times when he sounded way to the left of President Obama. Look at this interview he gave to CBS television and its anchor, Scott Pelley, about health provision in September 2015.

TRUMP: Everybody's got to be covered. This is an un-Republican thing for me to say because a lot of times they say, 'No, no, the lower 25 per cent that can't afford private.' But –

PELLEY: Universal healthcare.

TRUMP: I am going to take care of everybody. I don't care if it costs me votes or not. Everybody's going to be taken care of much better than they're taken care of now.

PELLEY: The uninsured person is going to be taken care of. How? How?

TRUMP: They're going to be taken care of. I would make a deal with existing hospitals to take care of people. And, you know what, if this is probably –

PELLEY: Make a deal? Who pays for it?

TRUMP: The government's gonna pay for it.

Now that sounds a lot like universal healthcare and rather like socialised medicine. Dare one say it, it sounds rather like a National Health Service. But phrases like 'I would make a deal with …' would suggest that the detail had not been worked out – but as a statement of intent it looks as though on certain things the Republican Party would find

Donald Trump more troubling than the Democrats. There has been a pledge to replace Obamacare, but how to replace it without creating millions of losers is something that the new Trump administration clearly struggled with, particularly as it was simultaneously seeking to advocate smaller government. In the end the Trump administration proposed a revised healthcare plan that, according to the politically neutral Congressional Budget Office, could have seen 24 million Americans losing their health insurance. It sent a shiver down the spines of moderate Republicans who feared the electoral consequences of that, and was rejected by the right-wing Freedom Caucus in Congress, which felt it didn't go far enough in removing the state from the provision of healthcare.

For Donald Trump, who had promised again and again that it would be so easy to fix healthcare, who said that he was a winner and that Americans would get bored of winning under his leadership, and that only *he* had the deal-making acumen to get this done, this was a cartoon, fall-flat-on-your-face humiliation. During the campaign Donald Trump had, it seemed, a coating of perma-tan, and a layer of Teflon. The perma-tan might have covered up the red face (a mix of fury and embarrassment), but there was no mistaking the chips in the non-stick that the Freedom Caucus had delivered.

The Freedom Caucus is the elected political wing of the body that has been most closely associated with 'small government' in the United States: the Tea Party movement – drawing its name from the incident in 1773 when the Sons of Liberty, protesting about the penal levels of tax the British government was putting on tea, threw an entire shipment imported by the East India Company into Boston Harbor. The cry went up – and it still echoes down the ages – that there should be no taxation without representation. The British colonists who would be subject to the Tea Act that had been passed at Westminster said they could not be subject to something they had had no say over. This act of revolt sparked a British government crackdown, and brought the two sides ever closer to war. Three years later would come the American Revolution.

When the modern-day Tea Party movement emerged in 2009, the perception was that it would prove to be a minor annoyance to the Republican Party, but it would be no more than that. It was much, much more than that. It was anti-government spending, in favour of lower taxes, and became a determined opponent of all Barack Obama's reforms. It was instrumental in the government shutdown of 2013, when because no appropriations bill could be agreed, federal agencies ran out of money – and so for two weeks in October of that year, 800,000 federal workers didn't go to work and nothing got done.

Without getting lost in the labyrinthine procedural tussles that were going on – this was, in effect, an effort by Tea Party members of the Senate and the House to starve funding to the Affordable Care Act, through complex mechanisms, votes and procedures. Polling would later show that Americans overwhelmingly disapproved of the government shutdown and felt that it damaged America's reputation abroad. More than half blamed the Republican Party for what had happened. The Tea Party undoubtedly got some of its political calculations wrong – it was largely seen as the villain of the piece. But if it wanted to leave people feeling more disenchanted than ever about Washington and government, it had probably succeeded.

Interestingly for a grouping whose pitch is to eschew big government and be a grassroots movement, winning the support of a lot of libertarians along the way, the Tea Party showed it was pretty adept at the good old-fashioned machine politics of smoky, backroom deals. Establishment Republicans were forced out of office, beaten in the primary races which determine who the party's candidate will be in an election. They seized control of a good many electoral districts, they formed their own mini caucus within Congress, and as a result were a continual thorn in the side of the Republican leadership. Barack Obama and Republican House leaders didn't see eye to eye on much. On their mutual dislike of the Tea Party they could.

For a long time in the primary process it was seen as likely that it would be a Tea Party candidate who might emerge to challenge Hillary Clinton for the presidency. Ted Cruz, who would come a distant second in the primary race, was a darling of the movement, and was far and away the most ideologically focused of the Republican hopefuls. There were many occasions in the run-up to the convention when the Republican leadership was engaged in a 'who do we hate the least?' debate as it faced the choice of Trump or Cruz. And the debate led to a popular joke. Q: Why do people take an instant dislike to Ted Cruz? A: It saves time.

In Donald Trump, it wasn't just health policy where the right-wing purists found themselves at odds with their candidate for president. In what was one of the most rancorous elections in American history, Donald Trump and Hillary Clinton agreed on one thing: they believed in government and spending. The year 2016 will become known for a lot of crazy things, but maybe it will also mark the moment when 'small is beautiful' went out of fashion in the US. Two candidates went into the election believing that spending was part of the answer to America's problems.

Donald Trump is after all first and foremost a builder – hotels, golf courses, condominiums – even vineyards. And as a man who has done business around the world all his life he could see for himself that American infrastructure was in a parlous, precarious state. So he was promising 'to build the next generation of roads, bridges, railways, tunnels, sea ports and airports'. And that takes a mighty big government chequebook.

Hillary Clinton had promised $275 billion in direct spending on infrastructure over five years, plus another $225 billion in loans and loan guarantee programmes. Trump's response to that? 'Her number is a fraction of what we're talking about. We need much more money to rebuild our infrastructure,' he told the Fox Business Network. The man representing the party of limited government went on to say it would require at least double that.

As ever with Donald Trump, detail was scant. But the direction of travel was clear. For six years Barack Obama had tried to persuade conservatives in Congress to support a public works programme, along the lines that Donald Trump was now advocating. Obama believed that investment in the nation's infrastructure would reverse decades of decay, and in the process create millions of jobs.

But that kind of Keynesian intervention is anathema to fiscal conservatives, who are horrified at the idea of massive federal spending. So when Barack Obama tried to pass his stimulus package in the wake of the financial crash, when the banks were teetering, the car industry was going bust and consumer spending had stopped, they fought him every step of the way.

Could it be that government is coming back into fashion?

The times in history when government has been most fashionable have been when the national position has been at its most precarious, and need at its greatest – and actually government at its most creative and inventive. Such a period came with the Great Depression.

The Wall Street Crash of 1929 was as calamitous as it gets. Tuesday, 29 October – Black Tuesday as it would subsequently become known – set off a chain reaction that would plunge America into a deep economic slump. People had started to believe that the stock market was a one-way bet, and the only way was up. So with credit cheap, and banks eager to borrow, millions of investors borrowed massively to pile into stocks and shares. And when the wind started blowing in the opposite direction (a number of companies posted poor results) people panicked, tried to limit their losses and sold at marked-down prices. Prices fell still further. Banks hadn't made proper checks of who they were lending money to, and thousands now defaulted on their loans, meaning the banks themselves went bankrupt.

The president, Herbert Hoover, didn't quite capture the mood of the times with his diagnosis. Unemployment was rising steeply, bankruptcies were rife and the howls of pain growing louder. But he dismissed the crisis as 'a passing incident in our national lives', one that the federal government had no part in seeking to resolve. He urged patience and self-reliance. As industries were laid to waste, unemployment soared, families went hungry, there was a sense that President Hoover was echoing the famous words of Marie Antoinette: let them eat cake. It sealed his political fate.

History rarely works neatly with one decade being one thing, the next decade being something else. But in the US the change from the 1920s to the 1930s really did mark such a shift. The optimistic laissez-faire economics of the 1920s, when the Republicans were riding high and the people were revelling in the economic bubble they were playing their own part in inflating, collapsed like the stock market, which by 1930 had lost 90 per cent of its value.

And with these straitened times came calls for a new type of politics. It wasn't just that people had lost money. There was grinding poverty and millions were struggling to put food on the table. In 1932 the American people elected the Democrat, Franklin Delano Roosevelt, who had vowed that he would use all the levers of federal government to lift America out of the slough of despair that it had entered. Relief, Recovery and Reform were the watchwords as he proclaimed: 'I pledge you, I pledge myself, to a new deal for the American people.'

The New Deal was born. A period when there was a mass of new legislation to achieve his 3Rs objectives, and a whole pile of new agencies were set up – there was the Tennessee Valley Authority, which created massive hydro-electric projects in seven of the worst affected areas, creating jobs; there were federal emergency relief projects to help the poor; attempts to regulate agriculture prices to stop overproduction, and on it went.

But two of the most interesting were the Civilian Conservation Corps (CCC) and the Public Works Administration (it would later become the Works Progress Administration). These bodies would employ millions of people, and at a stroke make the US government far and away the biggest employer in the country. This was a significant structural shift for the US economy. Whatever the shortcomings of the New Deal (something still keenly argued over), there could be no doubt that it permanently changed the federal government's relationship with the populace.

If you look at America's cities today, or its road networks, or travel across the great iron bridges that straddle America's famous rivers, or through the tunnels that go under them, if you look at some of the schools and post offices or even jails – you'll see that a huge proportion were built during this era. If you have an idle 15 minutes it is worth logging onto the Roosevelt Presidential Library website, where the list goes on and on of what was built in every state in the land. These are just a few of the projects from New York City – to do the whole state would take too long: there's La Guardia Airport, the Triborough Bridge that links Manhattan, Queens and the Bronx, the Lincoln Tunnel that stretches for a mile and a half under the Hudson, linking New Jersey to Manhattan. All of them when they were built were revolutionary. They were symbols of an America tackling poverty but investing in a future that would maintain the US as the pre-eminent capitalist economy in the world.

La Guardia is where I fly into when I travel up to New York from Washington. It is now undergoing refurbishment, but it had become dilapidated beyond belief. I cannot describe the numbers of delays there have been – not just due to adverse weather but because bits of the airport were falling apart. And travel through the Lincoln Tunnel – still a vital artery for getting onto the island of Manhattan – and it is crumbling. Or take the train up from Washington and you arrive at Penn Station – which again feels totally Third World. The New Deal may have seen massive investment in infrastructure, but it hasn't been maintained. And look at the infrastructure that isn't there. Fly into Heathrow and you have the choice of the tube or the Heathrow Express to get you into central London; fly into JFK in New York and you can take the Airtrain that will link you to the subway, but there is nothing direct. It is the same in Washington. A metro is being built that will go into the city, but it's not there yet. No wonder that on all the travel advisory websites the advice is simple and straightforward: take a taxi.

Incidentally, when people were looking at Bernie Sanders as a totally new phenomenon in US politics with his class-based approach to a lot of what he was seeking to achieve, it's worth replaying the words of FDR when he was campaigning for his second term. He was at Madison Square Garden in New York, which would later become famous for hosting some of the greatest boxing bouts ever held. But in 1936 it was President Roosevelt who came out of his corner swinging. 'The forces of "organised money" are unanimous in their hate for me – and I welcome their hatred,' he said, and went on: 'I should like to have it said of my first Administration that in it the forces of selfishness and of lust for power met their match, [and] I should like to have it said of my second Administration that in it these forces have met their master.'

The Roosevelt second term was more controversial – and difficult. The 'liberal' nature of his reforms upset many conservatives, and a split among the labour unions resulted in big gains for the Republicans in 1938, making legislation

143

that much more difficult to enact. Arguably the biggest single event that would propel the US economy out of recession was the Japanese attack on Pearl Harbor in December 1941. It brought America into the Second World War and gave a stimulus to key sections of the economy.

But if one is looking for what is the crowning glory of FDR's achievements, it is surely the work undertaken by the three million young men who over a ten-year period were put to work as part of the Civilian Conservation Corps. To qualify you had to be an unemployed, unmarried man between the ages of 17 and 28. This was for unskilled, manual labour. And the aim was to engage in conservation work and development of natural resources. For their efforts the young men were given food and shelter – and a salary of $30 per month, of which $25 had to be sent home to their families.

To describe the CCC's objectives will make it sound like something out of one of those Soviet-era paintings of muscled young men with chiselled jaws, heroically tilling the soil and building the new socialist idyll. Yet here, in 1930s America, these men were being put to work on the land with hammers and sickles to promote environmental conservation through vigorous and disciplined outdoor work. This civilian 'tree army' would relieve the rural unemployed and keep city kids off street corners where they would be getting up to no good.

The CCC was under the control of the army. And with that went military discipline – superiors would be addressed as 'sir'. And they would live on camps for between six months and a year at a time.

But let's leave to one side the utopian aspects of this. What these young men did was remarkable. There was soil conservation and reforestation. Millions of trees were planted on land that had grown barren, either through soil erosion or fires. Canals and ditches were dug, 30,000 wildlife shelters built; rivers and lakes were stocked with nearly a billion fish; beaches were cleared. And at the end of this herculean labour, in less than ten years the CCC had built more than 800 parks and planted nearly three billion trees.

It had also engendered in Americans a renewed love and appreciation of the great outdoors that persist to this day. That is why Americans drive so many more off-road vehicles than is the case in Britain. There are more shops selling fishing rods, camping equipment and hiking gear. Weekends are for getting out of the city and reintroducing yourself to nature.

And nowhere is that better done than in the spectacular, awe-inspiring, sensational national parks, which are the lasting legacy of the New Deal. Of course nature has played its part too. The spouting geysers in Yellowstone are not the handiwork of FDR's unemployed, nor did a group of CCC young men carve El Capitan in Yosemite National Park – or chisel out the Grand Canyon for that matter. It is a country where even nature seems to have been supersized. America is blessed with some truly amazing scenery. But the trails that you walk on, the fire roads that protect the parks, the three billion trees that were planted, the strict rules on what can be built there are all a result of the New Deal. Travel across America and the National Parks Service are working to ensure that the natural wonders are preserved but still available to all.

You may arrive in the US and be shocked at the state of the airport you land at, you may be bumped and shaken around as you drive on the nation's potholed and cratered roads, you may be inconvenienced by the bridge closures and the long lines at toll booths, but when you drive into one of the national parks which cover 84 million acres in 412 different areas, you will be awestruck at how a country which does some of the basics so badly, can do nature, monuments, historic battlefields, shorelines, rivers and trails so fabulously.

Americans may instinctively prefer small government and a less intrusive state, but what their country does exceptionally well – even though it may not be to everyone's taste – is the projection of power. By contrast, I remember one evening driving along the M4 heading west out of London and there was a Range Rover in front of me and I could see a Jaguar in front of that. They were going at about 75–80mph, which was clearly not fast enough for a boy racer like me. So I drove up fairly close behind the Range Rover and flashed my headlights.

And in return he put some blue flashing lights on and a sign that flashed in red from the rear window: 'Keep your distance.' I think it is fair to say I applied the brakes pretty sharpish and skulked at a respectful distance, way behind. It was the prime minister's entourage that I had foolishly buzzed.

One of my favourite John Major anecdotes (for a prime minister who was meant to be so grey, there are more good stories involving him than anyone else) was when he was travelling up to the Young Conservatives conference in Harrogate, and it was taking place the day after the IRA had tried to mortar bomb Downing Street in February 1991. Thick snow and ice blanketed the country, and in normal circumstances he would have cancelled the trip on account of the weather. But if he had cancelled, it would have looked like a victory for the IRA. So off they set, John Major in the armoured Jaguar, his personal protection officers in the Range Rover behind. This being John Major, after travelling some distance up the A1 from his constituency home in Huntingdon he decided it was time to stop at a Little Chef, just by the side of the road. They ordered cooked English breakfasts and sat at a table together. They were the only people at the Little Chef on this cold Saturday morning. But then the door swung open and a burly lorry driver walked in and, seeing how quiet it was, said to the waitress in a loud voice, 'This would be the perfect day to hold up a Little Chef.' As John Major's bodyguards slowly felt for their Heckler & Koch revolvers, the prime minister piped up, 'Not as good as you might think.'

Now the reason I recount this is that it would be inconceivable – just totally fantastical – for a truck driver or anyone else for that matter to be left in any doubt if the US president was in the vicinity. When the president moves it is not solely a question of security, it is also about the projection of might. The modus operandi of the British security services is to move the VIP around in a manner that draws as little attention as possible – whether it be a member of the royal family, a senior member of the government or a visiting VIP. For the US Secret Service it is the complete opposite. It is the full monty of sirens, blaring horns, motorcycle outriders and flashing lights.

And travelling with the president is a super-duper experience in the mighty projection of power – not just the convoy, but what goes into it. I travelled with POTUS (the president of the US) to Saudi Arabia, London and Germany and then back to Washington on the ultimate statement in big and powerful – Air Force One.

In Germany we went to the giant Hanover trade fair, the *Messe*, and I travelled in the presidential convoy through the city. I am not sure what word to use to describe it. Huge? Unbelievable? Ridiculous? What it certainly represents is a spectacle. The roads are closed at least an hour before we pass through, so there is no way we are going to confront any other traffic. And the whole population of Hanover seems to have turned out of their offices and houses to watch this procession of about 30 vehicles and probably twice that many police motorcycles. Everyone is filming on their smartphones. It is an event.

As the BBC's North America Editor, I travel all the time. From one regional airport to another on American airlines where the best you can hope for is a packet of pretzels. Americans fly for work the way Britons hop on and off buses or trains. Consequently it is utilitarian. Customer service is virtually non-existent. It is grin-and-bear-it travel. Though more grim than grin. Air Force One is not like that.

When you are travelling with the president you are in what is called 'the pool'. This is the group of journalists who, because space is so constrained on the plane, are representing all news outlets, not just their own. It is limited to 13 people; all material is shared and fed out simultaneously so no one has a competitive advantage.

The bubble is the secure, hermetically sealed force field in which you operate. Inside the bubble you are called 'clean'. Outside you're 'dirty'. So, on the day of the flight, we gather in the hotel where the president is staying. With our bags. First, a dog sniffs them, then two secret service guys open every piece of luggage and sift through everything. Yes, dirty underwear and all.

We then go through metal detectors and board a bus, which will move in the presidential convoy. From now on we are inside the bubble. An armed secret service agent is assigned to us. He is called 'the wrangler'. Think sheepdog and sheep. We are his obedient flock. There is also a White House press officer who has to yell at various times, 'Press pool, we're moving!' You are not allowed to leave the bubble at any point. Where the president goes, you go.

At the end of a day of meetings with Gulf leaders, at which we've had a ringside view, we join the presidential motorcade that takes us to the military airfield, and arrive at the foot of the plane. No further security is needed – we are the 'clean' pool inside the bubble.

The rule for moving about the aircraft is that everyone can wander around – but you can only move towards the back from the area where you are seated. The president sits at the front, so he can go anywhere. He has a bedroom, a gym and a huge conference room. Then there are his key staff and senior officials; there are the communication teams at banks of encrypted computers so that the president is never out of contact; there is a medical station, his security detail, the secret service. And as you go further back, reaching the bottom of this ecological food chain, there's the press pool. I don't have a boarding pass or an assigned seat number, but in the press section I find my seat by way of a neatly printed invitation-style card, saying, 'BBC, welcome aboard Air Force One.' It is perched on top of a comfy cushion with the presidential seal. The seats are way bigger than you'd find in the economy section of a normal jumbo, but they don't fold down into flat beds.

And then there's the vote. A vote on which film to watch on the two big screens. We are on our way to London, so the American journalists go overwhelmingly for a James Bond movie.

Now as I said we are nearly at the back. Behind us is the aft galley and it is a kitchen with a team of chefs who buy fresh ingredients to cook proper meals. There are ovens and a hob – not an aluminium foil container or trolley in sight. Christine, our head chef, is a fluent Arabic speaker and used to work in intelligence. But she wanted to see the world so joined the US Air Force. And now she's on Air Force One. Meals are served on the plane's crested bone china. Dinner is *filet mignon*, wedge salad and cheesecake, since you ask. The paper napkins have the presidential seal and the words 'aboard the presidential aircraft'. I'm amazed to find, when later that night I get to my hotel, that several of them must have fallen into my bag.

But the prized swag is the little boxes of M&Ms exclusive to Air Force One, replete with presidential seal and the president's signature. There used to be Air Force One playing cards and even cigarettes. I am also awarded a certificate, signed by the captain, saying that I was a guest of the president aboard Air Force One. And when we land at Stansted Airport there's no immigration or anything tiresome like that. Instead there are three Marine Corps Osprey helicopters, plus Marine One for the president, waiting to chopper us to the ambassador's residence in Regent's Park, next door to London Zoo. From touchdown to central London, it was maybe 25 minutes. I've often debated the best way back into town from Stansted after my less glamorous flights. Now I know.

Now just consider for a minute the logistics of all this. Wherever the president moves, a small army moves with him. In Saudi Arabia there was the full presidential motorcade – his vehicle the Beast, which has armoured doors eight inches thick so that it can withstand not just small arms fire, but a shell or chemical attack. There is a convoy of about a dozen other US armoured vehicles, all with the statutory blacked-out windows, some fitted with specialist communications equipment. Another vehicle is 'the armoury' in case things turn really ugly, and then there is the president's personal ambulance. All of these will have been flown in advance from America on giant US Air Force Galaxy transporters, along with the Osprey helicopters and Marine One. They needless to say have to be rebuilt by teams of aeronautical engineers once they come out the belly of these vast planes.

So in the Ritz Carlton in Riyadh, where he was staying, his entourage has taken over the entire hotel. It is like a small occupying army: his personal staff, special advisers, State Department officials, his personal secret service detail, the advance team, along with hundreds of other secret service officers who are keeping other dignitaries safe. They are securing the hotel compound, and they are guarding Air Force One (and on board Air Force One they keep their weapons with them at all time; if need be they have permission to open fire mid-air). There are the engineers maintaining the vehicles and aircraft, there are specialist firefighters who are beside the helicopters when they take off and when they land, there are the medical teams, there are teams of specialist police in khaki uniforms who are armed to the teeth – and a whole pile of other people whose role one can only begin to imagine.

And of course, because he has flown direct from Saudi to London, the same operation would have had to unfold there, with different transporter aircraft bringing in the fleet of cars and the squadron of helicopters – and the engineers and the support staff and so on.

At a guess the total number of US personnel involved in a presidential trip is not far shy of a thousand. When the prime minister travels, I would say the number of accompanying people is around 20. Maybe 30.

Just one other thing. When we eventually return to Joint Base Andrews in Maryland we get off the plane, and someone from the Department of Homeland Security approaches me and says, 'Are you the Brit?' When I say yes, he tells me I will have to accompany him into the immigration area at the top-security base. The reason being all the passports are on a support plane travelling behind us (why, I have no idea, but that is apparently standard operating procedure), and unlike the US journalists travelling with the president, I will have to fill in forms before I can leave.

Then I notice a whole pile of standard immigration forms that are on the desk next to him. He leaves for a second, and so it is a moment to snoop. And what joy! There at the top of the pile is the blue form of Mr Barack Obama. Address: 1600 Pennsylvania Avenue. Occupation: President. And no, he wasn't carrying fresh farm produce, or firearms, or any banned substances. I might have sneaked a photograph of said form, but am counselled very strongly by a startled White House correspondent I showed it to, not to put it on Twitter. I concur. The only part of the form that has not been filled in is his passport number, but at the bottom in his unmistakable, very round handwriting is his signature and the date.

Americans might like small government, and the president might project enormous power, but no one stands above the demands of a nation's bureaucracy.

Chapter 5

God

At one of the first dinner parties I went to when I came to America, we had all sat down, and the first forkful of food was about halfway on its three-foot journey from plate to mouth when something in the dining room's atmospherics caused me to pause – maybe it was the slightest clearing of a throat, maybe it was the sets of eyes looking nervously at me. I looked up and realised that I was alone. Grace had not yet been said.

If you were to put a compass point on our house in Georgetown, one of the most handsome districts of Washington, with its streets of late 19th-century houses that were built after the Civil War, and draw a circle around it with a radius of around 400 metres, you would incorporate well over a dozen temples – the Episcopal Church of Christ Church on the next block, the Epiphany Catholic Church down the street, the Mount Zion United Methodist Church, the parish of Christ the King. Behind our house is the Georgetown Baptist Church, not to be confused with the First Baptist Church of Georgetown just by Rose Park – oh, and that's not forgetting the Alexander Memorial Baptist Church on N Street, nor the Jerusalem Baptist Church on 26th Street. There is the Fifth Church of Christ, Scientist on 31st, which is not to be muddled up with Christ Church. The Dumbarton United Methodist is just across the street from us, and the Georgetown Presbyterian two blocks up on P Street, St John's Episcopal is on O Street – and there's one synagogue to throw into the mix too, the Kesher Israel. As I say, none of these is more than a four-minute walk from our front door. This country does a lot of God. And that is not a flippant point.

There's an old Jewish joke about a man rescued from a desert island after being trapped there for 20 years.

'How did you survive? How did you keep sane?' his rescuers ask, as he shows them around the small island.

'I had my faith. My faith as a Jew kept me strong. Come.' He leads them to a small clearing, where there's an opulent synagogue, made entirely from palm fronds, coconut shells and woven grass.

'This took me five years to complete.'

'Amazing! And what did you do for the next 15 years?'

'Come with me.'

He leads them around to the far side of the island. There, in a shady grove, is an even *more* beautiful temple. 'This one took me 12 years to complete!'

'But sir,' asks the rescuer, 'why did you build *two* temples?'

'This is the temple *I* attend. That other place? Hah! I wouldn't set foot in that other temple if you *paid* me!'

In Georgetown, and indeed the rest of America, never let it be said there is a lack of choice over which temple to pray in. On Sunday mornings the roads around our house are busy with people going to church, not just the elderly and infirm, but also young families – all ages, all ethnicities.

The figures are quite staggering. Nine out of ten American adults say they believe in God (a figure that has only dipped slightly over the past decade). Close on eight out of ten adults identify with a particular religion. But when people in the US are polled about the importance of religion in their lives, the difference between the US and Western Europe becomes even more striking.

In the US, half of all Americans deem religion to be very important in their lives, compared to only 17 per cent in Britain, and in France it's just 13 per cent.

All of which suggests that America is bucking a trend that can be observed throughout the rest of the developed world. If you look around there is an inverse relationship between wealth and religious devotion. The poorer a country is, the more religious it is, and vice versa. The promise of heaven and a saviour looks all the more attractive when you are struggling to feed your children. But when you have the big house and the double garage and the fancy holidays and the latest clothes, religion – generally speaking – seems to slide down the priority list.

But not in America.

Look at the battle within the Anglican Communion over women priests and gay clergy. The fiercest resistance has come from the African church, where the changes being proposed in the 'liberal' West are viewed as unconscionable. America is the glaring exception to the rule. A Pew Research Center report said that when it comes to religiosity 'the US is closer to considerably less developed nations, such as India, Brazil and Lebanon, than to other Western nations'.

But why? One fascinating possible explanation goes back to when the Founding Fathers were drawing up the constitution and it was deemed there should be a separation of powers between church and state. The First Amendment to the US Constitution, along with state laws, produced a sort of religious bazaar in which different religious traders set up their stalls to offer their wares – something you still see today in America with the proliferation of different faiths. There is almost a Heinz 57 variety pack of Protestants – as well as Catholics, Jews, Mormons, Seventh-day Adventists, Jehovah's Witnesses – and then Muslims, Buddhists, Hindus and adherents of other faith traditions. Contrast this with the other side of the Atlantic, where Europeans – broadly – stuck with their 'traditional' churches: Catholicism in Southern Europe; Calvinism further north; Church of England in Britain; Orthodox Christianity in the Balkans, Russia and Greece.

And as everyone (in America) knows, the marketplace outperforms monopolies, especially state-supported ones.

It's the old story of capitalism. Competition meant that denominations multiplied, religious entrepreneurs flourished: 'Roll up, roll up, visit my shiny new church.' This was a new country, not hidebound by one dominant religious tradition, with many of the early settlers themselves fleeing religious persecution at home. Immigrants would also play a hugely significant role in this proliferation by importing their own traditions.

There's a fascinating map produced in 2000 by the US Census Bureau. It shows the concentration of the different ethnic groups in different geographic regions. Far from it being a melting pot, it is a pot where the ingredients (the different national groups) stick to the bits of the pot where they first landed. The French are to be found in the Deep South in New Orleans; the Irish along the cities of the East Coast and Chicago. Then of course there are the millions of African Americans who came as slaves to the southern states but who would move north as industrialisation took hold. The map also shows big concentrations of Dutch, Finnish and Norwegian settlers around the Great Lakes.

There is the Amish community in Pennsylvania – with its Dutch and German origins – where its adherents live a life that is anchored in the 19th century. They use horse and cart for transport, they work the land, and wear the same clothes their forebears would have done 150 years earlier. It is a model of simplicity. And it was hard not to make immature jokes when I went to film there and found that one of the main towns where the Amish are concentrated is called 'Intercourse', with a big sign as you enter saying 'Welcome to Intercourse'. (When I signed off my report I simply said, 'Jon Sopel, BBC News, Pennsylvania.' Seemed safer.)

More recently there has been the influx of Mexicans and others from South America, who, not surprisingly, are found in their greatest numbers along the border. And there are the Cuban Americans clustered in southern Florida.

All of these different groups came with their own religious traditions, which they were anxious to maintain – and, in turn, bring into the mainstream. During the 2016 primary season I found myself variously listening to the New Jersey governor, Chris Christie, in a Greek Orthodox church in Manchester, New Hampshire, and to Senator Ted Cruz at his victory rally in Wisconsin at the Serb Center in Milwaukee – who knew there was a big Serb community in Milwaukee?

Plus a whole pile of other candidates who we would listen to in more mainstream religious settings.

Different churches for different traditions, with uneducated clergy attracting uneducated followers, educated clergy attracting educated followers. And then came the 'air war' as the different religious groups realised there was a whole new congregation to be reached who were sitting at home watching the TV or listening to the radio. The pulpit celebrities and televangelists snapped up FM and TV bandwidth to hammer home their messages, preaching from churches that in terms of size looked more like the sort of arenas that were meant to house The Rolling Stones, but reaching into millions of homes via cable TV.

Today there are interesting social attitudes wrapped in people's religiosity. According to Pew research, over half of Americans believe that to be a moral person you have to believe in God. The older you are, the more likely you are to adhere to that view. And this sense of faith is one of the most surprising things I have found about living in the US.

The one thing about America that strikes every visitor is the extraordinary politeness of the people. Maybe some who've experienced a New York subway in the rush hour would question this judgement (or who have found themselves in the midst of a full-on Twitter assault), but pretty well everywhere I have gone there has been a courtesy going beyond anything you would find in the UK. When you jump into a taxi you don't just bark out your destination. You exchange pleasantries with the driver first. On the streets in the neighbourhood where we live the norm is to walk past someone and say, 'Hello, how are you?' – well, more often a 'Hey, how's it going?'

There is also a formality here that in the UK belongs to a different generation. We were introduced to our neighbours' children and I said to the young boy, 'Hello, I'm Jon.' And his father quickly said, 'Charlie, say hello to Mr Sopel.' In my office a lot of the younger staff call me 'sir'. To me this is alien. A lot of our American friends asked what we found most surprising about living in America – and I think it is this. There is an old-fashioned civility and decency – and modesty in behaviour. I also think there is a good deal less swearing and cursing. Maybe it's the neighbourhood where we live.

One of my good friends who worked at the White House in the Obama administration was from a navy family at Virginia Beach, on the East Coast. Her father had been a helicopter pilot during the Vietnam War. It was a religious household in which she and her brother grew up. One day, needing to speak to her father, she went into the garage where he was working on something. They had a conversation, and then he put his hand on her shoulder and said, 'I think you should stop calling me sir now.' Taken aback, she said, 'So what should I call you?' 'You can call me Dad,' he replied. She was 25 years old.

This formality has so much to do with God and religion and the 'moral' way to behave to others, with a deeply ingrained respect for elders, and people in authority. What is most striking is how important a role religion still plays. Yes, there are oddities. In a country where so many people believe in one form of Christianity or another, Christmas is almost a forbidden word. You are wished 'happy holidays'.

Don't mention the birth of baby Jesus whatever you do. At Dulles Airport last December when I was about to fly back to London there was a big banner up in the terminal saying, 'We hope you like the holiday trees.' Err. They were Christmas trees. That is one of the pieces of political correctness that Donald Trump has promised to deal with. Quite right too.

America also has a convoluted relationship with alcohol. In the US today there is still a very different relationship to booze than you would find in the UK. I went to a dinner for 12 people at the Democratic National Convention in Philadelphia at a fancy restaurant. The guests were a mixture of business types, journalists and politicians. I think over the course of the whole meal just six glasses (yes, glasses) of wine were drunk (three of them by me). Now it is a few years since I've been to the UK party conferences, but my fogged memory tells me they are not quite like that.

In a restaurant, after we have looked at the wine menu, I will normally tell the waiter that we will have the Cabernet Sauvignon, and he will say, 'A glass?' And I will reply, 'No, a bottle.' And there will be an embarrassed pause, and then an 'of course'.

Go to a liquor store in the US and you will emerge with the bottle of scotch, or whatever it is you've bought, in a plain brown paper bag. It is treated the way that newsagents used to treat a certain type of magazine that would have been found on the top shelf. When I was in South Carolina at the airport in Charleston and we were having a beer at the airport before heading back to Washington, I even had to show my ID to prove that I wasn't underage. You have to be 21. I'm in my fifties. I mean, I know I look great and work out and all that, but really? Well, yes. It's the law and a hangover (not sure that is quite the right word) from what has gone before.

And those attitudes were imported to the US by the Puritans coming from England. But as time went on, attitudes relaxed. The Founding Fathers liked a tipple. Benjamin Franklin declared, 'Beer is living proof that God loves us and wants to see us happy' while Thomas Jefferson said, 'Wine is necessary for life' and George Washington said, 'My manner of living is plain … a glass of wine and a bit of mutton.'

But as that taste for alcohol developed, so the puritanism reared up again in the shape of the Woman's Christian Temperance Union, and the Anti-Saloon League. The combined forces of rural Protestants and social progressives would in the early part of the 20th century fight for the 18th Amendment to the US Constitution – a ban on the sale, production, importation and transportation of alcohol. In other words, prohibition. Communion wine was still just about OK, but practically everything else was a no-no. From 1920, for 13 years, alcohol was banned. And some of those attitudes persist.

Go to a dinner party in Washington (which, incidentally, will start most likely at just after 6pm and be over by 10), and a bottle of wine will be plonked on the table. I will start to drink at what I consider to be a pace short of guzzling, but at a reasonable lick. Quickly I come to the horrible realisation I have made a fundamental miscalculation. This bottle between the eight of us round the table is the *only* bottle that is going to appear. The other guests sip sparingly from their glass while mine sits throbbingly empty from midway through the starter course until the end of the meal. And the host, looking solicitously at me as I say my thank-yous on the doorstep, says, 'Are you OK to drive?' OK to drive, I think to myself – I could perform open-heart surgery …

All this in a country where religion is meant to have no role in the life of the republic. The key piece of Enlightenment thinking brought into the framing of the US Constitution was a strict separation between church and state. In 1773 a young, bookish James Madison became concerned about the plight of several Baptists in Virginia who had been imprisoned. Their crime had been to be dissenters from the Anglican establishment, and so he teamed up with a fellow Virginian, Thomas Jefferson, to challenge this. Madison argued that to promote any religion was outside the proper scope of limited government. Jefferson would later write: 'The legitimate powers of government extend to such acts only as are injurious to others. But it does me no injury for my neighbor to say that there or twenty gods or no God. It neither picks my pocket nor breaks my leg.'

That battle was won in Virginia, but then came the fight to get this incorporated into the US Constitution. A Constitutional Convention was called. Some anti-federalist critics of the proposed constitution warned that abolishing religious tests would allow Jews, Catholics and Quakers – even 'pagans, deists, and Mahometans [Muslims]' – to hold federal office, perhaps even to dominate the new national government. But their concerns were overruled. The First Amendment was passed. It was added to the constitution in 1791 as one of ten amendments comprising the Bill of Rights, and opened with the declaration that 'Congress shall make no law respecting an establishment of religion, or prohibiting the free exercise thereof.'

The separation of church and state would seem to be hard baked into the constitution, and President Kennedy expressed it most clearly in 1960 when he said: 'I believe in an America where the separation of church and state is absolute – where no Catholic prelate would tell the president (should he be Catholic) how to act, and no Protestant minister would tell his parishioners for whom to vote – where no church or church school is granted any public funds or political preference – and where no man is denied public office merely because his religion differs from the president who might appoint him or the people who might elect him.' But does that stand scrutiny against the reality?

Not so much. Look at the questions which still rage today in modern America – over prayer and the teaching of evolution in public schools, the posting of the Ten Commandments in courtrooms, and the launching of 'faith-based initiatives' by the executive branch. And in the election campaign, the questioning of whether it would be 'constitutional' for a Muslim ever to be president of the United States.

Before we dive into those controversies, one of the perversities I have found during my time living in America is that here, where there is no established church, religion plays a pivotal and central role in public life; while in Britain – where we have the Church of England as the established church, and the monarch is both head of state and supreme governor of the Church – religion seems to play next to no role. In our everyday lives it is marginal and peripheral. Yes, twice a year we will nod at what the Archbishop of Canterbury has said in his Easter message and his Christmas sermon, but established Christianity seems to be something that exists in name only.

Just look at the way British politics is conducted. Tony Blair was probably the most devout prime minister that Britain has had in recent decades. He went to church practically every Sunday and carried a copy of the Bible with him wherever he travelled. When he left Downing Street he converted to Roman Catholicism and, as I discovered when I wrote a very early biography of him, communitarianism and Christian teaching informed a lot of his political thinking. But to ask about his faith was akin to enquiring about a deeply personal health problem that was none of anyone else's business. His often brusque and combative official spokesman at the time, Alastair Campbell, when asked a question about Mr Blair's faith, replied curtly, 'We don't do God.' Theresa May, who became prime minister after Britain's vote to depart from the European Union in 2016, is a vicar's daughter who grew up in the Home Counties, and is still a regular churchgoer, but though I have heard her opine on a lot of topics, she has steered clear of talking about the role of God in her life and politics.

And after her woefully ill-judged decision to call a general election in 2017, the one casualty was not the leader of the Conservative Party (though her prestige was seriously dented), but the leader of the Liberal Democrats. The amiable Tim Farron had been given a torrid time during the campaign because of his openly and deeply held religious beliefs. He was repeatedly assailed over his attitudes towards homo-sexuality, even though he had always voted for liberalising legislation. In his resignation statement, he said that he felt 'remaining faithful to Christ' was incompatible with leading his party, and he went on: 'The consequences of the focus on my faith is that I have found myself torn between living as a faithful Christian and serving as a political leader.' Such a statement would be impossible to imagine from a political leader in the US.

In America maybe the famed separation between church and state is not a thick black line, but instead something much more splodgy in varying shades of grey. If I were to ask you now to pull a £10 note from your wallet, you would see a picture of the Queen on the front wearing her crown, along with the signature of the chief cashier of the Bank of England, and on the back a portrait of Charles Darwin. There is nothing to indicate religiosity. Now look at a dollar bill. There is a picture of George Washington, and there is the signature of the Treasury secretary, but on the back, above the big-lettered word 'ONE', are four words in smaller print – but unmistakably clear: 'In God We Trust'.

And it's more than just four words; in this country, where there is no role for the church, it is the national motto.

Or look at the pledge of allegiance that is sworn by every schoolchild each morning, and is recited at public events by everyone – something that every American knows by heart: 'I pledge allegiance to the flag of the United States of America, and to the republic for which it stands, one nation UNDER GOD, indivisible, with liberty and justice for all' (my capitals).

The original pledge, introduced after the Second World War, contained no reference to 'under God'. That came in 1954 and required a law to be passed in Congress before it could be adopted.

In both cases there was an argument that this was a breach of the First Amendment, but the concerns were dismissed. This was the rationale of the Supreme Court when the words were challenged in 1970: 'It is quite obvious that the national motto and the slogan on coinage and currency "In God We Trust" has nothing whatsoever to do with the establishment of religion. Its use is of ceremonial character and bears no true resemblance to a governmental sponsorship of a religious exercise.'

This thinking has a fabulous, fancy title. It is called 'ceremonial deism'. Oh, well, that's OK then. The idea that religious symbols have no meaning and are only there as 'ceremonial' is a curious piece of logic, when one considers the blood that has been spilt and the wars that have been fought over such things. Isn't it the same argument used by those who continue to demand to be able to fly the Confederate flag over the various state houses of the Southern states? It's only ceremonial, its defenders would say. And the fact that, historically, it was used by the states who went to war with the North over the right to keep slaves, and later became a symbol for white supremacists, is neither here nor there. It's just ceremonial, guv. Who could take offence at that?

You see, in America you can't do politics without also doing God. In the long drawn-out process of nominating a presidential candidate, the first state to vote is Iowa, in the Midwest. It is what they call a flyover state. One of those places you fly over when journeying from East Coast to West but never stop at, unless your plane develops mechanical trouble. Or, alternatively, it's a state you only visit when it's election season – and then the political campaigns set up shop for weeks on end and spend millions and millions of dollars on television advertising in their concerted attempt to win over this largely rural, agricultural population. The key to winning in Iowa is to know a lot about corn production, ethanol subsidies – and God.

Senator Marco Rubio from Florida, who at the outset of the primary race in 2016 was seen as one of the favourites to win, produced a TV advertisement that said this:

Our goal is eternity. The purpose of our life is to cooperate with God's plan. To those who much has been given, much is expected and we will be asked to account for that, whether your treasures are stored up on earth or in heaven. And, to me, I try to allow that to influence me in everything that I do ... To accept the free gift of salvation offered to us by Jesus Christ – the struggle on a daily basis as a Christian to remind ourselves of this.

And don't think this is exclusively a preserve of the Republican Party. In May 2015, Hillary Clinton, a lifelong Methodist, found herself in a South Carolina bakery. She was out canvassing and struck up a conversation with a customer about a passage he was reading in his Bible. Their talk was enough for Clinton to win his support. The former secretary of state's Bible knowledge 'is important in my world', the man, a Baptist minister, later told CNN. 'I'd like to know that my president has some religious beliefs in God.' Clinton may not have shouted about her faith from the hilltops as some candidates are prone to do, but she knows how to use it to connect with people.

OK – so it's hard to compare this to the UK, where you don't have paid-for television commercials, which are the cornerstone of US elections. But can you imagine *any* mainstream candidate producing material like this to support his or her campaign? This advertisement was played out across the state. It would have been a conscious decision by the Rubio campaign – born of faith, of course, but also born of necessity to show just what a good and devout Christian he was.

Now if I wanted to be flippant I might ask, is that the same Marco Rubio who later in the campaign would talk about Donald Trump's small hands being indicative of something else being small, but that is not my purpose (though surely it will go down in the history books as a peculiarly low point in political campaigning). In Iowa and a number of other states with very high numbers of conservative, evangelical voters, discussing *your* relationship with Jesus wasn't an optional bolt on, it was *de rigueur*.

Even Donald Trump emerged with a new prop at his rallies and prayer breakfasts – the copy of the Bible that his mother had given him when he was a child – one that would appear again at his inauguration, along with the Lincoln Bible (though his confusion over the name of a certain scripture reading at one early meeting suggested he might not be one who avidly reads it every night before turning the light out). More likely he had to blow the dust off and wipe away the cobwebs from it before bringing this cherished family heirloom out before the camera lights. Soon after he became president, Donald Trump was guest of honour at the annual Prayer Breakfast held in Washington, at which various senior clergymen gather, and prayers are offered. When he rose to speak he asked people to pray for Arnold Schwarzenegger's ratings on *The Apprentice*, which he had taken over hosting. It was – while we're on Germanic sounding words – pure *schadenfreude*. Oh, how the president loved that his successor was failing.

The eventual victor of the Iowa caucus was Senator Ted Cruz from Texas. He emerged onto the stage in Des Moines, camera lights flashing, cable TV channels ready to take his speech live across the nation, and he began thus: 'Let me first of all say, to God be the glory.' He then went on to proclaim that America's success as a nation was down to its Judaeo-Christian values, and then quoted from the scripture: 'Weeping may endure for a night, but joy cometh in the morning. Iowa has proclaimed to the world, morning is coming. Morning is coming.'

I was there in Iowa that night watching all this and was metaphorically tapping my political compass. But tap it as I might, I could no longer find magnetic north. In all my years at Westminster I had never heard anything like that. Politics, I realised, is played by different rules here.

What's interesting is that it wasn't always like this. Candidates didn't really begin talking about their personal faith in order to win office until after the 1970s. It was part of a conservative backlash in response to the perceived secularism of the 1960s, to abortion, and to measures that reinforced a clearer separation between church and state, such as the banning of school-sponsored prayer – and that galvanised the religious right. Evangelicals would boost the campaigns of Republicans like Ronald Reagan, George H.W. Bush and George W. Bush while John Kerry's perceived lack of faith was one of the reasons given for the failure of his bid to become president in 2004. Many would argue the role of evangelical Protestants is so strong that it shapes the entire presidential selection process.

All this is interesting but not of huge consequence. More interesting, and of more consequence, were the views expressed by Dr Ben Carson – at one stage leading in the polls to become the Republican nominee. He is a retired African American neuro-surgeon who was the darling of the evangelical right. He first came to prominence at a National Prayer Breakfast where he launched a ferocious attack on the record of Barack Obama. The president was in attendance at the breakfast, as Dr Carson spoke about the moral decay that had taken place under Obama, and how the country could face a Rome-like fate.

He was asked on the Sunday TV show *Meet the Press* whether a president's faith should matter. Here's the exchange:

CARSON: I guess it depends on what the faith is. If it's inconsistent with the values and principles of America. And of course, if it fits within the realm of America and consistent with the constitution, no problem.

MTP: So do you believe that Islam is consistent with the constitution?

CARSON: No, I do not. I would not advocate that we put a Muslim in charge of this nation. I absolutely would not agree with that.

Article 6 of the US Constitution is just about as clear a statement as you're ever going to find: no religious test shall ever be required as a qualification to any office or public trust under the United States.

But what Carson had said – and without arousing too much controversy – was that anyone can be president so long as they're Christian (or maybe Jewish). Never mind that the three or four million Muslims with US passports are law-abiding, well-integrated, living their lives according to the American dream – working hard, playing by the rules, serving in the armed forces and serving their communities.

So religion not only informs the conduct of politics and who can and cannot stand for elected office. It informs the social attitudes that guide life in the United States. Sometimes idiosyncratically; sometimes profoundly.

If you dig deep into the figures and statistics, things are changing – across a broad range of issues. Back in 2001 the Pew Research Center found an overwhelming majority of Americans opposed same-sex marriage. Now according to a poll conducted in May 2016 a clear majority *back* the measure. Yes, that is largely driven by young people – but a growing number of older people have come round to back the measure. That is a significant shift in social attitudes in – historically speaking – a comparatively short amount of time with a Democrat over twice as likely as a Republican to support same-sex marriage. As ever, the party divisions run deep.

One other important change in the religious landscape that is worth noting is the growing number of young people who profess adherence to no religious grouping. Pew in its November 2015 report found that, 'As older cohorts of adults (comprised mainly of self-identified Christians) pass away, they are being replaced by a new cohort of young adults who display far lower levels of attachment to organised religion than their parents' and grandparents' generations did when they were the same age.' A growing percentage of Americans now say they are religiously unaffiliated, which includes atheists and agnostics as well as many who describe their religion as 'nothing in particular'. Altogether, the religiously unaffiliated now account for 23 per cent of the adult population, up from 16 per cent in 2007.

But if you want to see something truly surprising, just look at attitudes towards atheism. According to recent research just 9 per cent of Americans would not vote for a Jewish candidate, 22 per cent would not support a Mormon, 32 per cent would not back a gay or lesbian candidate – but an atheist? Half of those questioned in this survey said they could never bring themselves to vote for a non-believer. In the pantheon of loathed groups, atheists are right down there with child molesters and estate agents.

Actually it's worse than that. A 2011 poll found that US citizens viewed atheists as being on a par with rapists. Why, is hard to fathom. As discussed, well over half of Americans would describe themselves as seriously religious, so to be a non-believer is seen as a challenge to that. Another part of it is demographic. Atheism is less acceptable the higher you climb in the age bracket. So the silver lining for atheists is they are not perceived to be so threatening among younger people. Which in turn implies that the answer for the future of atheist acceptance may simply be time, though it will probably be a very, very long time before an atheist could possibly become President of the United States.

One of the other really interesting questions the pollsters asked was about identity. American Christians are far more likely to think of themselves first in terms of their religion than their nationality. So according to a Pew survey taken in 2012, 46 per cent of Americans define themselves first and foremost as Christians; the same number as define themselves as Americans first. In Europe people overwhelmingly define themselves by their nationality.

Mike Pence, the man Donald Trump chose to be his running mate, and who is now the vice president, is a Midwest evangelical Christian. He was the serving governor of Indiana when he was chosen. He ticked a lot of boxes for Mr Trump.

First and foremost, there was never any danger that this slightly grey man (both literally and metaphorically) was going to overshadow the great showman. He was reassuringly Republican, so would give solace to all those party members who were holding their nose at the thought of a Trump presidency, and he was pleasingly religious – another important source of reassurance for the base.

When he was chosen, he described himself thus: 'I'm a Christian, a Conservative and a Republican. In That Order.' This is someone about to become the vice president, not hoping to rise up through the church hierarchy. And this wasn't just a neat soundbite; his words were borne out by his record in the state he governed.

Long before he was elected governor, a federal law was signed onto the statute book by the then president, Bill Clinton, called the Religious Freedom Restoration Act. The 1993 legislation brought diverse religious groups and bitterly divided political parties into the same fold. President Clinton would joke at the time: 'The power of God is such that even in the legislative process miracles can happen.' Essentially the law did what it said on the tin: it ensured that religious freedom was protected. In other words the state would be limited in the legislation it could pass because it could not impinge on someone's ability to practise their faith.

Interestingly, one of the main beneficiaries of this legislation was intended to be Native Americans. The land, which they held to be sacred, would be protected from the creeping expansion of government and commercial projects. Native Americans needed to be able to carry out certain ceremonies and rituals in particular locations because of their special historical significance. That land would now be legally ring-fenced.

Go forward a couple of decades, and the issue of gay marriage had come to the fore. Certain states had backed it; others opposed it. To the dismay of many Christians and conservatives (and remember, like Mike Pence, a good many see themselves as Christians first, and everything else second) same-sex marriage became recognised in Indiana in 2014, as a result of a court ruling. So Governor Pence and his Republican colleagues signed their own Religious Freedom Restoration Act into law. Its defenders said it was really no different from the federal law that had been passed 20 years earlier. And it does have an identical title to the one signed in Washington. And it sounds decidedly bland and uncontroversial.

But it was different. In two important respects.

The Indiana version had a clause, which specifically allowed any 'for profit' business to say that it had the right to the 'free exercise of religion'. The law also said this: 'A person whose exercise of religion has been substantially burdened, or is likely to be substantially burdened, by a violation of this chapter may assert the violation or impending violation as a claim of defense in a judicial or administrative proceeding, regardless of whether the state or any other governmental entity is a party to the proceedings.'

So, stripping away the legalese, this legislation looked very much like it gave the right to, say, my Indiana gateau emporium to refuse to make the wedding cake for a same-sex couple on the grounds of my religious freedom. Or to take the photographs. Or to provide the music. Or to do anything else for that matter if I didn't want to serve them.

And the second important thing this legislation did was give my gateau shop legal protection against any civil rights cases brought by the individuals. There is a telling interview that Mr Pence gave to the ABC News presenter George Stephanopoulos when this controversy was raging. In it he is repeatedly asked whether a shopkeeper would be legally allowed to refuse to serve gay people. Repeatedly Mr Pence sidesteps the question with a slightly desperate sounding 'That is not the point.'

Then some of America's biggest companies got involved. Tim Cook, the chief executive of Apple, said legislation like that mirrored the segregation laws of a bygone era. 'These bills under consideration truly will hurt jobs, growth and the economic vibrancy of part of the country where a 21st-century economy was once welcomed with open arms,' he said. Other large employers in the state, like Walmart, expressed their opposition to the legislation.

Within a week, Mr Pence called a news conference in which he blamed 'sloppy reporting', 'wilful misrepresentation' and lies for the furore, a little taste perhaps of how the media would be treated once the governor became the vice president.

Really? Did Tim Cook and all the people in the Apple public affairs team and press office not understand what the legislation was about? Ditto the pharmaceutical giant Eli Lilly? And what about all those other organisations and public bodies who were raising serious concerns? Perhaps more damning: if Mr Pence thought the law was being misrepresented, why didn't he get out and say so immediately? It would have taken him a nano-second to call a news conference. But the impression was allowed to persist.

The issue of same-sex marriage would finally be resolved in the summer of 2015 when the Supreme Court gave its ruling, to the ecstatic delight of gay-rights campaigners, and when, for a brief period, the White House and most of Facebook and a decent chunk of liberal America embraced the colours of the rainbow – while many Christians went a furious shade of purple.

Justice Anthony M. Kennedy wrote the majority verdict as the court split 5:4 in favour. 'No longer may this liberty be denied,' he wrote. 'No union is more profound than marriage for it embodies the highest ideals of love, fidelity, devotion, sacrifice and family. In forming a marital union, two people become something greater than they once were.' Marriage, he said is a keystone of America's social order; there would now be equal dignity in the eyes of the law. Outside the Supreme Court the chant rang out: 'Love has won, love has won.' Barack Obama from outside the White House would declare, 'Today we can say in no uncertain terms that we have made our union a little more perfect.'

As I have said, the court was divided. Bitterly. The Supreme Court justices who had opposed, railed against the decision. The late Justice Antonin Scalia – a man who was known for his bluntness – described the way the judgment was written as 'pretentious as its content is egotistic ... of course the opinion's showy profundities are often profoundly incoherent'. And the chief justice, John Roberts, took in a giant sweep of history to offer his denunciation: 'The court invalidates the marriage laws of more than half the states and orders the transformation of a social institution that has formed the basis of human society for millennia: for the Kalahari Bushmen and the Han Chinese, the Carthaginians and the Aztecs. Just who do we think we are?'

And both protagonist and antagonist would take sharply differing views about where this would leave religious liberty.

Justice Kennedy said the First Amendment would ensure that religious organisations are given proper protection; Chief Justice Roberts would counter that, saying, 'People of faith can take no comfort in the treatment they received from the majority today.'

A different issue but a similar fight would unfold in North Carolina. This time over 'the bathroom bill' – not the price for going to the toilet but a row, which again divided Christian conservatives from liberal opinion over Christian teaching and progressive social mores. In this case it was the attempt to regulate access to lavatories for transgender individuals based on the sex they were assigned at birth. The Public Facilities and Security Act would apply to students at North Carolina schools – it was legislation that overturned an LGBT anti-discrimination measure that had been passed in the city of Charlotte in the same state.

The idea that transgender people would be forced to use toilets that aligned with their sex at birth, not the gender identity they had adopted or become through realignment surgery, was seen by many as intolerant and an infringement of human rights. To many conservative groups and Christians it seemed that the world was losing all sense of moral compass. The law was introduced, passed and signed in a single day

Compared to gay marriage, this would be an issue that would affect far fewer people, but the backlash was quick, as it was seen as an attack on the LGBT community as a whole. And just like Indiana before, the state panjandrums of North Carolina found themselves under attack and being boycotted.

Bruce Springsteen and Maroon 5 cancelled concerts in the state, the NBA put off an all-stars basketball game.

The Greater Raleigh Convention Center lost millions of dollars in business and, more significantly, a number of other companies said they would suspend new investment in the state. PayPal, the internet commerce giant, cancelled investment plans; Deutsche Bank put on hold expansion plans in the state. And Washington waded in too, warning that federal funding for a number of projects would be put in jeopardy unless the state's legislature abandoned its policies.

The attorney general, Loretta Lynch, would later announce that she would take legal action over the law, which she said amounted to 'state-sponsored discrimination' that had caused transgender people to suffer 'emotional harm, mental anguish, distress, humiliation and indignity'. That in turn brought a counter-blast from the embattled lawmakers in North Carolina that the federal government was engaged in 'a baseless and blatant overreach' of its power. The Trump administration within weeks of coming to power would quietly reverse the policy.

This is just the latest manifestation of a battle that has been going in America for decades – the culture war. It is a war that lines up the forces of liberal America against the well-organised and well-funded army of Christian conservatives, and the battle has been waged variously on gay rights, global warming, recreational drug use and, perhaps most bitterly of all, on abortion rights. Back in 1992, at the Republican Convention, Pat Buchanan, who had fought George H.W. Bush for the presidential nomination, argued: 'There is a religious war going on in our country for the soul of America. It is a cultural war, as critical to the kind of nation we will one day be as was the Cold War itself.'

It was all the way back in 1973 that the Supreme Court ruled on Roe vs Wade, the historic decision which overturned a Texas interpretation of abortion law and made abortion legal in the United States. The Roe vs Wade decision held that a woman, in consultation with her doctor, could choose abortion in the early months of pregnancy without legal restriction, and with restrictions in later months, based on the right to privacy.

For over 40 years this has been the law of the land, and it is still the subject of the most rancorous division. It polarises opinion like few other subjects. Sometimes it is a matter of those opposed to the law waving banners and writing letters; often it is much more sinister. A shooting at a Planned Parenthood clinic in Colorado Springs in 2015 left three people dead and several injured. Now whatever you think about abortion, Planned Parenthood is an organisation far bigger and wider than just a place to get an abortion. The vast majority of federal money that Planned Parenthood receives goes towards preventive healthcare, birth control, pregnancy tests and other women's health services. And during the presidential election campaign, even Donald Trump praised much of the work it did. Anyway, back to the attack. The suspect, Robert L. Dear, had attacked other clinics in the past and declared himself a 'warrior for the babies' at his hearing. Over the years, doctors have been attacked and killed. There have been attempted murders, assaults are commonplace and there have been kidnappings too. Premises have been set alight, there have been hundreds of bomb threats – after one actual bombing on Christmas Day those behind it called the attack 'a gift to Jesus on his birthday'.

People oppose the abortion laws in the UK, but not like they do in the US. What I have found interesting about living in the United States is that you hear politicians endlessly talking about getting government out of the way, out of people's lives. Yet on this issue the – mostly male – political class has no qualms about wanting to legislate on what a woman can and cannot do with her body. These ardent 'pro-lifers' are invariably the same people who are most trenchant in their support of the death penalty. The US is the only advanced Western nation that still carries out capital punishment, and it is practised in 31 states – and by the federal government in cases that they try. Increasingly the preferred method of 'killing' is by lethal injection, but even here it has become oh so complicated.

The issue is that drugs companies aren't really all that keen to align their brand image and core values with – well – deliberately killing people. It just doesn't quite work as a selling point, nor with how they are trying to project themselves as a force for good in society. This has led to the few pharmaceutical companies involved in supplying the required chemicals announcing they are having nothing more to do with this side of their business. And that in turn in April 2017 led to this madness in Arkansas.

The state announced that because its supplies were about to run out, it would fast track executions at its main prison near Little Rock. Eight men would be put to death in 11 days – a rate unequalled since the Supreme Court reintro- duced the death penalty over 40 years earlier. The prisons were running low on midazolam, the sedative that puts the death-row prisoner to sleep before the administration of the two lethal chemicals that cause paralysis and stop the heart. Not only that, but the decision threw up a separate logistical difficulty. The state's prison department requires six independent people to witness the execution in order to see that it is carried out properly. And if you are carrying out eight in quick succession, then that's 48 people you need. So Wendy Kelley, the director of the Prisons Department, used her initiative. She wrote to the Little Rock Rotary Club with this bright and breezy little invitation. 'You seem to be a group that does not have felony backgrounds and are over 21. So if you are interested in serving in that area, in this serious role, just call my office.'

The pro-capital punishment pro-lifers are also often the same people who talk about the sanctity of the constitution, but then, when a ruling goes against their moral or religious standpoint, refuse to accept it.

Take what happened after the Supreme Court ruling on gay marriage. A 57-year-old woman, Kim Davis from Kentucky, worked for the social services department as a county clerk, and her job was to issue marriage licences. But following the ruling she very ostentatiously refused to issue a certificate to a gay couple. It was a made-for-television showdown. The gay couple arriving to collect their marriage licence, with the cameras rolling; Ms Davis standing in their way saying 'no'. She cited the sanctity of marriage and her religious beliefs (in her little statement about sanctity she must have forgotten to mention that she had been married four times, and had twins out of wedlock) as her reason for refusing them. Three months after Ms Davis was jailed she told the Associated Press in an interview that it was 'ironic that God would use a person like me, who failed so miserably at marriage in the world, to defend it now.' Ironic indeed.

So, just to recap – a case was taken to the Supreme Court, they have ruled, and a woman goes to prison for refusing to implement its decision. Surely if you are a constitutionalist your only response is to say that everyone has a duty to respect and obey the law of the land. But apparently not on this. Three of the Republican presidential hopefuls stood by her; Mike Huckabee even shared a platform with her after she was released from prison, saying, 'She has shown more courage than any politician I know.' Some of her supporters said she was the Rosa Parks of her day. During the days of segregation Rosa Parks refused to accept that as a black person she could sit only at the back of the bus, and for her resistance became an iconic figure in the civil rights movement. Not quite the same thing. Others saw Kim Davis as an intolerant bigot.

The Roe vs Wade and same-sex marriage judgments are important in themselves for the rights they confer on the affected groups. But they highlight again the extraordinary power of the Supreme Court of the United States to shape the social identity and direction of modern America. The nomination to be a member of the Supreme Court is made by the president, and the appointment is confirmed by the Senate. Justices are appointed for life. So a vacancy only arises if a member retires or dies.

Of course the purists would say the Supreme Court stands above such partisan analysis. Its members, having been appointed for life, should be immune from whichever political wind is blowing, and they should be protecting minorities from the tyranny of the majority. The judge is expected to embrace a duty of impartiality, making decisions that reflect 'neutral' legal principles, not partisan politics. But you don't get to go to the Supreme Court without having gone through a rigorous process of vetting – first by the White House, and then the Senate. And it is telling that when people discuss the sitting members of the Supreme Court, they are invariably mentioned in the same breath as the president who picked them. Justice X is President Y's man ...

For Christian groups and liberals alike, control of the Supreme Court of the United States – SCOTUS – became one of the most talked-about issues of the 2016 presidential election. Just look at what happened after Justice Scalia's death at the beginning of 2016. The president – as was his constitutional role and duty – proposed a replacement, Merrick Garland. He was already a federal judge, winning promotion during the Bush years – so hardly a liberal clone. But the Republican-controlled Senate refused even to hold a cursory confirmation hearing. Christian conservatives don't just want a neutral to be on the Supreme Court, they want to have someone of their ideological and political stripe. An ideological shift in the Court's membership would alter constitutional law on crucial 'moral' issues: affirmative action, abortion rights, immigration and healthcare.

Until the death of Justice Antonin Scalia in 2016, who was appointed to the bench by Ronald Reagan, there was – broadly speaking – a 5:4 conservative majority (going back to the same-sex marriage ruling, it helps to explain why there was such delight at the time – not just because of the ruling itself, but surprise that with the conservative make-up of the court it had reached that decision). There are three other justices who are also of advanced years – when the 2016 election came round the liberal Ruth Bader Ginsburg was 83, Anthony Kennedy (nominally conservative, but the critical voice in the same-sex marriage decision) 80, and Justice Stephen Breyer, who was appointed by President Clinton, just a little younger.

Look at the arguments put forward why President Obama should *not* seek to fill the vacancy. Senator Ted Cruz, a trained constitutional lawyer, said this: 'I don't think the American people want a court that will strip our religious liberties. I don't think the American people want a court that will mandate unlimited abortion-on-demand, partial birth abortion with taxpayer funding and no parental notification.'

Now I am no constitutional lawyer and I may be missing something subtle here, but that looks to me like a straightforward, unadulterated, 100 per cent pure political argument – a perfectly legitimate one, I hasten to add – but this view is political not constitutional: we want a solid Christian on the bench who will turn around these liberal judgments. He was equally candid when he said: 'We're not going to give up the US Supreme Court for a generation by allowing Barack Obama to make one more liberal appointee.'

Senator Cruz's view prevailed. Judge Merrick Garland was never given the courtesy of a single Senate hearing, and presumably his name will become a pub quiz question at some future date – who was the proposed Supreme Court justice who never got a hearing? One of President Trump's first acts was to propose Neil Gorsuch, another hugely respected judge, but one whose views were much more in line with what Senator Cruz wanted. Indeed Cruz was leading the chorus of praise from the White House on the night he was introduced to the American public, live on prime-time television.

Scholars talk about the 'firewall' between church and state in the United States. In modern-day America it looks more like a threadbare, moth-eaten blanket.

CHAPTER 6

Guns

When the call came from the White House late one evening at home, telling me I had an interview with the president in a week's time, it was as welcome as it was unexpected. OK. That quite doesn't do justice to my reaction. In fact while I was on the phone to a key aide to Barack Obama, I may have been jumping up and down with excitement, while trying to remain sounding carefully modulated to the man I was speaking to on the phone. BBC interviews with a serving president don't come along that often. But then came the torrent of advice and the sleepless nights over what issues to cover.

He was about to embark on a trip to Africa, and because of the BBC's pre-eminence on the continent – notably its Swahili and Somali services, the White House had come to us (although I obviously tried to spin it to my bosses that it was down to the astonishing reputation I had as a journalist). So that visit, and what he hoped to achieve, would take a good chunk of interview time. There was also the newly signed-off Iran nuclear deal. But then what else do you cover, when you consider the massive waterfront of issues that a US president has to contend with?

Before we sat down in the Roosevelt Room I spoke to a couple of people who knew him well, and I was warned of one thing in particular. If he was in a bad mood, or took against your line of questioning, you would get Professor Obama: clever, aloof, giving extremely long answers, refusing to be interrupted. Or, if the chemistry was right, you would get Friendly Obama: engaging, amusing, thoughtful and candid. We were lucky enough to get the second.

Normally when I do a big set-piece TV interview, I see it as my job to try to put the interviewee at ease – you know, don't worry about the TV lights, just look at me and ignore the cameras – but when you are speaking to the leader of the free world in the White House the boot is very much on the other foot. There was a crackle of expectation before he walked in – and then, there he was – relaxed, charming and shaking hands with all the team (when the interview ended he asked me whether I thought the film crew would like a team photo with him. 'My guess, Mr President, is that they probably would ...'). As it happened I made a mess of my first question, and said we would start again and go from the top. Without missing a beat the president said that was good, as it would give him a chance to wipe something from his eye. He had nothing in his eye, but it was a gracious move on his part.

I wanted to ask him a question about where he thought he'd failed – never an easy question to ask a serving politician. But I prefaced it with an unusual question. Eight months earlier the president had endured a horror show in the November mid-term elections. Commentators effectively wrote off the remaining two years of his presidency, saying he had become a lame duck. But in that time, moves were made to normalise relations with Cuba, the Iran nuclear deal had been signed, the Supreme Court had backed him on gay marriage, and his signature healthcare policy, the Affordable Care Act, had survived an assault there as well. And so I asked the unconventional question: what's gone right? He laughed. And gave me a version of Kipling's words about treating success and failure as the true impostors that they are.

But then I asked where he had fallen short. The answer he gave me on gun control was so raw and free of the usual filters that it was hard to believe it had come from the mouth of a politician:

> If you ask me where has been the one area where I feel that I've been most frustrated and most stymied, it is the fact that the United States of America is the one advanced nation on earth in which we do not have sufficient common-sense, gun-safety laws. Even in the face of repeated mass killings. And you know, if you look at the number of Americans killed since 9/11 by terrorism, it's less than a hundred. If you look at the number that have been killed by gun violence, it's in the tens of thousands. And for us not to be able to resolve that issue has been something that is distressing. But it is not something that I intend to stop working on in the remaining 18 months.

We recorded the interview at half past two in the afternoon. Five hours later in Lafayette, Louisiana, an audience had just taken their seats to watch the hilarious comedienne, Amy

Schumer, in the film *Trainwreck*. The movie had been running for about 20 minutes when a 59-year-old man, John Houser, pulled out a gun and fired 13 rounds, killing two people and wounding seven others. He then tried to leave with the panicking crowd, but realising that police were closing in on him he turned his .40 calibre handgun on himself and took his own life. And with that another mass killing incident in America was added to that long, depressing list.

The one consistent piece of punctuation from the Obama presidency has been the mass killings and shootings. Fort Hood, the Aurora cinema shooting which claimed the lives of 12 people, the attack on Congresswoman Gabby Giffords in Tucson, Sandy Hook Elementary where 20 children and 6 teachers were killed, the Wisconsin Sikh Temple killings, Washington Navy Yard, the attack by a lone white supremacist on a historic black church in Charleston, South Carolina, where nine people at a Bible study group were gunned down, the 'live on TV' killing of a reporter and her cameraman in Virginia by a disgruntled employee. San Bernardino. Orlando. The list goes on and on – and I am only mentioning the ones that have made international headlines. Every one of them a tragedy for those who lost loved ones.

One of the more grotesque discussions I've heard on the US news channels is to ask which is the most horrific of America's most recent spate of mass killings. Black churchgoers at a Bible study evening killed by a white supremacist? Revellers in a nightclub? Workers gathering for a Christmas party? People going to a family planning clinic? Settling down to watch a movie? Each has its own unique bit of hideousness. And for family members who lose loved ones, the pain is not relative to other crimes committed elsewhere, it is total.

But for sheer, horrific depravity and pointlessness, the killing of all those six- and seven-year-old schoolchildren at Sandy Hook still stands out as a nadir.

It was just before Christmas in 2012 when 20-year-old Adam Lanza got up on a Friday morning and started the day by killing his mother at their Newtown home. He then took the keys to his mother's car and drove to Sandy Hook Elementary School. He used a rifle to force his way into the school. He would eventually find his way into the classroom where Lauren Rousseau, a substitute teacher, and Rachel D'Avino, a behavioural therapist, had marshalled their first-grade students to the back of the room. They tried to get them to huddle in a bathroom. One six-year-old girl who played dead would be the sole survivor of what unfolded in that part of the school. When she was eventually reunited with her mother she said, 'Mommy, I'm OK, but all my friends are dead.' Twenty infants died along with six teachers. Lanza would turn the gun on himself and shoot himself in the head.

Newtown, Connecticut, which lies about 60 miles north of New York City, had been a quiet, relatively crime-free place until that day. In a town of 28,000 people there had only been one homicide in the previous ten years. One bit of 'journalese' that I have always hated is 'it could have been worse, but for …' – how could anything be worse than what unfolded in that school? But actually it could have been. Because mass-shooting incidents have become so common in the US, there are procedures and protocols in place, and schools regularly rehearse what to do in case there is an 'active shooter' – just like my parents' generation used to act out air-raid drills in the Second World War. When the principal and lead teacher realised what was unfolding, they went out into the hallway to call out 'Shooter! Stay put!' The teachers knew what to do and did their best to barricade their classroom doors.

One picture that went viral in 2016 was from Michigan and showed a beautiful little three-year-old girl in a yellow and blue dress at kindergarten standing on top of a toilet practising for an active shooter. She would tell her mother that afternoon when she got home that her class had been rehearsing 'mass shooting survival strategies'. It prompted an anguished nationwide discussion about how young is too young to expose children to the horrors of real life and modern American society.

But nothing like as anguished as the discussions over what the correct policy response should be to Sandy Hook in 2012. And just like in Britain after Dunblane, there was overwhelming support among the public for a tightening of the country's gun laws. Not a ban, but definitely a tightening. Within a week of the killings, 200,000 people had signed a White House 'we the people' petition demanding tough action. Barack Obama insisted, 'We're going to have to come together and take meaningful action to prevent more tragedies like this, regardless of the politics.' He would take a series of actions using his executive authority and wanted Congress to take measures to reimpose a ban on assault weapons, an expansion of background checks of people seeking to buy weapons, and a ban on high-capacity magazines, so that in future the magazine would hold a maximum of 10 bullets. Lanza at Sandy Hook had magazines that each contained 30 rounds. He wanted a total ban on the possession of armour-piercing bullets by anyone other than the armed forces and the police.

The Sandy Hook families came to the Senate to watch the votes – and to their horror see the proposals fall short – not just because the Republicans lined up against the changes, but because a large number of Democrats did as well. The latest attempt at federal gun control had failed. Senator Dianne Feinstein, who proposed the assault weapon ban, would say afterwards, 'I have watched these votes, and I must say I view them with substantial dismay at the lack of courage in this house ... Courage to stand up and say we've had enough of these killings.'

And then there are the shootings that just force you to raise a quizzical eyebrow. Take 31-year-old Jamie Gilt from Florida. She regularly posted on Facebook her support for the National Rifle Association, insisting that any change to existing gun laws would make her less able to protect her children from danger. But one day she had left her handbag on the back seat of her car, her four-year-old son had rummaged through it and guess what he found? Yes, her fully loaded pistol. And bang. 'She was sitting in the driver seat and he was in the back seat, behind her,' explained Captain Joseph Wells from Putnam County Sheriff's Department. 'He shot straight through. The bullet entered her lower back and exited through her abdominal area. It went through her and we recovered the round inside the vehicle. It was a .45 caliber [handgun].' The slug was pulled out of the dashboard. She survived the shooting. But every day – yes, every day – there is some new shooting horror, and a terrifying number who don't survive.

In 2005 I was sent to Louisiana to cover the devastating events of Hurricane Katrina. Much of the Gulf Coast of the world's pre-eminent superpower was not functioning.

The fall from First World to Third World took place at a frightening pace – electricity was cut off, there was no water because supplying it relied on electricity while air-conditioned buildings were designed never to have their windows opened. Hotels had stopped functioning because of this – so our enterprising fixer managed to hire a tour bus that had previously been used by Earth, Wind & Fire. Really. I got exclusive use of the circular purple leather bed at the back with the mirrored ceiling. Oh, if only those walls could speak, what stories they would tell ...

In Biloxi, Gulfport, and then in New Orleans, shop owners had graffiti'd their own shop fronts with the words 'If you loot, we shoot.' It was then that we found out that the driver of our bus was tooled up as well. Now even when we travel in Iraq or Afghanistan, where we will have ex-special-forces guys looking after our protection, they won't be armed. The thinking being that the last thing we want is to be in the middle of a firefight. There's also a danger that it makes us look like combatants. But here in Louisiana it was different. Our driver opened up his briefcase to reveal two revolvers and a pile of ammunition, and said that anyone who tried to hijack the bus or break in would get what's coming to them. His briefcase also contained bottles of pills and tablets. Wanting to change the subject away from the small arsenal, my producer, Declan, asked what the pills were for. 'I suffer from depression and anxiety,' he told us. Reassuring.

The statistics are roughly these. On average, 30,000 Americans are killed each year by guns. They are not all homicides – far from it. These are people who've gone into the woodshed and taken their own lives, people who've died after a gun has been fired by accident – but a lot are down to gun crime.

Take this catchy little statistic – on Christmas Day 2015 more people died from gun homicides in the United States than died in the UK throughout all of 2013. In America on 25 December, 27 people died and 63 were injured. This figure does *not* include suicides or attempted suicides. Or, to put it another way – that is equal to the total number of people killed in gun homicides in an entire year in Austria, New Zealand, Norway, Slovenia, Estonia, Bermuda, Hong Kong and Iceland, combined.

Now before you argue – correctly – that I am not comparing apples with apples, I accept that America is a far bigger country than the UK, so you would expect far more gun deaths. But on that basis the US would have five times as many gun deaths as the UK – not a thousand times more.

And just while I am on a statistical roll, how about this? Home Office figures reveal that between 2013–14 and 2014–15 the use of firearms by police in England and Wales went up 300 per cent. Shocking? Well, maybe, but from a very low base. Yes, police used their guns twice in the whole of 2014, and six times in 2015. In the US during 2016 it is estimated that a thousand people were shot and killed by the police. Actually what is remarkable in studying the Home Office statistics is the gap between the huge number of occasions when an armed response vehicle is deployed in Britain and just how incredibly seldom it is that a police firearm is drawn.

The US ambassador to London in Obama's second term, Matthew Barzun, was a determined champion of public diplomacy. When he was asked to take up the post, he asked the president what advice he had. President Obama said, 'Listen …' That was not the start of the sentence. That was the sentence. And so Ambassador Barzun travelled the length and breadth of the UK speaking to sixth formers and college students to gauge their views on America. And he produced a fascinating A5 word cloud. The young people were asked to list what they liked most about America – music, NASA, clothes, opportunity, food, iPhones, came the reply. And what did they dislike most? It was one thing overwhelmingly. Guns.

So where does this love of guns come from? One thing that the British school curriculum doesn't teach much of is the Revolutionary War, when Americans were seeking to fight off their colonial rulers. No discussion of gun law and the right to bear arms can take place without looking at the Second Amendment, passed over 200 years ago, and still the subject of controversy – perhaps even more controversy today. It states: *'A well regulated Militia, being necessary to the security of a free State, the right of the people to keep and bear Arms, shall not be infringed.'*

The idea of the 'right to bear arms' was not created by the First Congress, it was a concept deeply rooted in English history. For centuries, during the Middle Ages and up through the 17th century, every Englishman was not only allowed to have a weapon, but was *expected* to have one, or even *required* to have one. The kings of England had no large standing armies ready to go into battle at a moment's notice, so instead, whether he liked it or not, every man in the kingdom was considered to be part of the king's army – and it was the duty of everyone to protect the kingdom. That principle extended to the colonies where the British carried weapons.

But it was something they tried to deny to the Americans they ruled over. During the Revolutionary War period, the British recognised the local population would use their arms to defend themselves, so they made every effort to confiscate as many weapons as they could.

Once America declared its independence, the right to bear arms became an obvious issue for those framing the constitution. Yes, in part it was about self-defence – but the real motivation was much more revolutionary than that. When Thomas Jefferson wrote the Declaration of Independence he said that if a government failed to protect its citizens and instead *became* the enemy, the citizens had the right to overthrow it. So one reason the citizens wanted to be armed was not just for defence against external enemies. They wanted protection from their own government.

Noah Webster (later the founder of the eponymous dictionary) wrote: 'Before a standing army can rule, the people must be disarmed; as they are in almost every kingdom in Europe. The supreme power in America cannot enforce unjust laws by the sword; because the whole body of the people are armed, and constitute a force superior to any band of regular troops that can be, on any pretence, raised in the United States.'

Americans are, and have always been, deeply suspicious of federal authority and rule from Washington. In the 18th century the right to bear arms was seen as an important bulwark against an over-mighty government that the people might, one day, have to rise up against. And though today the standing army of the United States is the most powerful in the world, that symbolic desire to check the power of central government remains – if anything, it is felt even more keenly in the febrile mood of 21st-century America.

The sheer impossibility of forging political agreement on this would come to the fore again in the wake of the Orlando killings and what had happened in San Bernardino. Following 9/11 there was the creation by the FBI of a Terrorist Screening Centre. It is a single database used by all government agencies to keep tabs on those who might reasonably be suspected of having links to extremist groups. If you are on the terror watch list, there are serious restrictions placed on your ability to move around. For example, you will be banned from all internal and international flights. But, astonishingly, you are still able to wander down to the local firearms dealer and buy yourself a gun. Being on the FBI list is not in itself sufficient grounds for being banned from buying a rifle.

The renewed fears about the terror threat within the US after the IS-inspired attacks in San Bernardino and Orlando – Omar Mateen the perpetrator of the Orlando attack had twice been on the terror watch list – meant the president proposed to close that loophole. Commonsense measure? Well, no, as it turns out. The pro-gun groups said it would strip Americans of their Fifth Amendment rights of due process. If they haven't been charged with anything, and haven't had their day in court, how can they be banned from a lawful activity like buying a gun? The National Rifle Association of course agrees that terrorists should not be allowed to purchase guns, but has opposed using the watch list for that purpose. In a statement it said, 'Due process protections should be put in place that allow law-abiding Americans who are wrongly put on a watch list to be removed.'

Once you have made that argument, you quickly alight on the next one, that to impose such a ban would be in breach of a person's Second Amendment right to bear arms. That, combined with doubts about how accurate the terrorist screening database actually was, led to another impasse and a failure to pass the measure through the Senate – an unusual alliance between civil liberties groups and gun-lobby activists ensured that this measure would die the same death as previous efforts to change the law. And do they know how to flex their muscles!

The argument you will hear again and again is this: America is a vast sprawling country, with millions living in massively remote places, miles from anywhere. They still have a frontier mentality and won't – often can't – just pick up the phone and say, 'Can the state please come and sort this out?' They are out in the middle of nowhere, and when you are in the wilds you need to be able to fend for yourself. In Britain's small, overcrowded island that may be a difficult idea to comprehend; in America it is part of the psyche, and guns are an extension of who they are and how they live. Just as they are likely to have a basement shelter, full of tinned food and bottled water, a generator, fuel, blankets, tents and torches in case a hurricane or tornado rips through, so they view having a gun – or guns – as just another key element in being able to fend for themselves, a means to defend their family and community in the battle for survival. And when you see the epic weather that regularly bears down on the United States, that is not fanciful. But at the back of a lot of American minds is the belief that the only person you can trust to defend your family and your property is you.

And don't labour under the misapprehension that this is just a few swivel-eyed hillbillies living high up in the Ozark Mountains, or zany zealots of some religious sect who spend their nights howling at the moon. Many of our neighbours in wealthy Georgetown have their cellars stocked to the gunnels with enough tinned and dried food to deal with whatever catastrophic collapse in societal order may come their way.

But it doesn't end there. Survivalism, you see, is just as important to the super wealthy. So one of the industries that has seen a big upturn in interest since Donald Trump became president is the demand for blocks of flats built entirely underground – or, if you've got enough money, your own deluxe, high-spec, interior-designed, all luxury underground bomb shelter, either installed under the house or somewhere on your land. The idea is that thanks to shrewd investments and vast sums of money, you will be able to ride out the apocalypse, unscathed. The *National Geographic* ran a series called 'Doomsday Prepping'; the website for the programme had a quiz titled 'How prepped are you?' In Britain we think of Survivalism as being a hobbyish, boy-scoutish pursuit in which people like Bear Grylls go through the woods, teaching us how to rub sticks together to start a fire and make a delicious four-course meal out of grubs, fungi, moss, tree bark and worms. Actually, in the US Bear Grylls is a superstar because people like him are seen to hold the keys to surviving whatever the universe throws at you.

Just north of Wichita, Kansas, is a former missile silo which has been converted into a block of flats, 15 storeys beneath the surface of the earth. This is survival chic. All the apartments were snapped up in the complex. Each room in each flat has a wall-mounted flat-screen TV projecting pictures from above ground, so your television is performing the function of a window – not so much a window on the world, but on whatever is going on at ground level, Wichita. From sunrise to sunset. The flats are apparently designed to allow you to survive global pandemics, hideous weather events – and even a nuclear attack.

In Silicon Valley tech billionaires no longer sit around talking about property prices or which recherché school their kids will be attending – no, instead they'll be discussing which make of bunker to buy, what crypto-currency to use in the event of a collapse of the financial system, which countries would be safest to escape to. Probably quite a lot of money to shell out to last a month or two longer than everyone else, but, hey, this is a big, serious business.

And the group which sees itself as the champions of these individuals – whether the person with a leaky old generator and an assault rifle, or the person with a fully fitted bunker – is a body called the National Rifle Association, the NRA – unarguably the most powerful lobbying organisation in the United States. Go to any gun show and they are there recruiting new members, welcoming old, bringing people up to date with any changes to the law that might need opposing – but also organising training days and lectures on how to handle weapons and the like. The show I went to was in Chantilly, Virginia.

To give an idea of scale, it is like going to an out-of-town DIY store – except every table is loaded with weaponry: old, new, teeny little pistols that could fit in your handbag, hunting rifles that could probably dislocate your shoulder if you didn't know what you were doing with them. On one stand they were selling rifles in a fetching pink colour –

they're for the ladies, the male owner of the stand told me. And then there were the semi-automatic assault weapons that looked like they should only ever be used on the battlefield, or by Bruce Willis in a *Die Hard* movie. I asked the owner of this stand what the weapons were for. He shrugged his shoulders and said, 'Whatever you want to use them for.'

The first woman that I spoke to at the show had come with her husband and two children. To look at (and I know you should never judge people by appearances), she seemed to me as though she would be a stalwart of the Women's Institute, if she were living in the UK. Unflashy, sensible, neatly turned out, with scrupulously polite children, a slightly diffident husband. A cake-baking, churchgoing, homework-enforcing soccer mom if ever I saw one. She was about as far away as it was possible to get from my mental image of a gun owner.

So I asked her whether she had come to buy a gun. 'No,' she replies, 'I have a gun, I'm just coming to buy a laser sight for it.' Of course. And she patiently explained that ferrying her kids back and forth from school, she wanted to be able to rest easy that she would be able to defend them if anything untoward happened on the drive. Presumably the laser sight when fitted on her revolver would add to the accuracy that she would have in hitting her target. She also told me that her husband was away for work a lot, and they lived in a remote location. Having a weapon in the house made her feel safer.

There were one or two people at the gun show who you would definitely not want to meet in an ill-lit alleyway on a cold winter's night. A handful looked like they might be extras from the movie *Deliverance* – by which I mean dungarees, crazy hair, not a lot of teeth and a faraway look; others who looked like they were auditioning for the next Tarantino film. But overwhelmingly they were mundane, ordinary, bland-looking people who could just as easily have been buying bedding plants at the garden centre as semi-automatic assault rifles at the gun show. They were you and me.

And not for everyone is the gun a piece of vital security. For huge numbers it is a hobby. Just as people collect stamps or coins, so a lot of Americans collect guns. After the Islamic State-inspired shooting at the Pulse nightclub in Orlando, reporters went to the hometown of the killer Omar Mateen. He came from Port St Lucie in Florida. A fellow resident told us that he had seven Kalashnikovs in the house. 'Why do you need seven?' one reporter enquired. His answer was fabulously revealing. He said, 'No one asks my wife why she has seven pairs of shoes, so why do people ask me why I need seven Kalashnikovs?' As a piece of logic it is unarguable – provided, that is, you see no difference in owning shoes to owning high-powered rifles. And for a lot of Americans it is as unremarkable to own a number of different firearms as it is to own a pair of high-heeled shoes and a pair of pumps. There are shooting ranges everywhere and people go out hunting at weekends. Americans love their dogs and they love the flag and they love their guns.

In Britain after the Dunblane school shooting in 1996, where Thomas Hamilton killed 16 small children and one teacher before turning the gun on himself, the government moved, and moved fast. An inquiry was set up to look at what needed to change, and out of it emerged legislation a year later which, in effect, banned all handguns. It was an Act of Parliament that enjoyed massive support in the country. Britain was more or less united – there was no need for anyone to own or carry a handgun. And since then there has not been a mass-shooting incident on that scale, or anything close to it, in the UK.

There is a website in the US called massshootingtracker. org. According to its data – in which a mass shooting is defined as an incident in which at least four people are killed or wounded – there were 372 mass shootings in the US in 2015, killing 475 and wounding 1,870. In other words, just over one mass shooting a day.

One of the questions I am regularly asked on air after the latest mass-shooting incident in the US, when I am standing just behind a police line and the forensic teams are going about their work, and a small mountain of flowers is slowly taking shape as grieving families weep nearby, is will America enact similar legislation? I don't wish to do down our trade, but as BBC correspondents after a little while we become quite good at doing 'on the one hand, on the other' type answers, which always leave a little bit of wiggle room. But on this question there is no need. The only answer is an emphatic NO. It is not going to happen. Not now. Not in the future. There would be civil war before Americans give up their guns. It is enshrined in the constitution, it is an intrinsic part of American culture, and the NRA, which represents the gun owners, has awesome power. And there are few politicians prepared to stand up to the NRA.

Guns, you see, are not a minority interest. In 2009 a new record was reached. There were more guns in circulation than there were people to own them. That means just over 300 million weapons held in private hands. The inflection point came during the first year of Barack Obama's presidency. Although there are more guns than people, only around 40 per cent of households own firearms. And variation is great from state to state. In remote Alaska more than 60 per cent of adults say they own a firearm (a unique case in that danger can lurk not only in someone else carrying a gun with ill-intent but also polar bears who might see you as dinner), whereas that figure, according to the journal *Injury Prevention*, drops to 5 per cent in mostly urban Delaware, just north of Washington DC. As a gun owner you are also most likely to be a white male over the age of 55 who was once or is still married.

Laws vary from state to state on how openly you can wear your gun. One of the growing trends – and challenges to law enforcement – is the 'open carry' movement. More and more people now choose to have their gun openly strapped to their leg or around their waist, like in a cowboy movie. I was in a motorcycle shop in Virginia and was chatting to this charming gentleman, who, I noticed after I had finished speaking to him, had a revolver in a holster on his waist. It was Saturday morning in a peaceful and wealthy suburb, just a few miles from the centre of Washington DC. Gun-rights advocates see the practice as a way to normalise gun ownership and deter crime; those who advocate gun control believe that such 'open carry' in public places will encourage violence. And a number of the big restaurant chains have signs on the doors saying no firearms. There are only five states that ban 'open carry' outright – California, Texas, Florida, South Carolina and New York. The rest either allow it freely, or allow it providing you have a permit or licence.

The challenge this poses to the law enforcement authorities is obvious. At present many of the calls to 911 control rooms are from members of the public to draw attention to someone on the street carrying a firearm. But if everyone is carrying a firearm openly, then which calls are the police meant to respond to?

All states have to allow 'concealed carry' – though some only permit qualified individuals to bear their hidden firearms in public. In those states courses are run on how to safely carry a concealed weapon. States and districts that have tried to maintain a ban on even concealed carry have found themselves challenged in the Supreme Court. Illinois was the last state to allow concealed carry, but only after its long-standing ban was overturned by a federal appeals court. In Washington DC there were also very strict gun laws, but those too were struck down as unconstitutional.

President Obama has been one of the most determined opponents of unfettered access to guns, but inadvertently has been the gun industry's greatest friend. Honestly, some of the big companies should be putting him on the board as a non-executive director now that he's left the White House – because what he's done for their profitability and sales is off the charts. Let me explain.

When Barack Obama became president there was a huge spike in gun sales as people foresaw that he would try to limit ownership. He had committed himself to as much in his 2012 campaign. So for a brief period there was a 'buy now, while stocks last' mentality. And then history repeated itself. With every mass-shooting incident that was on a big enough scale to garner national attention, sales would leap again, with gun owners going out to stock up on weapons and ammunition for fear of a new federal clampdown.

Michael Fifer is the chief executive of Sturm, Ruger & Co., the largest handgun manufacturer in the US. Speaking at his company's annual meeting in May 2016, he noted that his company enjoyed a spike in demand that 'was strongly correlated to the tragic terrorist activities in Paris and San Bernardino'. Sales that would leap again in the wake of the Orlando shootings. And eyeing the possibility of Hillary Clinton winning the 2016 election – she had committed herself to further gun-control measures – Fifer called that a 'big opportunity for the distributors to step up and take on inventory' to be ready for election-related sales.

Earlier that year, in an investor conference call, he predicted that 'we'll see a step up of demand if a Democrat wins' the presidency. And if Democrats win control of the Senate, he added, gun sales will increase dramatically based on fears that a more liberal Supreme Court might restrict gun owner-ship rights.

It is one of the strange perversities of the gun industry that the worse things are, the better they are. What is fascinating is the correlation between the share price of gun manufac-turers and headline-grabbing mass-shooting events. Far from shares falling amid fears of new regulation, they rise sharply in anticipation of the surge in demand that will follow. So the Orlando killings happened late on a Saturday night, with the full scale of the horror only becoming apparent on Sunday. On Monday when Wall Street opened for business the price of Sturm, Ruger shares jumped 4 per cent in early trading; Smith & Wesson shares leaped 7 per cent. Look at any of the other infamous mass shootings and the pattern is repeated.

It's hard to get precise figures on firearms sales, because there's no industry-wide body that produces and reports these figures. So the best alternative way to chart demand and gun-buying activity is through the number of background checks carried out by the FBI's National Instant Criminal Background Check System (NICS). These are performed on anyone buying a firearm at a licensed gun shop. In the weeks after the June mass shooting in Orlando, gun-shop applications for background checks reached an all-time monthly high; and June was the third highest month on record nationwide.

So how easy is it to lay your hands on a gun in the US? Anyone buying a gun from a registered gun dealer will undergo a background check. It is a one-page form, or can be done over the phone to NICS. Most checks are resolved within a minute. Essentially the check is on whether you have a criminal record or are mentally ill. The FBI has up to three days to make a determination – and if it doesn't come back with an answer in that time the sale can proceed legally. In other words it's not very difficult.

In addition there are all sorts of loopholes and weaknesses in the system. Going back to the gun show I went to in Chantilly, there are individuals wandering around with rifles strapped to their backs, and coming from the muzzle of the gun is a 'for sale' sign. They are not registered dealers and are able to sell to whoever wants to buy, with no checks required.

While I was there I interviewed a chap who dealt mainly in antique weapons – and antique in this case was anything over 30 years old. He had for sale a high-powered Remington rifle from the 1970s, and I asked what checks he would have to make before he could sell it to me. He said he would need to see my driving licence and would need to ask me verbally whether there was any reason why he shouldn't sell it to me. Because it was an antique it would not have to be registered with the FBI. So although I had never owned or used a firearm (well I did shoot a .303 at the range when I joined the school cadet force when I was 11), and with just my word to go on, the dealer would have broken no rules if he had let me walk out with the gun and as much ammunition as I could fill my pockets with.

Then there is the birthday-present loophole. There is nothing to stop me perfectly legally buying and registering a firearm through the federal system, but then giving the weapon as a present to my wayward nephew. A number of weapons have found themselves in the wrong hands by this method of transmission. And then there is the black market.

Just after we had filmed at this gun show we went to the South Side of Chicago. Here, in the city where Obama cut his political teeth as a young community worker, gun violence is spiralling out of control. It is early January, and the temperature outside is -14°C, with the wind whipping off Lake Superior making it feel even colder. It is painful to be outside on the street for more than ten minutes at a time. We arrange to meet two former gang members who said they would take us on a tour. Joe and Will had both served multiple lengthy jail terms and were now trying to get younger gang members back on the straight and narrow. They call themselves violence interruptors. But the night before I meet them two of the teenagers they are mentoring die in a shootout at a liquor store they had tried to hold up.

In the morning, when we arrive, police have sealed off the area around the store with tape. By early afternoon it has gone, along with the investigating officers, and the off licence is back open for business. Incidents like this are two a penny in Chicago's South Side. And Will and Joe describe a situation where the market is awash with black-market guns. It is easier to buy a gun than cigarettes. Illinois has tight gun laws – but 60 per cent of the incidents reported by police involve guns that have come from outside the state. One of Illinois's senators, Dick Durbin, said that 40 per cent of guns used in Chicago crimes could be traced back to purchases made at gun shows in Indiana, where no background check is required.

As I say, we went to Chicago at the beginning of 2016 to film this report. By the end of the year 762 people had been murdered. There had been 3,500 shooting incidents. In other words two murders a day, ten shooting incidents a day. America's third city had become the most dangerous place to be in the USA.

So where does the argument on gun control stand? The last major measure that managed to get through Congress was piloted by then Senator Joe Biden in 1994 when Bill Clinton was president. It banned several types of assault weapon, which on the face of it sounds fine. But unlike the more or less total blanket British ban, this was much more selective. And it became rather like another piece of British legislation, the ill-considered Dangerous Dogs Act, which was practically unenforceable because there were so many issues about definition. The problem with the assault rifle ban was just the same: like the Dangerous Dogs Act, it was a bit of a dog's dinner.

For a start, what is an assault weapon? There are fully automatic weapons, where you squeeze the trigger and it fires continuously until you let go. Those machine guns have been banned since the 1930s. Then you are left with a 'semi-auto-matic'. They reload automatically, but fire only once, each time you squeeze the trigger. These weapons come as rifles and revolvers and are extremely common across the US. So Congress didn't want a blanket ban – because in effect you would be banning guns, so the lawmakers focused instead on 18 types of firearms, including some with military-style features on them. There were flow charts and diagrams. As the *Washington Post* would point out: 'Certain models of AR-15s and AK-47s were banned. Any semi-automatic rifle with a pistol grip and a bayonet mount was an "assault weapon". But a semi-automatic rifle with just a pistol grip might be okay. It was complicated. And its complexity made it easy to evade.'

When George W. Bush became president, the law was allowed to lapse. All of which means the AR-15s and the AK-47s are still freely available, with no more checks required to purchase one than for buying any other firearm. The AR-15-style assault rifle would be the weapon of choice in the Sandy Hook, San Bernardino and Orlando killings.

What would be a mistake, though, is to think that the gun lobby does not have an interest in curbing the carnage of gun violence. Of course it does – but its solution is for there to be more guns, not fewer. The argument was best articulated by the National Rifle Association's executive vice president, Wayne LaPierre, when he said: 'The only thing that stops a bad guy with a gun is a good guy with a gun.' For $17.95 on the NRA website you can buy that as a T-shirt in black or blue – the front of the T-shirt has the first part of the slogan; the second half is on the back.

Actually if you want to get a glimpse of the mindset of many NRA supporters, you could do worse than spend a few minutes on the website for the NRA shop. The best-selling cap has the legend 'stand and fight', and as well as lots of gun ephemera there is all manner of bits of survival kit: on the 'best sellers' page there is the NRA critical food supply, tactical waterproof blanket (not sure how a blanket can be tactical, but I quibble), five-day survival backpack, water purification kits. And on and on. Just as British people might find it incomprehensible that the gun plays such a pivotal role in US society, Americans can't believe that we are prepared to leave ourselves so nakedly unprotected, and so reliant on the forces of law and order to come to our rescue.

But going back to the T-shirt slogan, of course the counter-blast to that is that if guns make you safe, then why isn't America the safest place on earth? Presumably because the weapons are in the hands of too many bad people.

So let's be clear what this actually means. And it is said quite openly. In the context of Sandy Hook the argument is made that if only the first-grade teacher, Lauren Rousseau, had had a gun in her desk then she would have been able to cut down Lanza; if only the students on campus at Virginia Tech had had weapons then they could have killed Seung-Hui Cho before his rampage which left 32 dead, and if only the pastor, Clementa Pinckney, had had a revolver under his robes in the Emanuel African Methodist Episcopal church in Charleston, South Carolina, then he could have shot Dylann Roof before Roof shot him and his fellow worshippers.

In other words: let school teachers be armed, let students be armed, let preachers be armed to ward off 'the bad guy with a gun'. And the advocates of gun rights – and many others beside – lionise the 'have a go hero'. The person who fights back. The woman who is being sexually assaulted and is able to defend herself because she has a gun. The mother who can defend her children because of the revolver she keeps in the kitchen draw.

The organisation Gun Owners of America claims that far more criminals are shot and killed by civilians than by the police. And to the charge that the widespread carrying of guns results in chaos, they offer this riposte. 'No. Consider the case of Florida. A citizen in the Sunshine State is far more likely to be attacked by an alligator than to be assaulted by a concealed carry holder. During the first 15 years that the Florida law was in effect, alligator attacks outpaced the number of crimes committed by carry holders by a 229 to 155 margin.'

But where is the line drawn? Should the revellers in the Pulse nightclub have been allowed to carry weapons?

When you work for the BBC or any other major news organisation, and you are about to be sent out into the field where there may be serious personal risk – a disaster area, say, or a war zone – one of the courses that is obligatory is training for hostile environments. A good chunk of time is spent on first aid – and also ballistics. It is a part of the course that is simultaneously one of the most interesting and one of the most frightening. One of the things we are taught is to identify whether gunfire is incoming or outgoing. And is it contact left or contact right? Because identifying where the gun is being fired from helps you work out where to take cover. Incidentally, hiding behind a car door like you see in the cop films offers you no protection whatsoever. A bullet will go whistling through something as flimsy as a car door – and through you too.

We do our training in the open air where it is a bit easier. There's the bang and then the echo. But even then it is not that easy to work out where firing is coming from. Can you imagine trying to identify where a bullet is coming from in a nightclub – where the music is pumping, where it is dimly lit and people may have been drinking and taking drugs? Or what about in a confined space like a college lecture theatre? If lots of students – terrified and with adrenalin surging – are rushing around the college, bullets ricocheting in all directions, with their weapons drawn, isn't it a recipe for even greater carnage, as innocent people start opening fire on innocent people? And do you want a first-grade teacher to be having to worry about their close combat firearms skills in addition to how well they are teaching the children to read and write? Do you make it a stipulation that a new teacher has to be firearms trained?

In the context of the 2016 election, Donald Trump argued that schools should cease to be gun-free zones, at one stage saying that would be one of the first things he would do as president. 'The problem with gun free zones is it's like offering candy to bad people. They [the baddies] hear gun-free zones and they go in there with their guns blazing.' In the wake of a shooting at a community college in Oregon, Trump argued that 'if you had a couple of teachers or someone with guns in that room, you would have been a hell of a lot better off'. The woman who would be appointed his education secretary, Betsy DeVos, in her often painful confirmation hearings (to put it kindly, this billionairess had not quite got on top of her brief when she answered lawmakers' questions) argued that guns might be justified in schools due to the threat posed by grizzly bears. No, really.

Against the Trump approach, Hillary Clinton consistently argued for a tightening of gun controls – very much along the lines that Barack Obama had proposed – and failed to achieve. In doing so, Mrs Clinton put herself in the cross hairs of the NRA. It's not simply that they disagreed with her policies; they loathed her, and were determined to make their very loud voice heard. You are probably used to lobby groups discreetly advocating from the sidelines, acting as the 'hidden persuaders', hands cupped over their mouths – quiet-word-in-the-ear advocacy, while trying to stay out of the political fray – but that is not the style of this lobby group. It being the NRA, it's much more all guns blazing.

When the gun-rights group held their annual conference in May 2016 it was compelling. Remember this is a single-issue pressure group, not a political party. This is an excerpt from the speech of Wayne LaPierre, the NRA's leader:

> In rooms at the White House, political elites are changing our country, one policy disaster at a time. Failed border policies. Failed education policies. Failed economic and tax policies. Failed healthcare policies. Failed energy policies. Failed foreign policies. Failed criminal justice policies. Failed defense policies. And together, they're shredding the very fabric of our country and transforming America into an America we won't even recognize.
>
> To carry out that transformation and finish the job, there are rooms where hand-picked 'super delegates' have rigged the election and circumvented voters to coronate Hillary Rodham Clinton into the White House.

It is a dirty, inside game. A corrupt system. But no one should be surprised. Corruption has followed Hillary Clinton almost her entire life. So has failure.

From her room at the State Department, Clinton's history is littered with failures. The 13 hours of Benghazi. All of Libya on fire, Egypt on fire, Syria on fire, Iraq on fire. A nuclear Iran. A brazenly emboldened Russia. An expansionist China. A nuclear North Korea testing ICBMs capable of delivering that weapon to the United States while the Obam–Clinton administration slashed America's military. All in the face of the scourge of radical Islamic terrorism that Hillary won't even name.

I'm guessing you would agree that is not the most – umm – balanced, even-handed critique you've ever read. The organisation then followed this up with a series of TV commercials designed to hole the Clinton campaign below the waterline. In August 2016, it spent $3 million in just four swing states. The ad shows a lookalike Hillary Clinton boarding a private jet, flanked by armed guards while the voiceover says, 'She's one of the wealthiest women in politics – combined income $30 million; tours the world on private jets; protected by armed guards for 30 years. But she doesn't believe in your right to keep a gun at home for self defense.' Now it is certainly true that Mrs Clinton wanted to tighten the laws on gun ownership, dealing with the various loopholes that have already been outlined. But at no point did she say she wanted to take people's guns away. Fact-checkers, who play an interesting role in US politics assessing the truthfulness of political claims, dismissed this claim as a lie.

But don't think the NRA is just a bunch of blowhard rednecks either. The NRA is the most sophisticated, most brilliant lobbying organisation in America, and you underestimate the organisation at your peril. Just look at its record during the Obama years. It has seen off every attempted piece of legislation. So how did it get to be so powerful?

The NRA for much of its existence was a very different beast from what it has become today. It was originally set up in 1871 by a couple of former 'yankees' from the Civil War who felt the conflict went on far longer than it should have done because of the poor marksmanship of the men from the North who were fighting for the maintenance of the Union against the Confederates from the South. Army records showed that for every thousand bullets fired only one Confederate soldier was killed. That was not what you would call a good strike rate.

Indeed, in the organisation's early years, as well as encouraging people to be able to hit a target with a rifle from a reasonable distance, the NRA actually supported federal government gun-control measures. Its slogan then was 'Firearms Safety Education, Marksmanship Training, Shooting for Recreation' – there was no mention of the right to bear arms.

'Historically the leadership of the NRA was more open-minded about gun control than someone familiar with the modern NRA might imagine,' wrote Adam Winkler in his book *Gunfight: The Battle over the Right to Bear Arms in America*. 'The Second Amendment was not nearly as central to the NRA's identity for most of the organisation's history.' In the 1920s and 30s America would discover that the gangs of Al Capone and the like were better equipped – and more lethally equipped, with their machine guns – than the police. This led to calls for legislation, which the NRA backed. The then head of the association Karl Frederick told a Congressional hearing into the country's first National Firearms Act in 1934, 'I have never believed in the general practice of carrying weapons. I seldom carry one ... I do not believe in the general promiscuous toting of guns. I think it should be sharply restricted and only under licenses.' Those are words you would not hear today from an NRA leader.

The critical change of direction for the NRA came after the passing of another gun-control act – this time in 1968 by President Johnson, which required gun dealers to be federally licensed. The law put restrictions on certain classes of weapons. Stirrings of discontent among the membership grew. Gun dealers felt they were being harassed, rural states felt they were being forced to take the rap for the problems of America's urban violence. The split within the NRA grew wider, culminating in 1977 in a hostile takeover of the organisation by a new, much more politicised breed of gun activist. Forget target practice, the only target these right-wing libertarians were interested in was Washington. Instead of working with government, the new rulers of the NRA were deeply political – gun ownership was the epitome of freedom; Democrats in particular, with their penchant for gun-control measures, were to be mistrusted.

And just look at the story of the man who would take over. Harlon Carter grew up in a small town in Texas. Aged 17, he confronted a Mexican boy who he believed had stolen the family car. The Mexican pulled a knife, but Carter saw the knife, raised him a gun and shot him dead.

Harlon Carter was convicted, but that was overturned when the appeals court said the jury should have considered a self-defence argument. His is the perfect modern-day NRA narrative. As Winkler would point out, 'Who better to lead them than a man who really understood the value of a gun for self-protection?'

Some of those who staged the coup against the old guard had a keenly developed sense of paranoia – Harlon Carter's deputy not only thought that all gun laws ought to be repealed, including the denial of the right to own a machine gun; he believed that the deaths of Robert Kennedy and Martin Luther King had been staged to justify tighter gun-control measures.

The under-new-management NRA did two other things that are still relevant to understanding the organisation's immense power today. It took the words of the Second Amendment, which have always been highly ambiguous, and cast them anew. It omitted the first part of the sentence 'A well regulated militia being necessary to the security of a free state' because that part of the Second Amendment is nothing to do with an *individual's* right to self-defence; it is to do with the duty of the wider citizenry to keep the state safe. And the next key part of the sentence reads: '… the right of the people to keep and bear arms shall not be infringed.' Well, the use of the word 'people' is problematic too – because that also carries the implication it is not about the individual person, it is about the collective. That was how the Second Amendment was interpreted throughout the 19th century.

Many people thought that the new interpretation – that it was a constitutional right of the individual to bear arms for self-defence – was a brazen piece of historical revisionism. The NRA's revised view of the Second Amendment was scoffed at by no less a figure than a conservative, former US Supreme Court justice, Warren Burger. The man appointed by Richard Nixon would complain in 1991 in a PBS *NewsHour* interview that it is 'one of the greatest pieces of fraud – I repeat the word "fraud" – on the American public by special interest groups that I have seen in my lifetime.'

Fraud or not, the NRA's interpretation of the Second Amendment would 17 years later find favour with America's highest court in the nation, as it judged in a landmark ruling that the Second Amendment included the right to own a gun for self-protection in one's home – an interpretation that had travelled a long way from it being about the maintenance of a well-regulated militia.

The second decisive change was in the way the NRA 'lobbied' elected representatives. The NRA has around five million members, and not surprisingly wins strong financial backing from the arms manufacturers and the gun dealers who are understandably keen to support their work. How much better to have a membership organisation to make the argument for guns than just a self-interested industry body? During the 'coup' back in the 1970s, the plotters set up a 'Legislative Affairs' department – a key part of the shift in focus of the organisation was to move towards advocacy – but also a Political Action Committee (PAC) that would intervene directly in political campaigns.

The NRA rates every congressman and woman and every candidate, A+ being the highest rating, F the lowest. Rather than me trying to explain it, here's what it says on the NRA website:

A+. *A legislator with not only an excellent voting record on all critical NRA issues, but who has also made a vigorous effort to promote and defend the Second Amendment.*

A. *A solidly pro-gun candidate. A candidate who has supported NRA positions on key votes in elective office or a candidate with a demonstrated record of support on Second Amendment issues.*

B. *A generally pro-gun candidate. However, a 'B' candidate may have opposed some pro-gun reform or supported some restrictive legislation in the past.*

C. *Not necessarily a passing grade. A candidate with a mixed record or positions on gun related issues, who may oppose some pro-gun positions or support some restrictive legislation.*

D. *An anti-gun candidate who usually supports restrictive gun control legislation and opposes pro-gun reforms. Regardless of public statements, can usually be counted on to vote wrong on key issues.*

F. *True enemy of gun owners' rights. A consistent anti-gun candidate who always opposes gun owners' rights and/or actively leads anti-gun legislative efforts, or sponsors anti-gun legislation.*

Quickly, for those who think I am struggling with the alphabet, there is no grade E. So someone like Senator Ted Cruz is an A+, and Hillary Clinton is an F. Does it matter? Well, yes it does.

Because of the passion with which this subject is viewed, many members of the NRA are going to think that, come an election, where their local candidate stands on the Second

Amendment could be the biggest single determinant of how they are going to vote. The NRA will circulate to all its members a rating on everyone who is standing – and will use its political reach to encourage its members to back those who are 'on message' – and shun those who aren't. Simultaneously it will use its financial firepower to pay for TV commercials to burnish the reputations of lawmakers it likes, and run attack ads against those which it disapproves of. And while all that is going on, in Washington and state capitals up and down the country, there will be the NRA lobbyists saying to politician A or B, are you really sure you want to vote for this or that gun-control measure given all the unpleasantness that might follow?

Take this letter that was sent to members of Congress by the organisation's top lobbyist, Chris Cox, when in the wake of the Sandy Hook massacre senators were looking to expand background checks before people could buy guns: 'Expanding background checks, at gun shows or elsewhere, will not reduce violent crime or keep our kids safe in their schools.' And it went on: 'Given the importance of these issues, votes on all anti-gun amendments or proposals will be considered in NRA's future candidate's evaluations.'

All of which helps to answer a question that puzzled so many in the wake of Sandy Hook. In the emotionally charged air that followed the shooting at the school, successive opinion polls showed that a clear majority of the American people was in favour of moves towards gun control, but none was ever passed. One irresistible conclusion is that many of these mighty senators and powerful members of the House of Representatives had more fear of the NRA than concern for the public they served.

It was a British commentator on Twitter, Dan Hodges, who seemed to sum it up best in 140 characters. 'In retrospect Sandy Hook marked the end of the US gun control debate. Once America decided killing children was bearable, it was over.' This may be tendentious – of course Americans don't accept that killing children is bearable – but if an event like Sandy Hook isn't going to force a rethink on guns, or bring any consensus, what is?

Let's leave the final word on this to the man who starred as Moses in *The Ten Commandments*, Charlton Heston. The Hollywood superstar was also president of the NRA at one stage. With an actor's flamboyance, the then aging actor held a rifle above his head at the 2002 association conference and said, 'I'll give you my gun when you pry or take it from my cold, dead hands.'

Exactly. Over their dead bodies will Americans have their guns taken away from them.

CHAPTER 7

Anxiety

As headlines go, 'Maine nurse leaves house and rides bike with boyfriend' does not sound like one of those where you shout at your partner to drop whatever they're doing to come and watch the television for an urgent piece of 'breaking news'. But, believe it or not, this seemingly prosaic item made national headlines at the end of 2014 when Kaci Hickox saddled up and left her home. For those interested, they rode for about an hour, pedalled along a long country road, law enforcement vehicles watching her every move and hordes of journalists too. They returned home, shut the door and, for all I know, sat down and had a nice cup of tea.

The reason they were the centre of such attention was that Kaci had a few weeks earlier returned from Sierra Leone, where she had spent a month treating Ebola patients. When she arrived back in the US at Newark Airport with a slightly elevated temperature, she was forced into an isolation tent. The cameras filmed her through the clear plastic sheeting as though she was some exotic new addition to the local zoo. The governor of New Jersey, Chris Christie, was enforcing a policy that meant that anyone entering the country from the affected regions and showing symptons – and a raised temperature is one of them – had to spend 21 days in quarantine.

She then returned home having undergone two weeks of tests, which showed she was not carrying the virus. All fine? Well no, actually, because the governor of Maine, Paul LePage, then took it upon himself in effect to put her under house arrest and said he would 'exercise the full extent of his authority allowable by law'. She would not be allowed to leave home. Never mind that she had already been in quarantine, never mind that two tests had shown she was not carrying the virus.

What had brought us to this pass was not some revolutionary insight held by the governor into the treatment of the illness. No, it was that the population was borderline hysterical and believed that everyone was going to catch Ebola by merely looking at someone who had travelled to West Africa.

When the first cases were reported to have come into America, the cable channels went into overdrive. Round the clock, in big letters with whoops and whooshes and the BREAKING NEWS strap omni-present, the nation was told that the deadly, highly contagious disease was here. The extraordinary fuss that it provoked meant that I was suddenly on TV each night reporting the latest on the crisis stateside, until the BBC's head of news quietly asked his editors in London to remember that this was a West African problem, not an American one. But from the hue and cry in the States it would have been easy to overlook that. On American TV forget Sierra Leone, Liberia and Guinea, this story was now firmly stamped with the stars and stripes, and was getting the full treatment.

But before we dissect the news channels' contribution to making America anxious, allow me to take a brief detour into something called Betteridge's Law of Headlines. Because this is massively relevant. Admittedly not quite as significant as Newton's Law, or many other laws, but it is fun nonetheless. The law has an acronym to accompany it, which is QTWTAIN (I know – not *ever so* catchy). What these letters stand for is 'Questions To Which The Answer Is No'. Put simply, if you read in a newspaper a story with a headline which ends in a question mark, the answer is invariably NO. 'Is the Duchess of Cambridge expecting triplets?' 'Have scientists found a cure for cancer?' 'Are flesh-eating zombies about to take over earth?' 'Was Elvis just spotted in Walmart?'

If the writer or producer were sure of something, there would be no need for the question mark in the headline. So it is a very neat device that journalists have up their collective ink-stained sleeves for floating something that they are not sure of or have no way of knowing whether it is true or not. It allows journalists to unfurl a long piece of string and fly a kite masquerading as something more substantive. It allows you to say something which you know will grip the audience, but with your integrity remaining intact because you can point to that delightful little question mark at the end of the sentence and say, 'I never said it was true, I just wondered whether it could be ...'

The question mark was out in force during the Ebola outbreak. 'Should we ban ALL flights from Africa to the US?' was one of the headlines/discussion points on the news channels during the crisis. There was even discussion of whether all Africans could be banned from entering the country. And of course once a story like that is up and running there is no shortage of politicians and pundits wanting to fill the void with opinions – some of them better argued than others. There was discussion after discussion on how America was – potentially – standing on the edge of an Ebola epidemic. It wasn't and didn't.

As Kaci's attorney back in Maine argued, the lawmakers were not offering a proportionate response to the risk and the known medical science, just reacting to the fears of the public who were scared – and who voted these people in and out of office.

The legislators for their part said say they were acting out of an 'abundance of caution'. But often that abundance of caution can seem like over-reaction that does nothing but instil more anxiety and fear. Leadership would have been to say that Kaci was fine and posed no threat to those living near her in Maine – but that risked upsetting a fearful population. So instead the local politicians demand she be kept in quarantine – which in turn reinforces the feelings of anxiety of the local population. Even if she is being kept out of sight, who else is there out there who might be posing a threat?

It is a delicate line for the politicians to tread. The terror threat raises the classic dilemma: you want the citizenry to be aware of a risk – but not to be so paralysed by fear that they suspend their normal lives. When it comes to terrorism abroad, the way the state calibrates its response is via the travel advisories put out by each country's foreign ministries. And when the State Department, based in the delightfully named Foggy Bottom area of Washington, puts out such advice it has an immediate effect.

In many Americans there is a fearfulness of the outside world. And part of it is a question of geography – and the sheer size of their country. Fly a couple of hours from London and more or less any European capital is within your grasp. At a guess, 20 or so countries, with different cultures, speaking different languages, are on your doorstep. The one flight that always seems to me incredibly short, given the transformation you find when you get there, is the one from London to Marrakech. Just over three hours after you leave the damp and drizzle of Heathrow, where you have Staines and Feltham a short drive away, you enter a totally different world, with the Atlas Mountains and the Sahara Desert on your doorstep.

If I fly three hours east from Washington I am in the middle of the Atlantic; three hours west and I still have over two hours' flying time before I reach Los Angeles. If I go north, all there is is Canada, and if I fly south I only get as far as the Southern states of the US. Mexico would still be out of reach, but with a good tail wind I might reach the northernmost Caribbean islands. The point of this rather rudimentary (and not forensically precise) geography lesson is that America is geographically isolated, which does have an effect on the national psyche. And that is why the attack on Pearl Harbor by the Japanese in December 1941, and the attack on the Twin Towers in New York 60 years later, are such scarring events. They profoundly shook America's sense of inviolability and safety. Anyone trying to make sense of the America of today has to understand the profound, earth-shaking impact that 9/11 had on outlook, security, patriotism. The rest of the world, which for generations had been something that the USA could blithely ignore if it so chose, had suddenly impinged itself in the most unwelcome way imaginable with those planes flying into the twin towers and the Pentagon. The mainland United States of America was no longer immune from the conflicts and unrest of faraway countries of which the citizenry knew little.

When the US armed forces have fought in the last 150 years it has always been a long way from home. With Canada to the north, Mexico to the south and the Pacific and the Atlantic on either side of you, you tend to think that the outside world is quite a distance from where you live. So when you hear on the news or read in the papers that something bad has happened far away from home you make a mental note: 'Am not going there.' Alternatively you thank your lucky stars that you happen to be born in a country where these things don't happen. Speak to tourism bosses in London, Paris or Rome and the tourists they most want to attract are the Americans, but they will also tell you they are the most fickle, easily spooked travellers.

That said, I have also come across some of the most intrepid. And they were all elderly. We were waiting to fly from Miami to Cuba on the eve of President Obama's historic visit to the island. There was a three-way mix of passengers. Cubans going home – or Cuban Americans going back to see relatives; journalists like myself going out to cover the president's visit; and groups that fulfilled the strict criteria which allowed Americans to travel to the communist island – church groups, organised cultural visits, philanthropy, educational tours. This elderly church group waiting to board the flight were fantastic. They were intelligent, stoical, utterly determined – and totally unfazed by the flight delay. The plane had been due to take off at

19.30, but didn't actually leave until 02.45. We sat at the gate, with no information, no food and no water – all the shops in that part of the terminal having long since closed. I would like to report that the Cubans waiting to board were equally phlegmatic, but that would be a lie. People were going crazy. So much so that two burly armed police officers were sent to restore calm at the gate – which they did with only limited success. But whatever the indignities and discomfort of waiting, this group of pensioners, many with walking sticks and Zimmer frames, were the absolute picture of indefatigability.

Another trip I made with President Obama was to Saudi Arabia. The White House press party was picked up at the airport in Riyadh and driven to our hotel in the centre of the city. Partly because of the heat, partly so as not to draw attention to ourselves (I'm guessing), the curtains on the bus windows were drawn shut. This was my first trip to Riyadh and I wanted to see what the city looked like – I wanted to see what sort of cars people drove, what the architecture looked like, whether people were on the streets (they were) and women were walking about (not that I saw), whether the shops were Western or Middle Eastern, whether there were street vendors. So I pulled the curtains back and tried to get a feel. I was the only one on the bus to do so.

I fully accept the others might have been to Saudi many times before and had seen all there was to see, or they were tired after a long flight and just wanted to rest, or they had to file reports to their news organisations, so were busy with that. But no one at all interested in what it looked like outside? Not one? And many never left the hotel once we got there. Details of what the president was doing were fed in as well as the pictures, so there was no need to ever leave. But the souvenir shop did a good trade in selling miniature wooden camels to the travelling press party. I don't know whether it was partly born of fear, but there was a curious lack of curiosity among my fellow journalists on this trip.

After 9/11 we knew several people who cancelled long-planned trips to Europe – maybe out of an over-abundance of caution, maybe out of irrational panic. It really felt as if they were saying that because someone got run over outside our house, from now on it is too dangerous to cross the road there. It is not a rational response to risk. It is a neurotic, emotional response. Remonstrate though we did with some of the people concerned – that this was giving in to the terrorists, and delivering them exactly the type of victory they sought to achieve – our message of 'keep calm and carry on' was falling on deaf ears.

I remember going to a Donald Trump rally in Manchester, New Hampshire, after the primary in that state, which he had won easily. It was a beautiful winter's night with the snow falling fast, blanketing the city in no time at all and creating that wonderful eerie stillness, where all sound is muffled. Waiting for Trump to appear, I fall into conversation with two gentlemen who, having heard my accent, want to engage me in a discussion about the dangers of living in the UK. I tell them that, like any big city, London has parts where you would be wise to be a little cautious if wandering about there. 'But what about all the no-go areas?' one asks. 'What no-go areas?' I reply. 'Well, all those areas where the Muslim extremists have taken over in the east of the city, and in Birmingham, where even the police are scared to go.' There is some back and forth, with me remonstrating that there is nowhere like that in London or, indeed, the rest of the UK. I even tell them my sister's two daughters are living in the East End, and they are not Muslims, nor are they leading the quiet, modest lives that Sharia law might demand – and they go about their day-to-day activities without hindrance. But what do I know? Someone that they know who has been to England has told them this is the case and there is nothing I can say that will make them think otherwise.

But when the terror is on the US mainland itself, striking that balance between making the populace aware of a risk and maintaining equanimity becomes virtually impossible. Such a challenge came with the shootings in San Bernardino in December 2015.

It is 2 December and the office Christmas lunch is underway for staff and their partners at the Inland Counties Regional Centre, a government-funded organisation that provides support to some 30,000 people with developmental disabilities and their families. The building is set back from the road in attractive parkland. Tables inside are decorated with Christmas trees and there is a party atmosphere. But above the din of conversation and party poppers come more substantive bangs and muzzle flashes. One of the local health department employees, Syed Farook, has arrived with his wife and they have anything but celebration on their minds.

Over the space of a couple of terrifying hours they kill 14 people and leave 22 seriously injured. The death toll would have been far worse had the three remote-controlled nail bombs they had left behind detonated. But they fail to go off. The couple try to make their getaway in a rented SUV, but the police are now in hot pursuit. Four hours after the hell started they are killed in a hail of bullets as police surround their vehicle and a sustained gun battle ensues.

Syed Rizwan Farook was born in Chicago but later moved to California, where he attended the state university in San Bernardino. He would marry Tashfeen Malik, who was born in Pakistan, and they had a young daughter together. According to neighbours they were the classic, quiet, 'keep themselves to themselves' sort of people who were getting on with life having moved into a calm, rather nondescript house in Redlands, a couple of miles from San Bernardino. He had worked for the local health department as a driver for the previous five years.

This unobtrusive couple were drinking heavily from the jihadist poison that abounds on the internet, and were becoming radicalised. Fast. In private messages to one another they pledge their willingness to commit acts of martyrdom. To the outside world they look like a classic second-generation immigrant family who were playing by the rules, taking steps up the ladder. And in a country where weapons are so readily available there was nothing untoward about them amassing enough weaponry for their home to become an arsenal of pipe bombs, revolvers and ammunition. But far from living what appeared to be the American dream, they were living what law enforcement officials view as the American nightmare. Why nightmare? Because these were lone-wolf attackers, completely off the FBI's grid, one of them US born, armed to the teeth, able to live anonymous, unremarkable, mundane lives until the moment they decided to self-activate with devastating consequences.

What this fast-moving investigation is quick to reveal is that this couple had been acting alone. They had not received or been given instructions from a mastermind, they were not part of a wider network. This was not the start of a sustained campaign. But that was not how the American public saw it. It was just three weeks after the ghastly Paris attacks which left 130 dead, 89 of them killed at the Bataclan theatre, and the mood across America was fearful and apprehensive.

Back in Redlands, where we have now set up camp outside the family home, something utterly bizarre happens. The FBI completes its search of the house, and the nation's most important crime scene is finished with, and so the keys of the boarded-up property are handed back to the landlord. He then agrees to let the media in. Now this could go one of two ways. It could be an orderly procession in which the American networks respectfully go in one by one, after which it's the turn of the foreign media. Or it could be like the first day of the Black Friday sales where there is a Gadarene rush as journalists, camera crews and photographers jostle, more or less taking doors off their hinges, and barge their way into this small house to pick over the personal ephemera of a couple who two days earlier had killed 14 and – almost as unfathomably – left their baby daughter an orphan.

Needless to say it is the latter. It is chaos. And before I begin to sound overly pious, I am part of that melee. (As we are looking at the differences between the US and the UK – can you imagine any circumstances where anti-terror detectives would allow the press to wander through a house that had been the centre of such infamy?) After broadcasting live from inside the baby's bedroom, which also doubled as the study, I receive an email from my editor in London saying that was the most compelling bit of television he had seen in a long time, but how was he going to fend off the complaints of gross intrusion that were bound to come in? I am tempted to go for the Yossarian line of argument in Joseph Heller's *Catch-22* – if everyone else is doing it, I would be a fool not to. But that might have seemed glib.

The truth is it was entirely justifiable. In each room were old-fashioned carbon copies with handwritten lists of material the FBI had taken away. The FBI might be one of the best resourced law enforcement agencies in the world, dealing with the latest hi-tech cyber threats from sophisticated hackers, but how fascinating to see that someone is still manually writing out on carbon paper, 'One Nokia phone, no SIM card inside.' This they have to do, so the homeowner knows what property has been confiscated as part of the investigation. And what are the police doing while we are rummaging as if at a frenzied jumble sale? They are telling us where we can park our cars without causing congestion.

But away from the immediate vicinity of the investigation, the US media is turning to the wider questions – and, inevitably, the question marks. Is America under attack? Is San Bernardino just the start? Are we safe from ISIS attackers? Is there a lone wolf in your neighbourhood waiting to strike? All legitimate questions; all stoking anxiety and worry.

The president, seeking to reassure, does something he hasn't done for six years: he gives an address to the American people from the Oval Office. CNN reports it as follows:

President Barack Obama will try to reassure a nervous nation on Sunday that he has a plan to defeat the fast evolving threat of terrorism, as fears multiply of ISIS attacks on the homeland and public trust in his handling of the threat has dipped to record lows. Obama's rare

Oval Office address reflects growing anxiety that the global showdown with the extremist group has now spread to US soil. His appearance comes at a time of public disquiet over terrorism and a political debate over the threat, now consuming the 2016 campaign, raging at levels not seen since the aftermath of the September 11 attacks in 2001.

With Christmas fast approaching, the president promised that there would be a massive stepping up of security in public places, leave would be cancelled, more patrols would be visible in stations and airports. Sporting events would be under greater surveillance and the annual New Year's celebration in Times Square would be policed as never before. All went off peacefully.

A close aide to the president would later tell me this was a totally disproportionate response and not in any way evidence based. But it was politically essential. After all, as discussed, the FBI had no evidence there were further plots in the pipeline or that the attackers of San Bernardino had been part of something wider, or that the orders were coming from ISIS in Syria, or anywhere else for that matter. But if Donald Trump was playing fear and anxiety, the president had to play reassurance.

And I suppose I find myself feeling puzzled. Puzzled that San Bernardino has produced such a wave of revulsion, shock and horror among the American people. And if that sounds like a callous and heartless response, let me explain. There has been no shortage of mass killings in America over the past few years. And this at first looked like it wasn't a terrorist attack, but the act of a disgruntled employee of the

San Bernardino health department. If it had indeed turned out to be that, there would have been nothing like the intensity of reaction. Sure, there would have been alarm and disgust; and for a couple of days there would have been tentative discussion about whether tighter gun-control measures would have prevented it – and then it would have become just another statistic and people's attention would have moved on.

It is as though different types of murder produce different levels of tolerance – both in society and among legislators. So terrorism is zero tolerance, and every resource is thrown at it – if you think that's an exaggeration, look at the lengths to which the FBI went to unlock the phone recovered from the killers. They end up paying over a million dollars to a private security firm to access the hidden secrets of the Apple device, after the company says it will not help on a point of principle. If the killers were 'conventional' murderers, i.e. motivated by the more run of the mill 'deadly sins' – if it was a domestic dispute, a killing in the course of a robbery – would the Feds have gone to that trouble? Not a chance.

The impact of the San Bernardino killings on the political campaign was given turbocharged booster rockets a few days later when Donald Trump would stand up to declare: 'Donald J. Trump [someone should do a study of people who like to refer to themselves in the third person] is calling for a total and complete shutdown of Muslims entering the United States until our country's representatives can figure out what the hell is going on.'

Playing on people's fears had now become the currency of the realm of the Republican hopeful. And though at the time he never spelled out how this policy could ever be implemented, or whether it was in any way constitutional – which it clearly wouldn't have been – the idea gained immediate traction. I am not a constitutional lawyer, but it only takes a cursory reading of the 14th Amendment with its equal protection clause, or the First Amendment, which states that the 'Congress shall make no law respecting an establishment of religion, or prohibiting the free exercise thereof.'

And then there is the implementation question. I have a mental image of a Department of Homeland Security official standing at passport control at JFK with a bacon sandwich in his hand saying, 'Eat this to prove you're not a Muslim.' But that of course would catch the Jews trying to enter the United States as well, so that wouldn't work. Or maybe you just simply ask, 'Are you a Muslim?' – because that of course is going to catch out the determined extremist intent on committing jihadi mayhem in the US. In a country that receives 330,000 visitors each day, how on earth would this policy ever be effectively policed?

When he became president his efforts to fashion this into a workable, implementable and constitutional policy foundered badly. The White House knew it could not call it a Muslim ban, because that would be totally unconstitutional. So it was going to be a ban that would only affect a limited number of mainly Muslim countries. But it was so badly drafted, so wide-reaching in its impact, the courts struck it down. As the courts considered the case, spontaneous demonstrations were erupting at airports across the country. Lawyers were turning up at immigration to offer their services for free to people affected. It was chaos. And for the federal judges who heard these cases there was one other thing that weighed on their decision. The words that Donald Trump had himself articulated with such clarity during the campaign – that he wanted to ban all Muslims. It was tough for his lawyers to argue that's not what he wanted when he had announced with such crystal clarity it was.

It was a theme he would return to after the even more shocking killings in Orlando in June 2016 at the Pulse gay nightclub, which left 49 people dead. I have to say that flying down to Orlando early the next morning, just hours after the shooting, I have never been more aware of the dissonance between the nature and purpose of our journey, and what we are about to report on, and that of the rest of the passengers on the plane from Washington. They are all families on their way to Disneyworld. Wide-eyed, over-excited youngsters discussing with their siblings whether they will shake hands with Mickey or not, and begging their parents to be able to go straight to the park once they land. And there's the rest of us discussing the death toll, what sort of weapon, whether there was more than one person involved.

Even by Donald Trump's own standards, his first tweet after Orlando is quite something. Bodies are still piled up in the Pulse nightclub, when he puts out on social media this message: 'Appreciate the congrats for being right on radical Islamic terrorism. I don't want congrats, I want toughness & vigilance. We must be smart!'

These killings spark a fresh wave of fear and anxiety about the extent of the threat. And for the FBI, Omar Mateen represents another nightmare, echoing San Bernardino: a lone wolf, self-radicalised, US-born-and-educated citizen, outwardly normal, able to arm himself and wander into the softest of targets – a gay nightclub on Saturday salsa night.

Actually there are bits about his story which make it a little more complicated. Though married and Muslim, it emerges that Mateen was a regular at the nightclub. He had tried to pick up a number of different men, but they had all found him a bit strange. It leads some to ask whether this might have had as much to do with his sexuality as with jihad, and whether there was some element of him being a self-loathing closet homosexual.

Interesting though this is, it receives nothing like as much attention as the 911 calls that he makes in between the killings to calmly tell the police that this is being done in the name of Islamic State.

For the purpose of political campaigning the central narrative is that America is under attack again. And for Donald Trump, this is squarely where he wants the debate to be. In a country where fears don't need much stoking, the Orlando shooting has been akin to someone picking up a poker and giving the embers in the fire a good old prod. Mr Trump is able once again to portray himself as the tough guy who will make America safe again. Polls taken after his original statement show that 60 per cent of Republicans would back his proposal to ban *all* Muslims from entering the US. And at the Republican convention in Cleveland his speech would be an exercise in playing to people's fears and anxieties.

Whatever criticisms might be levelled at Mr Trump, he does visceral politics brilliantly. He taps into American anger, something he showed in Cleveland at the convention, and again in his inaugural address in January 2017. Ronald Reagan in 1984 produced a TV ad in which he talked about an America that was 'prouder, stronger, better'. It became known as the 'Morning in America' commercial because of its opening line, 'It's morning again in America.' It is as resolutely optimistic and hopeful as it is possible to be. Donald Trump, in stark contrast, served up midnight in America in his speeches at the Republican convention and the inauguration.

The picture he painted in Cleveland was of an America going to hell in a handcart: lawless streets with gangs gunning down police officers, people cowering inside their homes fearful to go out:

> Americans watching this address tonight have seen the recent images of violence in our streets and the chaos in our communities. The attacks on our police and the terrorism in our cities, threaten our very way of life. Many have witnessed this violence personally, some have even been its victims ... America is far less safe and the world is far less stable ... the people all across this nation have been ignored, neglected and abandoned. I have visited the laid-off factory workers and the communities crushed by our horrible and unfair trade deals. These are the forgotten men and women of our country, and they are forgotten, but they're not going to be forgotten for long. These are people who work hard but no longer have a voice. I am your voice.

In his inaugural address, spoken from the steps of the Capitol, he spoke of the carnage wrought across America by years of misguided policy. It was a vision of America as a dystopian hell, even if some of the statistics used and the assertions made didn't stand close scrutiny. But the effect was unmistakable. It engendered fear and alarm. And that's what it was designed to do. The former Speaker of the House and Trump backer, Newt Gingrich, made a shrewd point on CNN: 'The average American does not think crime is down, does not think they are safer,' he said. 'Liberals have a whole set of statistics that theoretically may be right, but that's not where people are. People are frightened.' This is the post-truth era of politics that is being seen not just in America, but around the world.

Does playing on fear work? All the evidence suggests it does. In 2002 the World Mental Survey found that Americans were the most anxious of all the countries studied. It's estimated that nearly one in five – 18 per cent – suffer from some kind of anxiety disorder, spending billions of dollars on drugs to help them. About one in three Americans can be expected to suffer anxiety at some point in their lifetime.

The underlying reasons why Americans may be more prone to anxiety are obviously complex and way beyond someone whose expertise in this subject is confined to a first-year undergraduate module in psychology. But it seems that you can lump in two the broad sources of anxiety. The first is that like many in First World countries you can become overburdened by choice – where choice also becomes entangled with who we are. Is our hair cut the right way? Are our jeans too skinny or flared? Is our smartphone too big or too small? Are our trainers hip or passé? Is that brand in or out? And so on. And then there is the pressure that comes from living the American dream. Am I achieving? Am I rising up the ladder fast enough? The efforts made to climb the social ladder, the desperate struggle for wealth and status – like that of Willy Loman in *Death of a Salesman* – are just leaving more and more people stressed, anxious and dissatisfied with their lot.

An economist writing for the *New York Times*, puzzled by why America is so anxious, did what we all do when we are in search of an answer. He went to Google. He discovered a lot of 'what', but didn't do so well on 'why'. Seth Stephens-Davidowitz discovered that over the past eight years, Google search rates for anxiety have more than doubled. They were higher in 2016 than they had been in any year since Google searches were first tracked in 2004.

He found that 2016 has been the record-breaker for searches about driving anxiety, travel anxiety, separation anxiety, anxiety at work, anxiety at school and anxiety at home.

It seems Americans have also become increasingly fearful of mornings. Searches for 'anxiety in the morning' have risen threefold over the past decade. But at night, when the demons come out to play, it's even worse. Searches for 'anxiety at night' have gone up ninefold.

Stephens-Davidowitz comments: 'The places where anxiety is highest are not where I would have expected. When I was growing up, if you had asked me which people were the most anxious, I would have said New York Jews. And a decade of interacting with our country's urban intelligentsia, Jewish and otherwise, has confirmed that pretty much all of us are a neurotic mess.'

One of America's most brilliant medical ethicists is Dr Ezekiel Emanuel (he comes from a modest achieving family – one brother, Rahm, was Barack Obama's first chief of staff; another is Hollywood's most successful and powerful agent, Ari). He has written a fabulously provocative article called 'Why I Hope to Die at 75' for the *Atlantic* magazine. It challenges the desire of Americans to kid themselves that they can go on for ever.

When I interview him at a BBC ideas conference in New York he holds up a full-page advertisement placed by the AARP (American Association of Retired Persons). There is a picture of an elderly couple hiking above a line of text, which reads: 'When the view goes on forever, I feel I can, too. Go long.' He argues that the vision of life stretching on endlessly into the distance is a con. 'As we add more years of life, we're adding more years of disability,' Emanuel told me. 'That just doesn't strike me as a great deal, and not the kind of deal I think most people have in mind when they are thinking about the future.' He said he wanted his grandkids to think of him as healthy and vigorous, not drooling and racked with dementia.

If the TV news channels play to Americans' fears about the threats of the modern world and the external forces that might impinge on and upend their lives, the advertising concentrates on the internal. Aside from the political advertising – that you would never see in the UK – commercials for prescription drugs are the backbone and the staple of American television. These ads foster the idea that life can go on and on, and that everything has a cure; and they are ubiquitous. And they range from the comparatively trivial with John McEnroe flogging drugs for toenail fungus that you can only get from your doctor (you guessed it: 'Unbelievable. Toenail fungus – seriously …') to the personal – the endless ads for Viagra and its competitors (which always contain the helpful advice 'If you have an erection that has lasted for four hours or longer contact your physician') to the highly specific. There are ads on TV for drugs that treat a certain type of lung cancer, which will prolong your life – they don't specify by how long.

The pharmaceutical industry spends tens of billions of dollars each year on advertising its heart drugs, its arthritis drugs. Drugs for Crohn's disease, drugs for kidney failure, drugs for respiratory problems. You name it, they flog it. I reckon I could quite easily con my way onto the set of *ER*, *Grey's Anatomy* or *Chicago Hope* as a leading physician having listened to all these incessant commercials.

What is interesting is that these advertisements are heavily regulated by the federal Food and Drug Administration. So a typical commercial will start with – ideally – someone famous (sports stars seem to have a particular cachet) saying how this drug has transformed his/her life. Then comes the line which is a variation of 'hit your GP over the head until he prescribes it for you' – but then the contra-indications have to be included.

I could have chosen any of dozens, but this is the transcript of an ad for an arthritis drug that is heavily marketed in the US. It is fronted by one of the world's most famous golfers and has a jaunty piano tune playing underneath:

Hi, I'm Phil Mickelson. I've been fortunate to win on golf's biggest stages. But when joint pain and stiffness from arthritis hit, even the simplest things became difficult, so I spoke to my rheumatologist and he prescribed Enbrel to help relieve joint pain and help prevent further joint damage.

[We now hear a woman's voice who is out of vision] Enbrel may lower your ability to fight infections. Serious, sometimes fatal events including infections, tuberculosis, lymphoma, other cancers, nervous system and blood disorders and allergic reactions have occurred. Tell your doctor if you've been some place where fungal infections are common or if you're prone to infections, have cuts or sores, have had Hepatitis B, have been treated for heart failure or if you have persistent fever, bruising, bleeding or paleness. Don't start Enbrel if you have an infection like the flu.

MICKELSON: Get back to the things that matter most. Ask how Enbrel can help relieve joint pain and help stop joint damage.

WOMAN: Enbrel. The number one rheumatologist prescribed biologic.

Hang on a minute. So I've got joint pain which is causing me discomfort and I hear an ad for this great new drug. But then I hear the warning: 'Serious, sometimes fatal events including infections, tuberculosis, lymphoma, other cancers, nervous system and blood disorders and allergic reactions have occurred.' Is that meant to ease my anxiety or intensify it? And this type of commercial is playing around the clock on all the channels.

In America the desire to go on and on, the marketing of eternal youth, the focus on everything being solved with a pill, means that health is not just a source of well-being, it's a source of stress. And of course affordability plays into all of that. Whether those drugs are available or out of reach will depend on what health insurance you have.

And it helps explain why Americans like a lot of medication.

Now I'll compare and contrast two stories concerning two very good American friends. One takes place in Miami, the other in London.

The tech genius, internet-freedom spear-carrier and all round great guy Jimmy Wales, who founded the not-for-profit Wikipedia, is in high demand around the world as a guest speaker, futurologist and savant. He was doing a keynote in Florida, but probably very unwisely went out on a big night with his English wife, Kate, and a number of her friends the night before his address. I think it is fair to say alcohol was taken. Rather a lot. Indeed, you could say without fear of contradiction, too much.

The next morning and day of his speech Jimmy is feeling decidedly off colour. And the worst happens. He is called to speak, and a few paragraphs into his address he passes out. Because this is a big prestigious conference, a medical team and ambulance is standing by behind the stage. Jimmy is taken off to Mount Sinai Medical Centre, and although he comes round he's now flushed with embarrassment rather than alcohol. The medics, out of an abundance of caution (yes, that phrase again), insist on admitting him and say that various potentially serious explanations have to be ruled out. They proceed to conduct any number of tests and scans; he is strapped to various monitoring machines; nurses repeatedly check his condition. He is installed in a suite overlooking the sea. Jimmy's assessment is that the total cost to his health insurance company would have been somewhere north of $100,000. And what did the finest medical minds of Miami conclude at the end of this exhaustive examination?

Go on, guess.

Jimmy had a hangover. Yes, a very expensive one.

All of which brings us to Lynsea. She is my American-born-and-raised producer in Washington who had come to London to study for a master's degree at University College London. Laid low with some kind of throat infection, she enrols at a local health centre and goes to see the GP on duty. She knows what she wants, because she has been here before: a prescription for a fast-acting, three-day course of strong antibiotics called Zithromax Z-Pak, along with painkillers and some lozenges that will make swallowing easier, and maybe something to help her sleep. The doctor shines a light down her throat, makes her say 'aaaahh', looks inside and then listens to her chest. He put his stethoscope away and sits back down in his chair. 'I think what you need is a nice hot lemon and honey drink, my dear.' And that was that. Next patient please.

Maybe that is exaggerated caricature. But not by much. The cultures are very different, not just the system by which healthcare is delivered but also in the manner in which medicine and healthcare are consumed.

But if we're looking for a real cause for anxiety, forget Ebola, which came and went – there is an epidemic in the United States, which the rest of the world is barely conscious of, and seems to be unique to America.

One drug that you won't see advertised on television in the US is naloxone hydrochloride. That's because there is no need. The five big pharmaceutical companies that are making it – Amphastar, Pfizer, Adapt, Kaleo and Mylan – are making a fortune from it. Demand is soaring and far from that driving the price down, the costs are soaring. A popular injectable version of the drug which cost $0.92 ten years ago is now selling at $15.00 a dose.

On patrol with the police in Maryland, it is striking that this is the new weapon that the police carry with them in their utility belts. And across the US, as well as more and more police, an increasing number of firefighters are equipping themselves with this wonder drug too.

So what is this magic substance that is captivating America? Well, it is not very sophisticated to produce and has been around for a number of years – but it has never been in such demand.

Naloxone is essentially an 'antidote' to drug overdoses – it blocks the brain's receptors from interacting with the opioids you've put into your body. It counteracts the effects of heavy drug use, which include slow respiration, coma and – possibly – death during an overdose. It almost instantly pulls the user back to a state of normality with a bare minimum of side effects.

For people overdosing on heroin it is of course a vital weapon. But heroin abuse is nothing new – either in the US or anywhere else in the world. Even though hundreds of thousands of people have been locked up in prison for drug dealing and possession of heroin, it is still readily available. When I was at the 2016 Democratic Convention in Philadelphia we went to film in one of the poorer areas of the city. And every few streets you would see hanging down from the electricity and phone cables strung across the street a pair of trainers. That denotes just where you can buy your fix.

No, the reason why demand for naloxone is going through the roof is that America has become addicted to prescription drugs. A report from the US Centers for Disease Control and Prevention found that, in 2014, 47,000 people died from drug overdoses. Opioids accounted for 60 per cent of those deaths. Just to throw a couple more statistics at you, the most recent National Survey on Drug Use and Health found that nearly 2.5 million people are addicted to opioids, with 1.9 million specifically addicted to prescription painkillers.

There are countless tragic stories wrapped up in those statistics. One man was so crippled by fear that he was unable to do his job without taking a cocktail of painkillers. Over a 25-year period he was hooked on opiates, sometimes spending thousands of dollars at a time to feed his addiction. His preferred painkillers were Dilaudid pills and fentanyl patches. His dealer said, 'He needed the drugs because he was so nervous – he could be nervous in a room with just five people in it. He was scared to go out in public, he was scared to talk to people.' He would eventually die at home in Minneapolis, Minnesota, after taking too much Percocet, a powerful opiate. His name was Prince.

His death brought world attention – not to the wider problem, but to the tragic end of a rock and roll icon. Another name to add to the list going back to Billie Holiday, Hendrix, Joplin, etc. Music stations played his music non-stop as millions were affected by the news. Among them was President Obama, who was flying to London from Saudi Arabia when he heard it. The next day, just before his news conference at the Foreign Office when he argued passionately for Britain to remain within the European Union, I'm told Barack Obama played 'Purple Rain' and 'Little Red Corvette' at full volume in the US ambassador's residence in Regent's Park. 'It got him really pumped,' an aide told me.

But though the money that Prince had to spend to feed his addiction was on a different scale from the other 1.9 million Americans, his story is strikingly similar.

One associates the president skipping up the steps of Air Force One with engagement in some important piece of global diplomacy, or to see some disaster-struck region of America. When President Obama flew to West Virginia in October 2015, it was to talk about this particular problem. Once famous for the coal brought out of the ground, high up in the Appalachian Mountains, the state is now notorious for its drug problem. Take a walk around the state capital, Charleston, and you will be struck by the number of people who are obese and wandering round the city's mall, seemingly with nothing to do. The president had come to signal an important shift in US policy, which dated back to when Ronald Reagan was in the White House. No longer would the administration be engaged in a war against drugs; it would be the battle against addiction. No longer just locking people up, but battling the causes of addiction and finding ways to assist those who become hooked. In West Virginia twice as many people now die from drug overdoses as car accidents. It was the right place to go.

Lindsay Morgan Smith is 27 years old and told us that when she was a child she regarded herself as a tom-boy – she played basketball and softball for the town in West Virginia where she grew up. She won a sport scholarship to college and said she then started taking painkillers to take away the stress that she was feeling in her life. She thought, hoped, they would take away all her problems. Soon she started experimenting with stronger tablets that she bought on the street. And then, to fund her habit of prescription drugs, she started dealing herself. And before long the police are knocking down her front door and she is put in prison. Lindsay is now 'sober', as she puts it. 'West Virginia has always had a drug problem,' she tells us. 'It hurts a little bit to know that we've waited so long till this problem has gotten so bad to even try to seek help for the state itself.'

Lindsay's was one route into prescription drug addiction. There are many others. And the most common requires cunning rather than illegality. Welcome to the practice of 'doctor shopping'. In essence you go to one doctor and because of some pain or injury you convince him or her to give you a prescription for a morphine-based drug. You then go to pharmacy A to collect the drugs. You then repeat, going to a different doctor and a different pharmacy each time. Repeat again and again. Now you have as many painkillers as you could ever safely want.

Or you mix it up a bit. At one doctor you order one type of powerful painkiller, and at another you order a different one, which combined together give you a super high. And without the need to go to a street dealer you have a cocktail that's hugely addictive – and often deadly. Though here's my one useful tip. There is some stuff that the pharmacists are smart to. It might be the easiest thing in the world to get yourself hooked on prescription drugs. But don't try and buy yourself two bottles of Sudafed, the nasal decongestant. They won't sell them to you. They are worried you might want to get drunk.

And the ever imaginative and resourceful pharmaceuticals industry is eyeing up the opportunities that this opioid addiction brings. Yes! There are whole new classes of drugs to flog to deal with the side effects of your addiction. Ever heard of OIC? No, me neither, until I was watching TV one morning and saw the advertisement for a drug dealing with Opioid Induced Constipation. Seriously. The first time I saw the commercial for Movantik I thought I had misheard what they were selling. But no. And because all drugs have to detail side effects, those associated with Movantik are pain, diarrhoea, nausea, gas, vomiting and headache. Presumably there is a good drug that will take care of those unwanted consequences.

There is of course an easy solution to this, and that is firstly to limit the number of painkillers any one doctor can prescribe to a patient; and secondly to set up databases so that doctors A, B, C, D, E, F and G can see what a particular patient is seeking to obtain. But even something as seemingly straight-forward as this gets tangled up in philosophical debates about privacy and the rights of the individual. So some states have implemented plans to set up these registers, others are stubbornly refusing. The American Civil Liberties Union is one of those bodies resisting such moves.

Could this happen in the UK? Possibly, but nothing like as easily. Doctor friends say the medical profession has long been aware of the addictive nature of certain painkillers, and at different times the Department of Health will change its guidance on which drugs to prescribe or not. But the fact that in the UK patients are registered with one GP practice, where all the doctors within that group have access to your records, makes it much more difficult to just go from doctor to doctor, town to town, filling your shopping bag with barbiturates.

With this mass abuse of prescription drugs it is hard to disentangle cause and effect. They are so intertwined. So, going back to Google searches to explain why America is so stressed, let's use Google Correlate – a service which, if you put in a search term, will find you something that has also been sought. If you put in 'panic attack' it will also come up with opiate withdrawal. So anxiety, which led a user into prescription drugs in the first place, is now the source of the most serious panic attacks for those coming off the tablets. And you can break this down region by region. Where do most people use the search term panic attack? In the places where opioid abuse is highest – in West Virginia.

And there's one other thing that is striking from the figures. And maybe it is in no way surprising. The places where people are most angry are also where they are most anxious. This is Trumpland – it's neither East Coast nor West, neither the Great Lakes nor Deep South. It's neither urban nor rural. His support is everywhere, but tends to be highest in those areas where unemployment has been highest, where the effects of globalisation have been felt most harshly, where educational attainment is lowest. The places where anger goes hand in hand with anxiety, and prescription drugs are the weapon of choice to dull the pain.

The *Washington Post* did an interesting piece of research. It found that during the primaries, the counties where Trump support was greatest were also those with the highest death rate for white men aged between 40 and 64. These are people who have lived such unhealthy lives – on a diet of too many Big Macs, doughnuts and fizzy drinks, presumably – and not enough exercise that death has come to them prematurely. Or they are people who popped one too many pills, and, intentionally or not, brought life to a premature end. The correlation was striking.

In his inaugural speech in 1932, the country's 32nd president, Franklin Delano Roosevelt, said, 'The only thing that we have to fear is fear itself.' He spoke as the country was buffeted by the Great Depression, when millions went hungry. In today's America the problems are very different, but the nation seems to be fearful of so much.

CHAPTER 8

Special

This is the stuff that political dreams are made of – well at least if you're a British politician. Not only are you being greeted at the North Entrance to the White House by the president of the United States, but you are the first foreign leader to get in through the door after his election victory. If the special relationship means anything, surely it means this. In fact let's give it capital letters: the Special Relationship – it is talked about so much, so often, that let's treat it as a proper, permanent thing as if it has a royal crest and the presidential seal. As if it is a part of the constitutional arrangements between the US and the UK. But it is also a complicated beast that can give as much pain as it can pleasure.

OK, that whole thing where Donald grabbed Theresa's hand as they walked along the colonnade in the Rose Garden was a little bit odd (yes, jokes went around the press room at the White House that it could have been so much worse …). Apparently he doesn't do slopes very well, and wanted someone to hold onto. But to the delight of Mrs May's team, even that seemed to contain its own internal bit of symbolism:

257

the fledgeling president reaching out an arm to his country's oldest and most stalwart ally. If you need a steadying hand, stolid, reliable and loyal Britain would be there. And was there ever a less likely coupling than the slightly austere woman from Sussex who grew up an only child to a Church of England clergyman, and the king of brash and flash from Queens. When asked at their very brief news conference how they would get along, the prime minister smartly replied, 'Sometimes opposites attract.'

Even Donald Trump seemed in playful mood as my colleague Laura Kuenssberg asked an absolute stinker of a question about all the reservations that Britons and Europeans had about him and his attitudes towards torture, women, minorities and abortion. For a man who is notoriously prickly when it comes to criticism he seemed to take it in good part, joking, 'There goes that relationship' – though afterwards, apparently, demanded to know why such a hostile questioner had been called.

For all that Theresa May can sometimes appear gauche and awkward, there was one moment of real poise in their appearance before the cameras. It came when she ambushed the new president, getting him to declare his support for NATO – a body which he had previously said he regarded as obsolete, that had failed to deal with the more modern threat of Islamist extremism, and into which America paid far too much money. What caused Europeans no end of anxiety was that those views were matched by a warmth towards Russia and its demagogic leader, Vladimir Putin. While she stood at her podium, and he stood at his, she fixed him with a stare and said that during their private talks the president had assured her that he was '100 per cent behind NATO'.

As she kept her eyes on him, he mouthed the word 'true'. The British side banked that. As did the rest of Europe.

In their private meeting she had apparently been extremely forceful on the importance of the alliance, and in particular Article 5 – the clause which states that an attack against one member is an attack against all. She may not have been able to force President Trump to change his view on Vladimir Putin, but had made progress.

This is the role that Britain has historically played, acting as the bridge between Europe and the US: Britain able to say things to the White House that others struggle to address. And she played her hand with aplomb during the two-day visit to America. On points of agreement she proclaimed them loudly; on areas of disagreement she spoke in a whisper – but nevertheless made those points of difference plain. It led me to wonder whether in some dusty Whitehall cupboard there is a slim tome called 'Etiquette for Prime Ministers when travelling to Washington'. If such a book exists Mrs May had studied it carefully.

The key to understanding this relationship is to accept that it is not a relationship of equals. It is decidedly lopsided, with one partner a touch insecure, the other not. Just take the need for a trade deal – one of the key reasons why Mrs May flew to Washington at the drop of a hat. A trade deal with the US, Britain's biggest single export market, was seen as her get-out-of-jail-free card in the post-Brexit environment. Coming back with words of reassurance from the president on the apparent simplicity of doing a deal, was her way of cocking a snook at the Europeans who thought that Britain might sink without them and their single market. But with Britain having voted for Brexit, ask this simple question: who needs whom more? Who is the supplicant, and who holds the whip hand? Yes, the PM came away with warm words or noises from her meetings – but America will be eyeing the opportunities of a one-off deal with Britain on its terms.

The whistle-stop trip to Washington had yielded everything a British prime minister could have hoped for and more. She had got in early and built a rapport; she may have helped shape the strategic thinking of the new leader of the free world; she had won some important concessions. And for the team at the British embassy, whose job is to burnish the special relationship, getting Theresa May into the White House before anyone else showed deft footwork on the part of the ambassador, Sir Kim Darroch. All the sweeter as shortly after the presidential election the newly elected president called ten other leaders before he spoke to the British prime minister. This gave several UK newspapers an attack of the vapours, with questions raised about whether the special relationship would survive such a grievous snub.

And then, to rub a tablespoon of salt into the wound, president elect Trump had fired off a late-night tweet that said this: 'Many people would like to see [@Nigel_Farage] represent Great Britain as their Ambassador to the United States. He would do a great job!' It was so extraordinary that I woke up the duty Downing Street press officer in the middle of the night London time to get a response. 'Oh fuck, he hasn't really said that, has he?' was his immediate response. I would report in my dispatch for that morning's Radio 4 bulletins that Downing Street 'seemed shocked'. Who says we can't do subtle? I had woken him up in the middle of the night, after all. But I think he did rather eloquently capture the mood in Whitehall.

Like the joke about crime in a multi-storey car park being wrong on so many levels, this one tweet seemed to achieve that. The leader of one sovereign nation telling the leader of another who their ambassador should be – wrong. The undermining of the current representative in Washington – wrong. The wading into the internal politics of another country – wrong. And making Nigel Farage so delighted that he was whistling a happy tune all day – well, let's give him that. Mr Farage has played the new president incredibly shrewdly, and could teach many in politics and the media a lesson on what makes the president tick.

But one can assume the former UKIP leader was not part of Mrs May's preparations for her meeting with President Trump. She didn't need him. She had something better to offer. She was able to pull from her back pocket the gilt-edged, 'it-never-fails-to-impress' trump card – the invitation that no president has been able to resist: the Queen offering all the pomp and pageantry of a state visit to Britain: gold carriages up the Mall, banquet at Buckingham Palace, overnight at Windsor Castle, a joint address to parliament.

The royal family is an abiding fascination for most Americans. This fiercely proud republic that shook off the British monarchy 240 years ago in its revolution still wants to know in microscopic detail the workings of the House of Windsor. The day-to-day happenings of UK politics will get zero coverage – when David Cameron won the 2015 general election, the most popular network nightly news programme gave it no air time at all. Not a word. But when the Queen misses church at Sandringham with a cold, or when a new photo is published of Prince George, there are hourly updates.

On the Friday evening when the prime minister left Washington to fly to Ankara, her entourage were almost giddy with excitement. You could imagine them all high-fiving along the aisle as the plane door closed. By the time they had landed the next morning on Turkish soil, there was not much delight to be had. No sooner had their plane taken off from Joint Base Andrews than Donald Trump had signed an executive order banning all Syrian refugees from entering the US indefinitely. Refugees from anywhere else would be banned for 120 days. Travellers from seven mainly Muslim countries would have their visas revoked. No one would be allowed to travel to the US if they had been issued a passport by those states. When Donald Trump had said during the campaign that he wanted to ban all Muslims from entering the US, he had clearly meant it. Except that would have been unconstitutional. So instead we were seeing what he meant by 'extreme vetting', which hit just as much legal turbulence.

There were disturbing tales of families being separated. A five-year-old Iranian boy was detained by himself for hours at Washington Dulles Airport, while his mother was questioned elsewhere. Asked to justify this, the president's spokesman, Sean Spicer, said: 'That's why we slow [the process] down a little. To make sure that if they are a five-year-old, that maybe they're with their parents and they don't pose a threat. But to assume that just because of someone's age or gender or whatever that they don't pose a threat would be misguided and wrong.'

People who had gone through the laborious process of securing visas had them revoked without warning. Spontaneous protests erupted across US cities; airports became the focus for demonstrations. Lawyers rushed to offer their services free of charge to those caught up in the chaos. The British Olympic legend, Sir Mo Farah, wouldn't be able to return to his training base – and home to his family – in Oregon because he had been born in Somalia, one of the seven nations affected by the ban. Nadhim Zahawi, a Conservative MP, representing Stratford upon Avon, would also have been barred from going to the US because he had been born in Baghdad.

Three times in Ankara the PM was asked to condemn this sweeping executive action; three times she refused or obfuscated. A wishy-washy answer that US immigration was a matter for the US president was as good as she could come up with. Later that night the position stiffened a little. The next day it was announced that the foreign secretary and home secretary would make representations. It was neither fish nor fowl.

And all this as poor Theresa May had just announced that Britain would be rolling out the red carpet to Donald Trump. The celebration of the special relationship was all turning into a bit of a nightmare. And the question was being asked – and she was probably asking herself: did I give away too much, too easily. One minute he's reaching out to hold my hand, the next minute my political virtue has gone. She was not the first prime minister, and probably won't be the last, to find herself in that position.

She returned to London later that weekend with condemnation ringing in her ears. Friday night's White House triumph a distant memory. A petition on the Downing Street website opposing the state visit very quickly garnering 1.8 million signatures. A former head of the Foreign Office would question whether the rush to embrace President Trump had put the Queen in an impossible position. Others pointed out that no US president had been granted a state visit so soon into their term of office. Oh, it's a mercurial old thing the special relationship, when the public is not as enamoured of the president, and the need to be close to him, as the prime minister of the day in Downing Street is.

And the president's popularity in London, it's fair to say, didn't exactly set itself on an upwards trajectory with his extraordinary intervention after the terrorist attack on London Bridge in June 2017. While the rest of the world was offering its condolences, Donald Trump had the London mayor, Sadiq Khan, in his cross hairs (the mayor had previously criticised Mr Trump's plan to ban all Muslims from coming to America, and the president nurses grievances like some horticulturalists care for a delicate rose). The day after the attack, he tweeted: 'At least 7 dead and 48 wounded in terror attack and Mayor of London says there is "no reason to be alarmed!"' Well yes. Mr Khan had said there was no reason to be alarmed – but what he was specifically referring to, was that there was no need for people to be alarmed by the sight of additional armed police on patrol. Not that there was no need to be alarmed by the terror attacks themselves. The president had completely misrepresented – either accidentally or deliberately – what the mayor had said.

This was then pointed out to Mr Trump by one of his aides, who gave him the context of the statement. But apology came there none. Instead of backtracking, the president – to use the American phrase – doubled down. This time tweeting 'Pathetic excuse by London Mayor Sadiq Khan who had to think fast on his "no reason to be alarmed" statement.' Quite extraordinary. In Washington, Republicans and Democrats alike shook their heads in disbelief – well, they would have done, but this had become the new normal.

Still, at least we learned quickly that one component of the state visit would likely be absent. The president would not be invited to make a joint address to parliament after all – at least, that is, if the House of Commons Speaker, John Bercow, had anything to do with it. He told MPs, 'I would not wish to issue an invitation to President Trump to speak in the Royal Gallery.' He added that he would also be opposed to an address in Westminster Hall, saying: 'I feel very strongly that our opposition to racism and sexism and our support for equality before the law and an independent judiciary are hugely important considerations in the House of Commons.' Well, that told President Trump.

But hang on. Is this the same Speaker Bercow who formally invited President Xi of China just a year and a half earlier to address both Houses of Parliament in the Royal Gallery of the House of Lords – an honour 'reserved only for those people we hold in the highest regard' – as the then Lord Speaker, Baroness Frances D'Souza, gushingly pointed out. Now Donald Trump is a controversialist, a man who relishes a fight. But he is the fairly and duly elected president of our closest ally. Whether wisely or not, under the advice of the government of the day the Queen had extended an invitation to him to come to London. So question one is what was to be gained by a deliberate, public grandstanding snub like this? And question two is, by implication, are we saying we find the leader of China – who I don't remember coming to power through free and fair elections, and where the human rights record is, how shall we put it, a little sub-optimal – a preferable figure? If the invitation had been premature, the reaction from the Speaker had to some in Washington seemed immature.

Or is there something else going on? Because of our love affair with that big, bright country across the Atlantic, we hold the United States to a different standard. Like any other relationship it comes with expectations of how the 'partner' should behave – and particularly the president. Unlike any other leader on the planet we tend to have strong feelings on who is occupying the White House. As a former Paris correspondent I have debated at various times the relative merits of presidents Chirac, Sarkozy and Hollande. But do we have any real emotional feelings about any of them? Do we think of them as heroes or villains, impostors or visionaries? No, probably not. Even though France is our nearest neighbour, the country we visit most often and the country we compare ourselves to most often. But if we were to change the names to Reagan, Clinton, Bush, Obama and Trump I suspect round any dinner table you will have love and loathing expressed in equal measure for the most recent US presidents.

When I accompanied President Obama on his last trip to Britain he held a 'town hall' meeting in Westminster. The expectation, the crackle of excitement before he came on stage, was the same as before a great sporting fixture or a rock concert. And he was treated by the audience who'd managed to get tickets like a total rock and roll star. Young and old alike. He was cool, urbane, thoughtful – and very European. It was easy to relate to him. If George W. Bush had held a similar event would it have evoked a similar response or sentiment? Or President Trump? To many British and European palates they seemed far too foreign for their tastes. Yes. They are American! And why they both succeeded was that millions of Americans identified with them.

One piece of diplomacy that went as smoothly as smooth can be when Theresa May came to Washington was the restoration of the Churchill bust to the Oval Office. The Jacob Epstein sculpture had been loaned to President George W. Bush by Tony Blair, but removed by Barack Obama, who chose instead to have statuettes of Lincoln and Martin Luther King in his famous office. The decision caused a slightly *faux* outrage. It was used as a stick to beat the new president in 2009. It was a snub to America's closest ally. President Obama even had to defend himself later at a news conference with David Cameron by saying, 'I love Winston Churchill. I love the guy.'

But the restoration to the White House of a bust of Britain's wartime leader is not without irony. It was history coming full circle. It was Churchill who first coined the phrase 'special relationship', when he called in his famous speech in Fulton, Missouri, for a 'special relationship between the British Commonwealth and the Empire and the United States', who could 'work together at the common task as friends and partners'. It was also there that he spoke about an 'iron curtain' descending between the West and the Soviet bloc.

Yet in the early days of Winston Churchill's leadership at the outset of the Second World War, America was doing anything but stand at Britain's side. This was the darkest hour, and the view in the United States was that it was a conflict that was nothing to do with them. This was a nation of America First (sound familiar?), of isolationism, of the need for America to sort out its own problems and not worry about the rest of the world. America must remain neutral, not get involved. The US ambassador to London, Joseph Kennedy (father of JFK), was firmly of the view when he arrived in London in 1938 that appeasement of Hitler's Nazi Germany was the best way forward. He disagreed with Churchill's insistence that there could be no compromise with Germany. And even late in 1940, with the blitz about to begin, and so much of London about to be razed to the ground by the Luftwaffe, Kennedy was still trying to make plans to visit Hitler 'to bring about a better understanding between the United States and Germany', as he told the State Department. He also sent telegrams back to the US saying that no military or economic aid should be offered to Britain. 'Democracy is finished here,' he declared. The antipathy the British establishment felt towards him was not lessened by his scarpering to the countryside the moment the blitz began – while the political leadership and the royal family steadfastly refused to leave London.

Churchill's every waking hour was spent either working out how to fight and resist Hitler, or how to win over the American President Franklin Delano Roosevelt. As the 1940 US presidential election campaign was reaching its climax, the stance of FDR could not have been clearer. At the end of October, just days before polling, he told an audience in Boston: 'I have said this before, but I shall say it again and again and again: your boys are not going to be sent into any foreign wars.' It was a message he would repeat on a daily basis, as he travelled the battleground states, seeking simultaneously to reassure and tap into the wave of isolationism sweeping America. 'The first purpose of our foreign policy is to keep our country out of war,' he would tell an audience in Cleveland three days later.

And every day (more or less literally), Churchill would write to the US president beseeching him to supply arms, money and eventually US soldiers for the fight against Nazism. He would later write: 'No lover ever studied every whim of his mistress as I did those of President Roosevelt.' The relentless pressure from Churchill was wearing and annoying – but ultimately effective. One sign of the change was the replacement of Joe Kennedy as US ambassador to London by John Gilbert Winant. There is a fascinating photograph taken at Windsor railway station. It is March 1941, and standing tall wearing an overcoat is the new ambassador 'Gil' Winant. Next to him is a man in British Army uniform, baton in hand. The chap in the khaki is none other than the King, George VI. Normal protocol insists that when a new ambassador is sent to the Court of Saint James, an invitation will come from Buckingham Palace for the new representative to come to meet the monarch to present his credentials at St James's Palace. Such was the importance to the British state of Winant's arrival that there was an unprecedented reversal of the normal rules of behaviour. The King came to present his credentials to Winant, and to welcome him to Britain.

The newspaper the *News Chronicle* captured the jubilation that not only had Kennedy gone but that Winant, a former governor of New Hampshire and fierce critic of appeasement policies, was now coming in his place. 'There is no name that could have been more welcome ... he is an American for whom an Englishman feels an immediate liking, and few Americans have a warmer admiration and regard than he for this country and its people.'

Churchill, who had grown so frustrated by American foot-dragging, had in Winant a man with whom he could do business. And at a lavish reception to welcome him at the Savoy, the old bulldog was nothing but charm. In the speech, which was broadcast to the nation by the BBC, Churchill turned it on. 'Mr Winant, you come to us at a grand turning point in the world's history. We rejoice to have you with us in these days of storm and trial, because in you we have a friend and faithful comrade … You, Mr Ambassador, share our purpose. You'll share our dangers. You'll share our interests. You shall share our secrets. And the day will come when the British Empire and the United States will share together … the crown of victory.'

Now it was Winant's turn to speak. Not a natural orator, certainly when compared to the wizardry of Churchill, he nevertheless had the room – and the nation – spellbound. He made no attempt to defend the policies of his prede-cessor, or of America's isolationism. Instead he said: 'The lost years are gone. The road ahead is hard. A new spirit is abroad. Free peoples are again cooperating to win a free world, and no tyranny can frustrate their hopes.' The Allied nations, he said, 'with the help of God shall build a citadel of freedom so strong that force may never again seek its destruction.'

What is interesting is the little domestic difficulty that Churchill became aware of at this time. He was straining every sinew to bring American support to Britain's side, but British public opinion was slightly ambivalent. One of the constant sources of dissonance in the special relationship is the public's sometimes far less enthusiastic embrace of it than the politicians. Ask Theresa May about the Trump state visit, Tony Blair about support for the Iraq War, Margaret Thatcher about the siting of US cruise missiles at Greenham

Common. So Churchill recruited the government's propaganda arm, the Ministry of Information, to counter any prevailing hostility and negativity towards the Americans. In April 1941 a strategy paper was submitted to the MOI called 'Outline for a Plan for the Presentation of the USA to Britain'. Its goal: 'At the present stage of the war it is a matter of urgency to bring about the closest possible collaboration between the British Commonwealth and the United States of America. With this end in view, mutual misunderstandings and suspicions which tend to hamper a co-operative war effort must be done away with.'

There would be radio broadcasts on American life and culture. American music – folk and jazz – would feature heavily. Advertisements would be taken out in newspapers to highlight prominent Americans living in the UK. The picture to be painted was that America was a very similar nation to Britain, built on a way of life that was almost interchangeable, with broadly shared values. They were our friends, they wanted to help in our hour of need, and we should welcome them with open arms.

By the end of the war, as any number of GI brides were heading back to start new lives with their American *beaux* on the other side of the Atlantic, that particular part of the policy would have to be deemed a success. The Yanks not only came and saw. They conquered a lot of British hearts, with their easy swagger, their music, their chewing gum, their shiny white teeth – and their gifts of 'nylons' for the ladies in austere, rationing-constrained, drab Britain. This was the start of the love affair with America for the British. American popular culture was being adopted wholesale: the music, the movies, the clothes, the food.

The game changer for American involvement in the war came at the end of 1941, with the 'day of infamy': the day that Americans' sense of inviolability was destroyed, the day that left a scar on the national psyche, when the Japanese bombed Pearl Harbor. In her wonderful book, *Citizens of London*, Lynne Olson records how Churchill had been dining with Ambassador Winant and Averell Harriman, who was then President Roosevelt's special envoy to Europe. These were two men who passionately believed that America must join Britain in the fight against fascism. So far from being distraught about the sinking of a number of vessels from the US Pacific fleet, resulting in the loss of over 2,000 American lives, there was euphoria when news of the attack came through. For it could only mean one thing: the United States would be entering the war. Olson notes that in an early draft of his memoirs, Churchill recalled that the two Americans were in a state of 'exaltation – in fact they nearly danced with joy'.

This now was the start of the special relationship in earnest, the vestiges of which survive to this today. It was the start of extremely close military cooperation, the pooling of intelligence and strategic planning as these two giants of politics sought to turn the tide in the battle against the Axis powers.

The tools to get the job done would be finally coming Britain's way. But at a price. And this is another important part of the special relationship. In the business dealings between the US and the UK, there was no such thing as 'mates rates', and never was that more apparent than in the 'Lend-Lease' deals struck. This was a cunning ruse by Roosevelt to maintain America's position of neutrality before her entry into the conflict while still supplying

Britain with the military hardware it so desperately needed. In effect it was a trade. No money would pass hands. Britain would hand over military bases in the West Indies and Newfoundland on a 99-year lease to the United States, in return for America handing over some 50 destroyers to the British. The problem was that these naval vessels were old rust-buckets. Only nine were fit to go into immediate service. In a letter marked 'most secret' written in March 1941, Churchill would complain: 'As far as I can make out we are not only to be skinned but flayed to the bone.' Some Americans would later comment that Britain 'was shaken down to the last dime'. But Britain's wartime leader knew that he was in no position to complain. So despite the deepest reservations, he sold this to his cabinet as not ideal, but completely necessary. The terms on which the UK did business with the US would be a persistent problem.

In December 1941, just after Germany had declared war on the United States, Churchill came to Washington to spend Christmas with FDR, and while in DC gave a stirring address to both Houses of Congress, concluding:

Lastly, if you will forgive me for saying it, to me the best tidings of all is that the United States, united as never before, have drawn the sword for freedom and cast away the scabbard ... Hope has returned to the hearts of scores of millions of men and women ... In a dozen famous ancient States now prostrate under the Nazi yoke, the masses of the people of all classes and creeds await the hour of liberation, when they too will be able once again to play their part and strike their blows like men.

What followed was a period of unbelievable cooperation at head-of-state level, ministerial level, military command level. Were there clashes of egos and personalities? Yes. Did some of the disputes get ugly and have to be adjudicated higher up the chain? Of course. The Supreme Commander of Allied Forces in Europe, Dwight Eisenhower, didn't exactly have the easiest time with Field Marshal Bernard Montgomery – a man whom even Churchill regarded as 'insufferable'. But was there a singleness of purpose about the task at hand? Absolutely. If one military operation came to epitomise the extraordinary closeness and cooperation at every level it was surely the D-Day landings.

When I left Paris in 2003 at the end of my tour there, we took our then 11- and 13-year-old children to Normandy to visit the beaches and the gun emplacements where those thousands of heroic young men – mainly American and British – gave their lives for Europe's freedom. To walk through the Commonwealth War Graves and the US cemeteries was to see true sacrifice. While we were there we met a fabulous American family at the hotel we were staying in near Bayeux. The mother, Janet, was – how can I put this – not exactly quiet in her loathing of President George W. Bush. She was fun and she was loud. And she was there with her children, husband and father-in-law Bernie, now in his late eighties, who had been part of the 82nd Airborne which had parachuted into Normandy on 6 June 1944.

We all ate together that night at a restaurant in Bayeux, and he quietly and modestly told us the story of those days. The life expectancy of paratroopers was extremely short. But, incredibly, he had participated in all four of the combat jumps that the 82nd were called into action for. So as well as D-Day, he was involved in the parachute jump into Sicily, in Salerno as part of Operation Giant on mainland Italy and finally, at the end of 1944, in the Battle of the Bulge – the most costly of all engagements for the Americans in the Second World War. He was never wounded in service, but served for over two years in Europe's bloodiest conflicts as a machine gunner.

At the table next to us were a bunch of British young men wearing replica football shirts. They were boisterous and laddish – and had been drinking. But they suddenly fell quiet as they eavesdropped our conversation. One by one they came to our table and asked if they might shake Bernie's hand, and each of them with the utmost respect thanked him for his service and their freedom. It was a moment that will stay with me for ever. There wasn't a dry eye in the house. Carafes of wine were brought to the table, as the French restaurant owners realised they had a liberator in their midst. History had conspired to make a young man who had grown up in a poor family on the outskirts of Chicago, caddying at the local golf club because there were no proper jobs in the Great Depression – and who knew nothing beyond his home state of Illinois, let alone Europe – become a figure to be venerated some 60 years on, by all who were in that Bayeux *brasserie* that night. We, a generation of French and Britons, had never known military conflict but knew what sacrifice meant. And he was the embodiment of it.

The blood spilled by those British and American young men would underline the profound sense in which the two nations had an inseparable and forever shared history. There may have been times when the British have wanted to say to America 'mind your own business', but America has a simple rejoinder: our blood and treasure were spilled for your freedom. When I travelled with Barack Obama to Britain just before the Brexit vote in 2016, there had been some debate about how far he would go in seeking to intervene. There was a mood in Britain that this was nothing to do with a US president. A sovereign nation should determine its own affairs. But in an article for the *Daily Telegraph* he wrote this: 'I will say, with the candor of a friend, that the outcome of your decision is a matter of deep interest to the United States. The tens of thousands of Americans who rest in Europe's cemeteries are a silent testament to just how intertwined our prosperity and security truly are. And the path you choose now will echo in the prospects of today's generation of Americans as well.' It's estimated that on 6 June 1944 alone, around 4,500 Allied troops lost their lives – 2,500 of them American – as their troops fought their way up those treacherous Normandy beaches.

Another observation that Churchill made in his speech at Westminster College, Fulton, in 1946 was this: 'The United States stand at this time at the pinnacle of world power. It is a solemn moment for the American Democracy. For with primacy in power is also joined an awe-inspiring accountability to the future.' No longer was there the pretence that the once great British Empire was in any way a co-equal of what was now the pre-eminent superpower and far and away the richest country on the planet. In the 1930s and 40s, when the Americans were driving hard bargains with the British, it was because the Empire was seen as a competitor. No longer. And any lingering doubts about that were laid to rest by the Suez Crisis.

In the mid-1950s if you studied the colour of the globe you would still see much of it shaded in imperial pink. From the Caribbean, over to Singapore, Hong Kong and Malaya, and across to Africa, the Union Jack still fluttered on top of colonial governors' mansions. But the tide of history was running in the opposite direction, as nationalist politicians sought to follow the example of the Indian sub-continent and chart a new, independent destiny for their countries.

Given the parlous state of Britain's finances after the burdensome debt accumulated in the war, and with the economy still trying to get back on its feet, a military adventure in Egypt would seem to be the last thing you would imagine politicians considering. But there were those who still believed that the 'great' in Great Britain needed to mean something – we were a nuclear power, and one of the five permanent members of the United Nations Security Council. We were also a great trading nation, which benefited hugely from the unhindered movement of goods. The Suez Canal, since its completion on Egyptian soil in 1869, had been run by an international company, mainly British and French in composition.

So when those 'upstart' revolutionaries in Egypt, under Colonel Gamal Abdel Nasser, threatened to take back control of the strategically vital waterway, the British – who had a strong military presence in the zone – bristled. Once Nasser announced the nationalisation of the canal, the most extraordinary plan was cooked up by Israel, France and Britain. In complete secrecy it was agreed that Israel – which had a legitimate grievance through being denied access to the waterway for any of its goods – would invade. Then under the pretext of needing to separate Israeli and Egyptian forces, French and British paratroopers would move in – and thus protect the freedom of navigation of the canal. America was kept in the dark. The two fading colonial powers of Europe didn't need permission. They could do what they chose.

Except quickly, and extremely humiliatingly, they learned they could do no such thing. President Eisenhower was enraged. The special relationship would count for nothing over this. In effect America ordered the British Prime Minister Sir Anthony Eden to halt forthwith. The *Guardian* newspaper described Eden as a 'curiously inadequate man. He had the vanity that often accompanies good looks, and the querulous temper that goes with innate weakness.' The silky mandarin, who had been Churchill's foreign secretary through the war, seemed not to have learned the lesson that the world had changed. But, boy, was President Eisenhower going to show him who was the boss. Washington moved against Britain diplomatically, forcing through a UN resolution demanding a ceasefire, but the critical bit of *force majeure* came with the run on sterling that the crisis – and some historians would say the Americans quite deliberately – provoked. America was turning the financial screw. The Treasury reported to Eden that the country would need urgent financial support from the US to stave off financial collapse – to the tune of a billion dollars. The answer from Washington was swift – no chance of you getting a cent from us unless you get your forces out of Egypt.

A disgraced Eden had no choice but to resign. Britain would no longer talk about its global imperial reach, except in smoky old gentlemen's clubs in Pall Mall, where former brigadiers and colonial masters could reminisce about better days over a large brandy and a fat cigar – and sepia-coloured memories. The *realpolitik* was unambiguous. America was in charge.

A few years later, the US secretary of state from President Harry Truman's administration would cause massive upset in the UK by questioning the very point of Britain and whether the special relationship meant anything at all. Dean Acheson had been invited to give a keynote speech at the West Point military academy. The speech was a broadly conventional canter round the big geo-strategic questions of the day – the Soviet threat, the role of Europe in countering it – and then this:

> Great Britain has lost an empire and has not yet found a role. The attempt to play a separate power role – that is a role apart from Europe, a role based on a 'special relationship' with the United States, a role based on being head of a 'commonwealth' which has no political structure, or unity, or strength – this role is about played out. Great Britain, attempting to be a broker between the United States and Russia, has seemed to conduct policy as weak as its military power.

Those views find an echo from some on the eastern side of the Atlantic. On the left, there has always been a strong streak of anti-Americanism: people who disliked America's brash, free enterprise policies, its sometimes bullying foreign policy: Vietnam, Chile, Nicaragua – and more recently Iraq. But there was criticism from the right, too. The eminent British historian Correlli Barnett has argued forcefully that the special relationship is a myth, a fantasy that existed only in the heads of British politicians. Because Britain was a nuclear power and was allowed to sit on the UN Security Council, it was delusional about the levels of influence it had over the United States. It was love unrequited.

He gives the example of America selling Britain the Trident nuclear weapons system. The words were 'independent, nuclear deterrent'. But what imaginable circumstances were there, or would there be, when Britain would give the order for one of these fearsome weapons of mass destruction to be fired without the blessing of Washington? This was an extension of the American nuclear arsenal, but Britain continued to pretend otherwise. It was, Barnett told a conference in Cambridge, 'the supreme example of overstretch stemming from *folie de grandeur*'.

But there is a Goldilocks and the Three Bears problem – at least from a British vantage point – in the special relationship. The temperature is never just right. Just take what happened with Tony Blair and Gordon Brown, and the different treatment that each received.

Tony Blair stood four-square behind George W. Bush over the Iraq War. The British prime minister had persuaded his American counterpart – initially – to go via the UN route to give Saddam Hussein one final chance to comply with the demand that weapons inspectors should be given unfettered access to the country. That Resolution 1441 was passed, at the end of 2002, was in no small part down to British influence. But to sanction an invasion the British wanted the US to go back to secure a second resolution. That wasn't going to happen. The president was frustrated by the United Nations; he had committed US troops to Kuwait, and in the desert the average daily temperature was rising and rising. He also had two hugely powerful and overbearing lieutenants, in Defense Secretary Donald Rumsfeld and Vice President Dick Cheney, who wanted to get going, and were frankly not interested in the British sensibilities on the subject. There could be no question of just letting the troops sit there in the baking sand for another few months. So Britain went along, without a second resolution – and with much tortured debate afterwards on the legality of the advice that the UK government relied on for its decision. The disastrous Iraq entanglement began, in what became known as the 'coalition of the willing'.

From that moment on, in every depiction, Tony Blair was George W. Bush's poodle. A gift for cartoonists. The narrative was set: he was taking orders directly from Washington, incapable of independent thought and action. Of course that is a travesty of the truth. Blair was a believer in so-called 'liberal interventionism' before Bush became president. And after the successful operations in Kosovo to halt ethnic cleansing, and to put an end to the appalling brutality of the rebel army, the RUF, in Sierra Leone, it really wasn't that surprising that he backed the overthrow of Saddam Hussein. But that didn't matter. Blair was seen as a spineless follower, the lapdog – and sometimes far worse. The British people seemed to hate how close and how supine he appeared to be to the Americans. Going back to Goldilocks tasting the three bowls of porridge on the table, that is the too-hot scenario.

Now for too cold. Gordon Brown went through – surely – one of the most humiliating episodes for a British PM when he was in New York for the United Nations General Assembly in 2009. There is broadly speaking a hierarchy of meetings. At the very pinnacle of the tree, when you are loved beyond belief, is the invitation to stay in the White House, and you are put in the Lincoln bedroom. One down from that is the stay across the street from the White House in the government-owned mansion, Blair House. The invitation to spend the weekend at Camp David is a sign that you are well in favour. Then we go a bit further down the food chain to a working lunch and a joint news conference; below that is the quick camera shot of you and the president sitting in the Oval Office, with the press allowed to capture the moment for 30 seconds – while at the bottom of the diplomatic protocol league table is the 'brush past'. That is when two leaders at some event have a quick chat passing each other in a corridor. That is only one better than the true pits of diplomacy, the brush-off – which is more or less what Gordon Brown got.

Five times British officials, at Downing Street's behest, had sought a one-to-one meeting with the US president. Diplomats were quoted as having had to beg for the 'bilateral'. The meeting would have meant at the very least a photo-call; ideally the two men would have held a joint news conference. The British prime minister, whose approval ratings were not exactly stratospheric, would be filmed looking purposeful and a linchpin of global democracy next to the still very popular US president. But five times the White House batted away the idea. So, after much nagging, the president's team said if the British were that anxious to secure a meeting, then Mr Brown could walk with Mr Obama as he left the UN with his secret service detail via a back exit. Not what Britain's PM had in mind. The press were told they had 15 minutes together walking through the UN's kitchens. It was the kitchen summit. And it was a sleepless night for Brown's apparatchiks who spent the hours of darkness trying to hose down the 'Brown snubbed by Obama' story that would be lighting up the front page of every British newspaper. And what fun was had. This is from the *Daily Telegraph*.

It is the stuff of GCSE maths nightmares: How long does it take two world leaders to walk round a 9,455 sq ft kitchen after a dinner of roast lamb, strawberry tart, Patagonian Malbec and sparkling conversation about climate change? The surprising answer, according to Downing Street, is 15 minutes. The calculations assumed some significance yesterday after Gordon Brown unsuccessfully badgered Barack Obama for a face-to-face meeting at the United Nations General Assembly summit.

A former Foreign Office minister, Lord Malloch Brown, said British officials had been over-anxious in their efforts to arrange a meeting with Mr Obama. 'I don't know whether they were frantic or not, they should not have been frankly so desperate.' Hmm. Really. One suspects it wasn't the officials that were desperate. It was their political master. Another diplomat, speaking anonymously, and therefore more candidly, said that he was 'pathetically needy'. Mr Brown would later issue a statement that brimmed with the confidence of a football manager whose team are rooted to the bottom of the table, talking about his relationship with the club chairman: 'President Obama and I have the strongest working relationship and the strongest friendship. I am not only very confident about the strength of the relationship between our countries and I am very confident about the relationship between the two of us.' Of course you are …

David Cameron aimed for a middle course and a temperature 'just right' plan, when he very sensibly told people to stop obsessing about the special relationship. He wrote in the *Wall Street Journal* at the outset of his premiership, and ahead of his first meeting at the White House with Barack Obama: 'No other international alliance seems to come under the intense scrutiny reserved for the one between Britain and the United States. There is a seemingly endless British preoccupation with the health of the special relationship. Its temperature is continually taken to see if it's in good shape, its pulse checked to see if it will survive. I have never understood this anxiety.' He also acknowledged openly that Britain was very much the junior partner, and that they wouldn't agree on everything. He also said that America would have other extremely close relationships. It was spot on.

Indeed it was a silky operation at the Obama White House as they found inventive ways to make *everyone* feel special. So when the French were in town it would be described as 'our oldest relationship'. If the president was meeting the German chancellor, Angela Merkel, the phrase used would be 'the most trusted relationship'; and if he was meeting the leaders of Mexico or Canada, 'our closest relationship' would be the preferred form of words.

In terms of background and political ideology David Cameron and Barack Obama were from different worlds, but despite that they really did get along well. Cameron, with his Eton and Oxford background, had not been called 'Bro' too often, one suspects. But that is the term the US president used for him. They flipped burgers together in the Downing Street garden, they munched on hot dogs together at the basketball, and played table tennis. There was warmth and respect.

But there were big differences that would underline who gave the orders. When it looked like Britain was about to cut defence spending, so that it would fall below the 2 per cent of GDP target required of NATO members, there was fury in the White House. It was a message that was not getting through to Downing Street. I remember the first time I was invited to play tennis with the then British ambassador, Sir Peter Westmacott, at the spectacular residence on Massachusetts Avenue as part of a doubles match. One of those participating was a very senior White House adviser. At the change of ends there was a candid exchange on what was at stake over NATO, and how vexed the president was by Britain's stance. Though I would not be able to report directly on what was said, this was gold-dust intelligence to have. As I listen intently, my mobile phone rings. It is my daughter in London. I pick up just to say that I can't really talk. But she is sobbing, having just crashed the car. I ask whether she is injured. 'No,' she says, 'I think I'm OK.' I reply, 'Good. I'll call you later,' and throw my phone down to go back to the conversation. Maybe not my finest hour in concerned parenting ... but, hey, the tennis was great.

The vote in the Commons in 2013 which rejected David Cameron's call to back American action in Syria after that country's use of chemical weapons caused a good deal of anger and astonishment in Washington. In the *New York Times*, Roger Cohen wrote: 'When Britain opts for the sidelines with Germany, leaving an American president to look to France and Turkey for support in holding Bashar al-Assad account-able for breaking the world's taboo on chemical weapons, there is little or nothing special left. Rather than standing shoulder-to-shoulder with its ally, Britain has turned its back.'

But there is a piece of untold history here, and it is a fascinating reflection on UK ambition and the reality of the UK's position. Barack Obama the week before the Commons vote had wanted an urgent conversation with David Cameron about the Syria situation. It was a Saturday lunchtime, London time; early morning in DC. Senior advisers to Cameron who wanted to sit in on the call would have to go to Whitehall and the British version of the White House's Situation Room. This was the only place that a secure call like this could be heard.

One of those present told me that Barack Obama started by saying that President Assad had crossed a red line by using chemical weapons, and he felt he had no option but to start bombing immediately. Could he count on Britain to be alongside? David Cameron affirmed his 100 per cent support. It was agreed that the first air raids would commence the next day on the Sunday evening. Obviously because of the urgency there would not be time to consult parliament. But after the PM came off the call a more practical problem came to the fore. Where on earth was the UK going to find any planes to participate in the raids? Eventually, after much scrambling around, it was established that a couple of Tornadoes that had been involved in Iraq could be prepared. On this occasion Britain was willing; it just wasn't very able.

Now, from untold history to an accident of history. It was either a bizarre coincidence, or details of the US and British plan were leaked to the Syrian regime, because the next morning UN inspectors were suddenly told they could have unfettered access to the sites that the Americans and British were about to start bombing later that day. Obama said they would have to delay. The frantic work to get the two British Tornadoes ready could be halted. But that meant David Cameron now felt he had to consult parliament, and so MPs were brought back for this crucial debate. One interpretation of what unfolded was that this was Britain moving away from its ties to the US and aligning itself much more with Europe (a difficult interpretation when the French were absolutely with the Americans on this). But it felt much more as though parliamentarians were subconsciously re-arguing the case for and against the Iraq War – with many of those who had voted for the disastrous Iraq campaign switching sides.

There were some seriously tense conversations between the president's national security advisor, Susan Rice, and various British officials. Worse was the reaction the British military were on the receiving end of. Senior American commanders were saying to their counterparts, 'And we thought we could rely on you.' That hurt. But the president's reaction? Well, that is harder to fathom. In a long interview he gave a couple of years later to the *Atlantic* magazine, you could almost sense his relief that he didn't take action against the Syrians. He had assumed the presidency in an attempt to disentangle the US from foreign engagements, not seek out new ones.

But if there is one truth about the 'special relationship', it is that America will always – ultimately – do what it sees as in its interests. First and foremost. Just look at the relationship between Ron and Maggie. The links between Ronald Reagan and Margaret Thatcher were always held up as the closest since Roosevelt and Churchill. They were the Cold War warriors who were determined to face down the threat of the Soviet Union; they were the ideological soul mates who agreed on rolling back the frontiers of the state. He would purr in delight at her forcefulness and no-nonsense style; she would clearly be charmed by the former film star's 'oh gee shucks' manner. They were the most forceful double act on the world stage. But when America decided that it didn't much like the government that had taken over in that tiny speck of an island in the Caribbean called Grenada, there was no hesitation: President Reagan ordered the invasion of this Commonwealth country without letting his friend in Downing Street know.

On the penultimate day of the Obama second term, I went to a breakfast with the president's spokesman, Josh Earnest, who was reflecting on the challenges of doing the job. He spoke eloquently about how once you occupy that great office words are live ammunition. The argument he was making was a version of the wartime 'careless talk costs lives'. And it was a none too subtle dig at the extravagantly loose talk of Donald Trump. But the example he gave was not of something that was said, but something that was *not* said. When Barack Obama first became president, the then press secretary, Robert Gibbs, spoke about Great Britain – and at no point mentioned the two magic words 'special relationship'. It caused an unwanted furore. The British press had a bit of a hissy fit. This, combined with the removal of the Churchill bust, was now conclusive proof that the relationship had never been so bad. Of course all utter nonsense, and meaningless.

The relationship is strong, far stronger than with most other countries. But it is just something that you don't pay that much attention to if you're an American. There are so many other global players wanting your attention, and Britain is not always at the forefront of every thought. But at the White House that omission came to be seen as a serious mistake, and something from which a lesson could be learned. What you do is one thing; what you say is something else. So long as you are paying lip service to the special relationship, that is fine – then you can do whatever you like. And America will.

CHAPTER 9

Truth

About two miles from where we live is a pizza restaurant, called Comet Ping Pong Pizza. It's in a fairly trendy, affluent area of Northwest Washington just beyond the zoo up on Connecticut Avenue. Two weeks after the election, a 28-year-old man got up one morning and drove from his home in Salisbury North Carolina to this pizza restaurant. It's a 720-mile round trip, which any way you cut it is a long way to go for a slice of pepperoni pizza.

In fact he hadn't gone for pizza at all. Edgar Maddison Welch walked into the pizza restaurant armed with an AR-15 assault rifle – the same weapon used in some of America's most notorious mass shootings – on Sunday lunchtime, at the restaurant's busiest time, to rescue youngsters who were part of a horrifying child sex ring, and who were being kept in the restaurant's cellar-cum-dungeon and were being routinely abused. And wait for this: this vile paedophile network was being run by none other than Hillary Clinton, her chief of staff, John Podesta, and the restaurant's owner.

Welch fired one shot into the ground to show that he meant business. A terrified waiter managed to raise the alarm, and SWAT teams were quickly on the scene.

Of course there was no sex ring, there were no paedophiles, no Hillary Clinton, no enslaved children – the restaurant didn't even have a cellar. It was all total, 100 per cent pure, unadulterated nonsense. Rubbish. Complete and utter garbage. And there never had been a scintilla of truth in it whatsoever.

So what made Edgar Maddison Welch think there was? Well, in the slew of leaked emails from the account belonging to John Podesta, one message among the hundreds of thousands that were dumped by Wikileaks discussed the possibility of holding a fundraising event at the restaurant.

The restaurant is next door to a wonderful bookshop called Politics and Prose, owned by a former close aide of Hillary Clinton, and this part of the city is about as rock-solid Democrat as you are going to find anywhere. Only 4 per cent of DC's residents voted for Donald Trump. So the idea of a fundraiser in the restaurant was about as unremarkable an idea as you could reasonably imagine.

Except for this: someone, somewhere, decided to turn the unremarkable and banal into a hideous conspiracy. Stories started to appear on right-wing websites that 'pizza' and 'pizzeria' were code for something much more sinister. They signified paedophilia on a grand scale. These totally fake stories were given a push by right-wing supremacists. One of the 'reports' had the headline: 'Pizzagate: How 4Chan Uncovered the Sick World of Washington's Occult Elite.' Or how about this one, which gives it all a veneer of respectability: 'FBI insider: Clinton Emails Linked to Pedophile Sex Ring.'

What seems to have happened is that on a white supremacist message board, which is a haven for trolls and where the most outlandish and theatre-of-the-absurd claims get propagated, people start to talk about this. From there, others on the fringes of conservative media begin to speculate on the story. And before you know it, it has jumped a respectability gap and appears on Reddit, which is a social media aggregator. This is a community where people post what they like; whatever is on their mind.

Think of it if you like as a giant car-boot sale. The farmer who owns the field just lets the cars in and makes his money from the admittance fee – he or she isn't responsible for the quality, quantity or genuineness of what is being sold from the trunks of the different vehicles. But car-boot sales don't have algorithms – well, not any that I have been to. The pizzagate story gets championed with 'likes' by Trump supporters – and so it gets pushed out to all sorts of people whose previous user history suggests they are interested in this type of material, or are admirers of Donald J. Trump.

So a malevolent falsehood and a computer algorithm combine to give the story apparent substance – and wings. But it is worse than that. It starts to be propagated by people who really should know better. General Michael Flynn, who after the election was appointed national security advisor by Donald Trump, tweeted during the campaign itself: 'U decide – NYPD Blows Whistle on New Hillary Emails: Money Laundering, Sex Crimes w Children etc … MUST READ!'

Remember this wasn't a casual retweet from a nobody. This was the former head of the Defense Intelligence Agency choosing to write his own utterly false and malicious tweet. There was no NYPD investigation, they didn't blow a whistle, there was no money laundering. General Flynn's son, Michael G. Flynn – who was due to be joining the new Trump administration as an aide to his father – even *after* the shooting incident at the pizzeria wouldn't let it go, tweeting 'Until #pizzagate proven to be false, it'll remain a story. The left seems to forget #PodestaEmails and the many coincidences tied to it.'

What? Until it's proven to be false? Hold on a minute. What about providing evidence that there is a single grain of truth to it? Have we now entered an era where I can accuse anyone of anything and the burden falls on the accused to prove it's not true? It is the most basic tenet of justice turned on its head. In the post-truth world someone accused is guilty until proven innocent.

When people ask how could poor Mr Welch have been so deluded as to think there were children trapped in the basement of a pizza restaurant being sexually abused by Hillary Clinton, here is your answer. Easily.

A friend of mine who worked at the White House as the Middle East adviser to President Obama, and would have been an obvious pick for a senior position in a Hillary Clinton administration, tells how he took his son fishing in the most far-flung corner of America. They flew to Anchorage in Alaska, and then had to drive four hours north to get to the town where they would hire their boat. This is the state where Sarah Palin used to be governor. On the journey all he could find on the radio was a succession of right-wing talk-show hosts – each vying with the other to be the most provocative. The formula was simple – you say something wild and unsubstantiated, invite on an 'expert' from a university or journal that no one has ever heard of and get them to validate the opinion you first expressed.

His punchline to the story is that by the time he and his son got out of the car four hours later, they too hated Hillary Clinton and thought she ought to be locked up. If this is the only diet you are being fed on, is it any wonder that millions of people like Mr Welch believe this?

In any election, truth is always an elusive thing to grab hold of. It is as slippery as a wet bar of soap in a shower. Politicians will seize on a statistic, or an allegation, or a quote made by an opponent and mischievously take it out of context, and fashion it into a missile to be hurled at an opponent. Tendentious is what politicians do. But traditionally the barb or the insult or the claim will have a grounding in reality, a hint of something plausible. You start with a kernel of truth and then wrap it in sly and provocative layers – and then you weaponise it.

But not in 2016 in America. The day after the election I had to go and record what we call a 'piece to camera' – or what Americans call a 'stand up' – for my report that would go on that evening's news. It was a drab and rainy day, so to give it a bright and jazzy backdrop we went to Times Square in Midtown Manhattan. Barack Obama had earlier that day recorded a message on Donald Trump's victory saying that no matter what Americans were feeling the 'sun would still rise in the morning'. This is what I reported in my piece to camera. In other words the world would carry on spinning as before, even if it felt like the globe was now on a different axis.

But post-election proved to be no different from pre-election; the lies would keep spewing out. Having recorded the 20-second segment we got in a yellow taxi to take us back to the BBC office on Ninth Avenue. The driver was an old African American guy. He had the news on the radio in his cab. Everyone in America was transfixed by what had unfolded the night before. I asked him to turn the volume up. In earnest tones (are there any other?) the correspondent was reporting that the Clintons had organised a private jet and were preparing to flee the US. The forces of law and order were closing in around them, and were about to raid their home in Chappaqua, just outside the city. They had shipped their stolen fortune of $1.8 billion out of the country, most likely, he said, to Switzerland or to an offshore tax haven in the Caribbean. But they themselves were heading to the Gulf state of Qatar where they would live out their days – because the US had no extradition treaty with the oil-rich state in the Persian Gulf.

I asked our cab driver whether he believed this stuff. Absolutely, he said. He then backed it up by reciting previous untrue stories about Hillary Clinton. Once you go down this route each new absurdity reinforces the previous one, and makes it seem utterly plausible.

During the Brexit campaign it was commented on that Britain was going through an era of 'post-truth'. Perhaps it was best summed up when one of the leading lights of the 'leave' campaign, Michael Gove, railed that 'people in this country have had enough of experts'. For someone who prides himself on his intellectual rigour, this was a curiously anti-intellectual thing to say. Indeed such was the grip that post-truth had on our politics, that the Oxford Dictionaries declared it the word of the year (though with a hyphen). They defined 'post-truth' as 'relating to or denoting circumstances in which objective facts are less influential in shaping public opinion than appeals to emotion and personal belief'.

There was plenty of that in the US too. Donald Trump's appeal was all about going for the gut, appealing to people's instincts, drawing on feelings of discontent and alienation. And to try to counter this post-truth world, some publications made a valiant attempt to call the politicians out on their more fanciful claims and allegations. The *Washington Post* introduced a 'Pinocchio' test, so a teeny little white fib would get one Pinocchio, while a howling, great whopper of a lie would be given the full four Pinocchios.

The *Post* put 92 of Trump's statements through the fact-checking machinery. And as the cogs and wheels clunked and clicked away a verdict was reached. Of the 92 statements, 59 were awarded four Pinocchios. If you were being unkind, or merely statistical, then 64 per cent of what he said was a total fiction.

So, to go through a few straightforward ones, Trump claimed the Mexican government was sending thieves and rapists to the US. But evidence shows immigrants commit no more crimes than those born in America. He claimed again and again that the true unemployment rate in the United States was 42 per cent, at a time when the official rate was just over 5 per cent. Trump repeatedly stated that there was a plan by Barack Obama to admit 200,000 Syrian refugees to the United States. The official figure was 10,000. He said that he had always been opposed to the Iraq War, while the only recording of him talking before the 2003 invasion has him offering his support. In the wake of 9/11 he claimed that he watched on television as 'thousands and thousands' of Muslims in New Jersey cheered and celebrated the collapse of the twin towers at the World Trade Center.

No such footage has ever been found to support that claim. And so it went on.

But in a post-truth world, it's not the lies that get told, it is the indifference – or lack of awareness – of the people who are hearing them that is most remarkable. Or the willingness to believe anything you are told if it fits with your world view. Books much weightier than this will be written about the abject failure of the conventional media to comprehend fully the parameters of this new world, but a Pittsburgh-based journalist Salena Zito summarised it most succinctly when she noted, 'The media take Trump literally but not seriously, while the public take him seriously but not literally.' In other words, because so many of his statements were demonstrably nonsense, the conventional media thought along conventional lines: once you expose the falsehoods, the public will thank you and see him as a bit of a charlatan. There was collective 'group-think' that would reinforce the old saying that trust arrives on foot but leaves on horseback. The thing is, it didn't. A big slice of the American electorate was totally undeterred by the untruths. They knew that he told 'porkies'; in their appraisal of the character of the man they had that factored in. What mattered to his supporters was that he had serious things to say about turning the US economy round, to make America great again. And they trusted him to get that job done. On that, they took him seriously.

Some of this is analogous to what happened in the UK with Brexit. Pretty tall claims were made about the gusher of cash that would soon be slopping around the most cash-starved corners of the NHS if only Britain were to free itself from the suffocating embrace of the European Union. It was the same with getting control of Britain's borders and putting a halt to immigration. You didn't need to sign up to the detail of these claims to decide that you thought the future of our island nation was best served by severing ties.

While a lot has been made of the similarities between Brexit and the Trump victory in the USA – and the concerns over immigration, taking back control and economic nationalism were undoubtedly similar – there were very big differences too.

It is also worth saying there is a big difference as well between a referendum and a general election. A referendum, as I'm sure David Cameron and the former Italian prime minister, Matteo Renzi, would agree, can be a fatally risky thing to do. It rarely focuses simply on the question before the people. Voters see it as a chance to express dissatisfaction about a whole range of other issues, totally unrelated to the matter on the ballot paper. It was astonishing to hear people explaining their vote the day after Brexit. People saying they voted to leave because their local swimming pool or library was under threat of closure by the council, as if that had anything to do with the EU.

The post-war British Labour prime minister Clement Atlee described referendums as the last resort of demagogues and dictators. Complex issues are boiled down to a simple question. So with Brexit, it was simply do we stay in or leave the EU. Fine, but what the 'leavers' were desperate to avoid doing was spelling out what departure looked like – because it is hugely, migraine-inducingly complex. And in post-truth politics attempts to scare the living daylights out of voters – as the Remain campaigners sought to do, with backing, it should be said, from some very credible economists around the world – fail. The siren warnings fall on deaf ears.

But the referendum vote in the UK came only a year after the British people had eschewed some of the populist politics that were on offer at the general election. Arguably the British people had taken the most small 'c' conservative choice open to them. A tried and tested Conservative government that had sought to manage the deficit, that had governed with the Liberal Democrats in a reasonably effective way, won re-election on a fairly traditional, right-of-centre manifesto. They won against a Labour Party that was perceived to have drifted too far to the left, and hadn't come to terms with the reasons for the parlous state of the economy when it left office in 2010. My reasoning here is not to revisit the 2015 general election, when I was happily 3,000 miles away from the action. It is simply to make the point that the British people were hardly saying to the politicians, 'To hell with the lot of you.' In the 2015 general election it was pragmatism not populism that won.

In the 2016 US general election it was populism that won the day. And there was a very strong 'to hell with the lot of you' sentiment. It was a rejection of Hillary Clinton, sure – but it went wider than that. It was the whole state apparatus that seemed to be distrusted. Anything official was to be given the same degree of credence as something totally made up.

The most striking example of that came a week after the election. Throughout the campaign and in the run-up to it, there had been a damaging dump of emails on a daily basis from within the Democratic National Committee and from the private email account of Hillary Clinton's chief of staff, John Podesta. The emails which had been passed to Wikileaks had been seized on, as you might imagine, by the Trump campaign. They had a corrosive effect. Seven days after the election, intelligence officials let it be known that the CIA had concluded its formal assessment of Russian activity during the campaign and found that the government of Vladimir Putin was not only behind the hack to interfere in the election of another sovereign nation, but was actively working to help one candidate over another.

This was the view of the CIA, the FBI and assorted other agencies whose job it is to keep America safe and secure. You would imagine the only reaction that a politician could give to the revelation that a foreign government – of whatever political shape and hue, friend or foe – had sought to undermine the democratic process of the country is it needs to be investigated, and the 'truth' must out. Donald Trump's reaction was very wide of that. His office mocked the very people who he must now rely on to give him his intelligence briefings. 'These are the same people that said Saddam Hussein had weapons of mass destruction,' he said, adding that the election was over and it was time to move on. President elect Trump went further. He quoted Vladimir Putin approvingly, who had accused the Democrats of being bad losers at his end-of-year news conference in Moscow. In other words the CIA, the FBI and all the rest of them were either talking rubbish or were making stuff up.

For a weekly podcast I did in the run-up to the election and in the aftermath of it, we went and talked to people in a bar about the judgement from the intelligence community that Russia had sought to influence the election. This was in a conservative area. And remember historically throughout the Cold War 'the Ruskies' were – and remain – the greatest threat to the US, with hundreds of nuclear weapons of varying shape and size still pointed at America. And conservatives have been the most alert and anxious about the threat. Well, in this bar we couldn't find one person who believed the intelligence agencies. They all thought it was sour grapes on the part of the Clintons, and from those who supported her. When asked why the intel guys would make this up, they couldn't answer. But that didn't matter. Like Beppe Grillo they were sick of facts.

And here is another critical difference between the UK and the US. Britain may through the 2016 referendum have gone through its moment of 'post-truth', but America went through the 'no-truth' election.

Winston Churchill is credited with the quotation that 'a lie travels half way round the world before the truth has got its pants on'. I love the quote, even though I find it hard to believe the greatest phrase-making draughtsman would have used the word 'pants'. Just sounds too American. Anyway. That is a minor quibble. What he says is undoubtedly true. Except that in today's world of social media, the impact of a lie is instantaneous. Even as recently as 20 years ago, a politician needed a conduit to get a view 'out there' into the public domain. And the mass media was the only means of doing that. You would rely on friendly journalists or newspapers to do your bidding. They might afford you room to publish an opinion piece. You could start a hare running about an opponent and see if it sprints. When I covered successive general elections in the UK there were always 'rumours' about some scandal that would break about this one or that one: a careless sexual encounter here, a corrupt bit of money-making there. But they rarely hit the mainstream media because we have libel laws, and unless you got your facts right you would be sued. And the fringe bits of media were so tiny that they could be dealt with by a shrug.

But in the 2016 US election, we saw the arrival in earnest of something new: fake news. The story about the paedophile ring operating out of a pizzeria in Washington was but one example of a proliferation of completely false stories that would pop up on the newsfeed on people's Facebook page. Fake news became a burgeoning industry. And it was part driven by ideological warriors who wanted to bring their dark arts to the presidential campaign and by young computer whizzes wanting to create 'clickbait' – stories that people would click on – guaranteeing the person who posted it a small piece of the advertising revenues that would accompany the post.

It is worth looking at this a little more closely – but allow me just a minor digression. Donald Trump's big campaign promises were America First, controlling immigration and stopping unwanted interference from outside. But look at the origins of post-truth, fake news. We had Wikileaks: an organisation registered in Iceland, with its Australian head, seeking refuge from the Swedish police on sexual abuse charges in the Ecuadorian embassy in the UK, pumping out material that had been hacked by the Russian government. And then on further investigation, it turns out that one of the biggest fake-news 'factories' on stories about the election is in the former Yugoslav republic of Macedonia. That is quite an international cast list for a US general election, where only citizens of the United States vote.

This all sounds so unlikely that I thought I was reading fake news about fake news. But 100 or so fake-news websites, that were by a huge majority pro-Trump, operated from the Macedonian town of Veles on the Vardar River. Where? Hitherto, this town had only been known for its production of beautifully painted porcelain. Well the porcelain factory has closed, but the art of embellishing clearly hasn't as millennials there sought to make a quick US buck.

One of the stories they produced was a report containing an entirely fictitious quote from Hillary Clinton, in which she was reported to have said a few years ago that Donald Trump should run for president. She had never said that. But the story received half a million shares. These Macedonian youngsters were feeding on the gullibility and susceptibility of the American voter.

Covering the presidential election had moments that were entirely surreal. One of them came in February 2016 when I saw a 'news alert' on my computer at work saying that the pope had launched a blistering attack on Donald Trump. I thought there was just no way that Pope Francis was going to wade into the US election campaign. But on his way back from Mexico, where he had prayed with pilgrims on the US border, he *did* launch a pretty uncoded attack on the Republican hopeful. He spoke of the need to build bridges, rather than walls, in a way that could have left no one in any doubt about where he stood.

So imagine my surprise when I saw this during the campaign itself, just a couple of weeks from polling day: 'Pope Francis Shocks World, Endorses Donald Trump for President, Releases Statement.'

The report came from the website of Radio WTOE 5 News. A statement from His Holiness accompanied it: 'I have been hesitant to offer any kind of support for either candidate in the US presidential election but I now feel that to not voice my concern would be a dereliction of my duty as the Holy See.' The statement accompanying it then goes on to talk about the pope's displeasure that the FBI did not proceed with a prosecution against Mrs Clinton for her use of a private email server when she was secretary of state. However, the Holy Father then pulls back a tad, saying he is not endorsing Donald Trump as the pope, but 'as a concerned citizen of the world'.

The only problem is that there is no Radio WTOE 5 News. It doesn't exist. The whole thing is a complete fiction from beginning to end. In the cold light of day, far away from the sound and fury of the election campaign, maybe one can look at it and laugh, and treat it as the risible nonsense that it is. But two weeks before the election, this page had just shy of a million views, making it the number-one fake story of the campaign.

I feel that the next couple of sentences should be accompanied by the music to Alan Freeman's radio chart show *Pick of the Pops*. So let's go through the rest of the fake-news chart: in at number two with 790,000 views was this: 'Wikileaks CONFIRMS Hillary sold weapons to ISIS.' In third place is: 'It's OVER: Hillary's Isis email just leaked and it's worse than anyone could have imagined.' Three-quarters of a million people read that. At number four on the Ending the Fed website was 'Just read the law: Hillary is disqualified from holding any federal office.' And at number five – and frankly I'm surprised it didn't do better – was 'FBI agent suspected in Hillary email leaks found dead in apparent murder-suicide.' That seemed to me a surefire winner. This story claimed that Hillary Clinton had had an FBI agent killed for being involved in the leak of her emails. OK, there was no sex in the story, but it's got everything else, yet this one only got 567,000 clicks.

The website Buzzfeed carried out an analysis of the 20 best performing fake election stories, against the top performing ones in the conventional media. The results are slightly terrifying. The fake stories generated 8.7 million shares, likes and comments on Facebook. But the top 20 on websites like the *Washington Post*, the *New York Times* and CNN lagged behind with 7.4 million over the same period.

The *Washington Post* tracked down one of the most prolific authors of these stories, a man called Paul Horner. He said the US election had been extremely good for business, and reckoned that he had made $10,000 per month. What gave wings to his efforts to spread falsehood was when Eric Trump and the then campaign manager for Trump, Corey Lewandowski, started tweeting links to his stories. One was a bogus report that Hillary Clinton had been paying protestors $3,500 to disrupt Trump rallies. He told the newspaper: 'My sites were picked up by Trump supporters all the time. Trump is in the White House because of me. His followers don't fact-check anything. They'll post everything, believe anything.'

Just before the election I had a fascinating dinner with Jim Messina. He was the man who ran Barack Obama's 2012 election campaign, and for 2016 was the chairman of one of the main support bodies for Hillary Clinton. He is a number cruncher and data analytics person. But he quickly realised that if you were doing individual polling and canvassing, just asking someone how they intended to vote was not sufficient. People lie. They might not want to admit they are voting for candidate X or candidate Y – so his team sought to identify another question which would give an indication of intended behaviour.

In the UK his team used 'Are you a homeowner?' – your likelihood of voting Conservative grew enormously if you were. So people who replied yes to that question would be canvassed more thoroughly and interrogated about their views. In the US the question was: 'Where do you get your news from?' If you were a reader of the *New York Times* and *Washington Post*, or watched a cable channel like MSNBC, then there was a much greater likelihood you were a Democratic voter; if you said Fox News, talk-show radio or some of the more right-wing websites you were most likely going to be in the Trump corner.

Incidentally Messina also told me the story of how Obama had persuaded him to run the 2012 campaign. The president invited him to Hawaii, where he was on holiday with his family. The leader of the free world then suggests they go for a swim in the sea – an offer that is hard to decline. And so there they are in the Pacific Ocean, a hundred or so yards offshore, treading water, when Barack Obama asks him to head up the campaign. But Messina becomes distracted. He is suddenly aware of a mass of bubbles coming up to the surface where they are splashing about. 'What's causing that, Mr President?' he asks. 'They're coming from the secret service frogmen underneath me in case I start to drown,' he replies matter-of-factly. 'Wow. And what if *I* start to drown, Mr President?' 'You sink, Jim. You sink.'

But back to fake news and the impact it had. Paul Horner, the grand master of fakery, expressed some remorse. Yes, his motive had been to take money by providing 'clickbait', but he said he was also driven by a desire to make Trump supporters look like idiots for being dumb enough to believe what he'd written. This is his mea culpa: 'I thought they'd fact-check it, and it'd make them look worse. I mean that's how this always works: someone posts something I write, then they find out it's false, then they look like idiots. But Trump supporters – they just kept running it! They never fact-check anything! Now he's in the White House. Looking back, instead of hurting the campaign, I think I helped it. And that feels … bad.'

But not all of this contentious material was created by geeky, young, apolitical opportunists seeking to earn a bit of extra cash, or by anarcho-satirists trying to make others look stupid. There were players in the 2016 election who had a very clear political agenda – and that was to get Donald Trump elected, by means fair and foul. The *New York Times* conducted an investigation into the Patriot News Agency, which first made an appearance in July 2016.

The website is pro-Putin but is actually run by a Briton, James Dowson. He was a founder of the far-right Britain First movement, having also been involved in the British National Party. He'd played a largely insignificant role in Britain's Brexit campaign, but like Paul Horner he found a more receptive – and more gullible – audience in the US for his output. He was clear about his mission, posting on one of his sites that his goal was to 'spread devastating anti-Clinton, pro-Trump memes and sound bites into sections of the population too disillusioned with politics to have taken any notice of conventional campaigning'. And with a touch of vainglory he went on to say that 'Together people like us helped change the course of history … every single one of you who forwarded even just one of our posts on social media contributed to the stunning victory for Trump, America and God.'

And without wishing to give Mr Dowson undue prominence, what he expresses as his rationale finds an echo with many conservative voters in the US. 'The simple truth is that after 40 years of the right having no voice because the media was owned by the enemy, we were *forced* to become incredibly good at alternative media in a way the left simply can't grasp or handle.'

It is worth remembering that Fox News in the US was established – massively successfully – because of the perceived liberal bias of so much of the rest of the US media, that left millions of conservative voters feeling dissatisfied, with their voices unheard. But Fox News – for the most part – conforms to what you would expect of a news station. Rock solid reliable reporting but just with a different 'slant' to, say, CNN. So when Donald Trump was getting castigated during the election for 'pussygate' (the tape that emerged from a decade earlier in which you hear him boasting of being able to do what he liked to women because he was famous), Fox focused on other aspects of the campaign that were either damaging to Hillary Clinton – or more favourable to Mr Trump. Yes, they were 'in the tank' for the Republican candidate – no mistake – but they were not 'fake news'.

One of the other great fake stories that gained credence after the election was that Donald Trump actually won the popular vote. I remember receiving a volley of abuse from Trump supporters on Twitter for being ignorant about the electoral facts – not only had their man won the electoral college, he'd received more votes than Hillary Clinton. The author of this tweet helpfully sent me a link to a fake news website to prove his point. This would be a subject Donald Trump would return to when he was sworn in as president.

Now it is easy to exaggerate the role the purveyors of fake news played in this election – and there is no way of accurately measuring how many Americans had their vote changed by one or more mendacious articles they read on the internet. Voter behaviour is not an exact science. All manner of different variables go into determining how people will behave when they pitch up at the polling station. And if it were a precise science then political analysts and psephologists would be able to tell us the results accurately beforehand – which they palpably are unable to do. But did these stories help shape perceptions? Did they reinforce views already held? Did they help decide some people dithering over voting for Clinton to switch to Trump? Almost certainly. And for all the bluster there has been since the election, this was an incredibly tight result where it mattered: in the electoral college.

The closest thing to a study examining the impact of fake news on the 2016 campaign was carried out by pollsters working on behalf of the *Economist* magazine. YouGov asked voters which 'fake' stories they believed, and did this according to party affiliation. The broad conclusion is that Americans believed a lot of nutty things in 2016. The more nuanced 'take out' is that if the crazy stuff was being said about the person you *weren't* going to vote for, you believed it; if it was about the person you *were* going to vote for, you didn't.

So let's go back to where we started: Satanism, paedophilia and what is now called *pizzagate*. Nearly a half of Trump voters believe it to be true. I should add this polling work was carried out from 17–20 December 2016 – long after the election, and a long time after the man had gone into the pizza restaurant with his rifle. Among Trump supporters 62 per cent agreed with the statement that 'millions of illegal votes were cast in the election'. There is no evidence to back that up. Donald Trump would claim post-election that around five million people voted for Hillary Clinton who were ineligible to do so. But when his spokesman was challenged to explain the empirical basis for this, we were told it was what the president believes.

On the cyber-espionage carried out by the Russians, the question was about the statement 'Russia hacked the email of Democrats in order to increase the chance that Donald Trump would win the presidential election' – which 87 per cent of Democrats believed to be true; 80 per cent of Trump supporters said that it was false. And just so that I don't give the impression that it was exclusively Trump supporters who were susceptible to believing whatever they wanted to, more than half of Clinton supporters said they were convinced the Russians had actually tampered with voting machines to boost Trump's numbers. Barack Obama repeatedly said there was no evidence to support that.

One other question the pollsters dug into was the ethnic origin of Barack Obama. More than half of Trump supporters questioned said they believed that their president had been born in Kenya. This may sound innocuous, but has been one of the most persistent and disgraceful conspiracy theories that has done the rounds in the US these past eight years. Because what it does is seek to delegitimise America's first African American president. If you are not born in the US, then you cannot rise to the highest office in the land. On that Article Two of the US Constitution is crystal clear.

The 'birther movement' first of all demanded that until such time as Barack Obama produced his birth certificate, his assertion that he was born in Hawaii could not and must not be believed. Then the naysayers moved on to question whether the certificate – which was released in 2011, and proved that he had indeed been born in the US – was a forgery. Others then shifted their fire onto whether he was really an Indonesian citizen. And so it went on. To many this seemed like naked racism wrapped up in a beguiling cloak of constitutionalism.

The greatest advocate of this movement was Donald Trump. He repeatedly questioned Barack Obama's eligibility to be president, supporting those who raised questions about it. Just before the publication of the birth certificate in April 2011 he said, 'Why doesn't he show his birth certificate? There's something on that birth certificate he doesn't like.' The next week he was back at it. 'He doesn't have a birth certificate, or if he does there's something on that certificate that is very bad for him. Now someone told me – and I have no idea if this is bad for him or not – that where it says "religion", it might have "Muslim". And if you're a Muslim, you don't change your religion, by the way.' In another interview, there was a new line from Mr Trump claiming that Obama's grandmother had confirmed he was born in Kenya. He said she was on tape saying that, and it was going to be produced 'fairly soon'. It never was.

So was the publication of the birth certificate the end of it from Mr Trump? Not a bit of it. It wasn't authentic, he argued in one interview, and on Twitter in 2012 wrote: 'An "extremely credible source" has called my office and told me that @BarackObama's birth certificate is a fraud.' Then this a year later: 'How amazing, the State Health Director who verified copies of Obama's "birth certificate" died in a plane crash today. All others lived.'

What is so fascinating is that this is far more than just a passing topic of interest for Mr Trump – the relentless way he pursued it suggests a borderline obsession with the subject. He was a dog with a bone when it came to this, a bone he would only give up six weeks before the election – not, it should be said, because of some road to Damascus conversion to reason, but because it was starting to adversely affect his campaign. It was preventing him from broadening his appeal to minority voters; it was getting in the way of the messages that he wanted to push on jobs, trade and security. And so at the launch of his new hotel on Pennsylvania Avenue he finally uttered the words 'President Obama was born in the United States.' There was no apology for his role in the 'birther' movement, and he didn't explain what had led him to change his mind. His aides tried to paint it as a victory for Mr Trump, as he had forced Barack Obama to release his birth certificate. But the president had done that five years earlier. Why had it taken Mr Trump so long to move on?

It is easy to go all pop psychologist here to try to explain what was going on in Mr Trump's mind and what was feeding this. Was it just a cynical and calculated attempt to undermine the position of America's first African American president, or did he really believe it – indeed does he still, despite the politically expedient volte face? One of the striking things about Donald Trump throughout the campaign is that he was willing to believe in conspiracies on scant evidence. When the campaign was going badly for him after the release of the 'pussygate' tape, Donald Trump repeatedly charged that the election was being rigged because of a conspiracy involving the mass media, Wall Street, Hollywood and the Washington establishment, who were all meeting together, plotting and planning to deny him the presidency.

It sounded rather like the Jewish conspiracy of the 1930s without the word 'Jewish' being used. And a bit like what assorted Trotskyites and Leninists used to assert when they were trying to explain why the proletariat hadn't yet cast off their false consciousness to embrace the revolutionary determinism of Marxism.

And here is a huge difference between the UK and the US. In the UK I think our default position is to think cock-up; in America it is to think conspiracy. The view that tends to prevail about our political masters is that they are a pretty hapless bunch. At the height of the expenses scandal, maybe we thought they were pretty avaricious. But conspiring? Nah. What are the great conspiracies that people believe about the UK in the last few decades? Twenty years ago there was the death of the Princess of Wales with her boyfriend Dodi Al-Fayed. That prompted a whole bunch of stories about the role of the security services, the mysterious white Fiat in the Alma tunnel in Paris, and the role of the Duke of Edinburgh in this as well. But the truth turned out to be much more prosaic: an off-duty chauffeur who'd drunk too much, who'd also been taking prescription drugs; the two not combining well. He took a bend in the tunnel way too fast in his bid to shake off the paparazzi. His two passengers weren't wearing seatbelts. How many people still believe it was a conspiracy?

There was the death of the government scientist David Kelly, who committed suicide after he had been 'outed' as the source of a report on the danger posed by Iraqi weapons. But he had faced a humiliating encounter with a Commons committee, which he clearly found agonising; this anonymous, rather retiring person had become a figure of infamy in the politically charged post-Iraq environment – and in a state of depression and anxiety took his own life. Some tried to point the finger at the security services, but who is still talking about this? When Harold Wilson stood down as prime minister in the 1970s, some again pointed to a plot by the security services to topple a Labour prime minister not much to their liking – but it turned out Wilson was suffering the start of Alzheimer's disease, and stood down for health reasons.

I have scraped the barrel to come up with these examples. But just compare them to the massive and buoyant conspiracy-theory market in the US. It is an industry, not just a fringe concern. Books are still written, films are still made, argument still rages on the assassination of JFK – whether Lee Harvey Oswald was acting alone or whether there was a second shooter on the grassy knoll. Then of course we had the murder of Oswald two days later. In fact anything to do with the Kennedys has spawned a thousand theories. One book that came out in 2005 sought to link the deaths of JFK, his younger brother Robert, Marilyn Monroe and Mary Jo Kopechne, the girl who died in Edward Kennedy's car at Chappaquiddick in 1969, in one great overarching all-encompassing conspiracy theory. Wow. In fact anything to do with the FBI, the CIA and the presidency are all subjects ripe for endless conspiracy theories. So clearly Roosevelt conspired with the Japanese to allow the bombing of Pearl Harbor to facilitate the US's entry into the Second World War. Henry Kissinger was a

Soviet spy. And 9/11 was actually a plot carried out by the US government at the behest of George W. Bush – or was it the Israelis? One of the two anyway. Of course on that day American Airlines flight 77 never actually crashed into the Pentagon. There was no Pentagon crash, though how that is explained away I can't quite remember. The Clintons also spawned a mass of conspiracy theories that were germinated and lovingly tended by the disillusioned right in American politics. The left then nurtured their own conspiracy theories about Dick Cheney, Rumsfeld et al. when they appeared to be pulling the strings in George W. Bush's White House.

And I haven't even mentioned UFOs and what was going on when there was the mysterious air crash just outside Roswell, New Mexico, in 1947. It was for many – and remains – the first proof of aliens from outer space crash landing. Then there is Area 51 in the Nevada Desert – undoubtedly a top secret US military base where experimental aircraft are tested. But, say it very quietly, there are also alien spacecraft there. And aliens. Lots of them. No, of course there is no proof, but an awful lot of people believe that to be the case. And then there are the moon landings, which were clearly faked. Old Neil Armstrong was probably in a warehouse somewhere in a remote part of the US or on a Hollywood studio lot when he was taking his small step for man and that giant leap for mankind. And on, and on, and on. America thrives on conspiracy theories and the nefarious activities of its political leaders.

The brilliant political columnist David Aaronovitch wrote a wonderful book called *Voodoo Histories*, debunking with forensic precision and great wit the many conspiracy theories that have abounded over the years and assessing the role they have played in shaping modern history. He argues that such theories are 'formulated by the politically defeated and taken up by the socially defeated'.

But Donald Trump is now the politically victorious, and seems to have lost none of his taste for conspiracy theories, with a vast army of followers, who love what he has to say, retweeting with gusto whatever the 140 characters are that he has just fired out. And a lot of what he does is attacking the media – in general. But also specific targets – he loves to attack the *New York Times,* the *Washington Post*, CNN and MSNBC. And this is having an effect.

Some argue – even on the right – that what Donald Trump is doing is acting as a catalyst to delegitimise, or undermine, established, fact-based journalism. I cannot tell you how many times at Trump rallies, midway through a train of thought, he would look over to where we the press had been corralled and penned in – and accuse us of being the most dishonest people ever; saying we were a bunch of sleazy liars. And the audience would take their cue from Mr Trump, and boo and jeer and hurl insults at us. Journalists covering the Trump campaign were threatened and spat at. I'm not reporting this to evoke sympathy or anything of the kind. Rather it is to make the point that truthful reporting, fact-based discovery, did not win much admiration in this post-truth world.

The wartime American writer and satirist H.L. Mencken wrote that the relationship between a journalist and politician should be the same as between a dog and a lamp-post. Well it's starting to feel that that has been reversed. We are now the lamp-post. Of course there is nothing new about politicians becoming infuriated with the media.

It is by its nature an uneasy relationship – we each have different jobs to do.

An exasperated President Lyndon B. Johnson once commented that if he left the Oval Office, sauntered down to the banks of the Potomac River and then managed to walk across it, the headline in the newspaper the next day would be 'President Can't Swim'. No politician is ever happy with the coverage they receive. I remember the British PM John Major on a flight to Prague telling me and a couple of other colleagues that he no longer listened to the radio in the morning, or read the papers, as leadership was about forging a path and not being distracted by what we, the fourth estate, were writing about him. His protestations would have had more force if he hadn't then, a couple of minutes later, taken us to task for what had been in our news reports that morning.

There was a period when Tony Blair had become exasperated with conventional political journalism, and wanted to be able to reach the public more directly. So to daily briefings, non-Westminster journalists would be invited. He was always looking for new ways to get his message to a wider audience. The holy grail was to be able to communicate directly to the public, unmediated by anyone. It drove his press secretary, Alastair Campbell, mad that if the PM was giving a speech, the news media might play a 30-second clip of it, and give the remaining two and a half minutes to the political correspondent (i.e. people like me) to give their interpretation or spin on what it all meant.

We are now in a totally different era. Donald Trump on Twitter has over 30 million followers; his Facebook page is available to anyone who wants it. Put that in old money.

He has more 'subscribers' than any newspaper or media outlet could dream of reaching at any one time. It was a tool he used to great effect during the campaign, and he will continue to do so. The frustrations of previous generations of politicians, that they lacked a mechanism to get their message across unmediated, have now disappeared. Yes, Donald Trump will still rail against the 'biased' conventional media, as he describes it – but that is an easy way for him to present his version of the truth, and to cast further doubt on what the old-fashioned news organisations are doing.

This presents a huge challenge to the established media and to politics in general. The cautious President Obama, who would make evidence-based decisions only after weighing the facts and the options, has railed against the rise of fakery. At a news conference in Germany on his final overseas trip he said this:

> If we are not serious about facts and what's true and what's not, if we can't discriminate between serious arguments and propaganda, then we have problems ... In an age where there's so much active misinformation, and it's packaged very well, and it looks the same when you see it on a Facebook page or you turn on your television, where some over-zealousness on the part of a US official is equated with constant and severe repression elsewhere, if everything seems to be the same and no distinctions are made, then we don't know what to protect.

All of which puts focus on the providers of social media, like Facebook. According to the Pew Research Center, 62 per cent of US adults now turn to social media for some or all of their news. The founder of Facebook, Mark Zuckerberg, initially dismissed as a 'crazy idea' the suggestion that his platform had played a part in giving Donald Trump his election victory. It is an argument that goes to the heart of what the internet and social media are about. Do Facebook and Twitter have any responsibility for what is posted on their sites? Is it an open microphone where people can say and write whatever they like? Or are there barriers? Should there be curators of the content? If so, what should their role be? Is it their job to weed out fake news?

In the early part of the 2016 campaign, Facebook came under fire from the right for what was seen as over-zealous interference by curators of the 'trending topics' chart. The site stood accused of censoring stories which favoured the right. As a result of that, Zuckerberg got rid of the team that filtered the trending stories and replaced them with an algorithm – and, hey presto, before you could say 'Hillary Clinton is a rapist,' fake news was proliferating.

In response to the criticism that was coming their way both Google and Facebook announced plans to starve the hoaxers of revenue, by not allowing them to place their stories in areas which also generated advertising income. That's fine – but it still doesn't prevent the purveyors of fake stories from peddling their wares, and posting whatever they like. And not all of those people who were doing this were motivated by money.

The benign view of this is that what happened in America was a spasm – it was a perfect storm of a disillusioned, angry electorate willing to believe anything, a genius communicator in Donald Trump, a Democratic candidate in Hillary Clinton of whom people wanted to believe the worst, social media caught by surprise by fake news and the alacrity with which it would be taken up, and a conventional, liberal elite media that was flat-footed and out of touch with so much of America. And the most Panglossian view: yes, there was a lot of fake news around – but it had no real effect. It was only at the outer fringes that this stuff had any kind of impact.

And then there is the more pessimistic outlook. Lies, fake news, Russian interference, a weak media, a supine social media and an alienated public made a Donald Trump victory. And next time round the lies will multiply and intensify – and all rational and reasonable argument, all debate over policy will go out of the window.

But surely the lies would stop once Mr Trump had scaled the mountain, his enemies slain, and could look out from his perch on high? Well, no.

The tall stories/falsehoods/tendentious figures/lies would carry on pretty much unabated. But nothing brought this into sharper focus that the testimony to the Senate Intelligence Committee of the sacked FBI Director, James Comey. It is hard to think of two more temperamentally different people. The old saying is that 'revenge is a dish best served cold'. After his humiliating defenestration, Comey had kept quiet. But now, before the Senate, he calmly set out how uneasy their relationship had been, and most damning of all, how much he mistrusted the 45th president of the United States. The head of the FBI is, of course, meant to operate independently of the president, but Donald Trump had wanted a number of one-on-one meetings with him. At one such encounter, Comey told senators that Trump had 'demanded loyalty', a highly inappropriate thing to ask of someone who is meant to be independent of the executive branch. Such was

Comey's unease about this, he revealed that he had kept a detailed memorandum, written contemporaneously after each conversation. In a court of law, notes of this nature from an FBI officer are admissible as evidence.

The committee vice chairman, Mark Warner, asked why he felt the need to document his meetings with Trump, when he didn't do the same with past presidents. Comey responded: 'I was honestly concerned he might lie about the nature of our meeting.' One commentator noted 'politicians – and those longtime members of the political swirl like Comey – would rather cut off a finger than call another political person a liar. And yet, Comey has now done so five(!) times.' Not only by implication, but in explicit terms, this lifelong public servant called the sitting president dishonest.

Just before Donald Trump's inauguration an astonishing report surfaced – and who knows whether it was fake news or not. Looking at the background of the author it would seem not. It was an 'intel' report by a former MI6 officer on what the Russian intelligence services had apparently discovered about Donald Trump. And it had been commissioned by Republicans opposed to Trump. It made for fascinating reading in the most part, and just occasionally lurid reading (the president completely denied its veracity). The story broke overnight and I was in London having gone to bed blissfully unaware of what was unfolding. I remember being woken at 5am by a well-meaning producer from Radio 4's *Today* programme. I picked up the phone and blearily said hello. 'We want you to come on the air in the next hour to talk about Donald Trump and his golden showers.' 'Sorry,' I said. 'Just repeat that one more time a little more slowly. I thought you said golden showers for a moment.' Later that day there was an enquiry from my 89-year-old mother-in-law, via email, about what a golden shower was. There was a lively discussion on the family WhatsApp group about who wanted to have that conversation with her ...

At the news conference he gave later that day, he rounded on the US intelligence services for having been responsible for leaking (sorry) this. Extraordinarily, he was charging the men and women whose job it is to keep America safe of behaving like Nazis. He tweeted the same. But then the weekend after his inauguration he went on his first official visit to Langley in Virginia, the headquarters of the CIA, to try to rebuild the relationship. And his argument was this: he had always supported the intelligence services, and it was the lying, dishonest media that had made the whole thing up. This despite his tweets and his words making it clear that the media had had nothing to do with it. The president had gone to war with the CIA all by himself.

The relationship with the media had become toxic. He used his first proper news conference as president to wage war on journalism. It was 'fake news' that was being published and broadcast by the *New York Times,* the *Washington Post* and CNN. We were all inveterate liars, he said, while standing at the podium and claiming that the number of electoral college votes he had won was the highest since Ronald Reagan. One of the journalists at this unforgettable news conference pointed out that both Barack Obama and George H.W. Bush had won way more, and the president just shrugged and blamed it on duff information he'd been given.

In his early weeks in office he also waged war on the judges who had overturned his travel-ban executive order. This far-reaching measure, which had sparked protests across the country, had been drawn up by two aides with little input from other areas of government. The ruling was challenged in the courts as chaos unfolded, and rather than blame those responsible for its drafting, the president went after the judges. That looked like an attempt to undermine one of the much vaunted co-equal – and independent – branches of government, the judiciary. His attacks on the media, and attempts to ban from briefings certain publications he found disobliging, seemed like an attack on the First Amendment guaranteeing free speech – and a robust and free press. One of his key lieutenants went on television to say that the president could do whatever he wanted and no one had the right to question him.

Just going back to his visit to the CIA at Langley for a minute, one other thing he did when he stood before the famous memorial wall, studded with stars to represent each CIA officer who had died serving the country, was to complain that the media had underplayed the crowds who had turned out to see his inaugural address. Needless to say, in his mind, it was the biggest ever – even though the photographs decisively proved otherwise. The crowds on the Mall were nothing like those at Barack Obama's first inauguration in 2009. But he wasn't going to let this go.

That Saturday evening, just 24 hours after the inauguration, the White House correspondents were summoned at short notice to an early evening briefing. With so much else going on there weren't many of us there. What followed was nothing short of a tirade. Sean Spicer, the president's spokesman, came in and read us the riot act: 'This was the largest audience to ever witness an inauguration, period.' We needed to be held to account; we were dishonest; there would be consequences; and when he got to the end, he turned and walked out, refusing to answer a single question.

I had been sitting next to the *Guardian* correspondent, David Smith, who had previously been the newspaper's man in Southern Africa. 'It's like being back in Zimbabwe,' he said with a cheery smile. I said I felt as though I was back at school. The occasionally self-important group that is the White House Correspondents' Association had never been spoken to like that. There was a profound sense of shock in the briefing room: not just that there had been such an onslaught, but that what he said was palpably false. Photos from 2009 and 2017, both taken from the Washington Monument looking towards the Capitol, make that abundantly plain.

But this wasn't the end of it. The next day it was the turn of the president's former campaign manager – and newly installed counsellor to the president, Kellyanne Conway – to take the fight to the media. She went on the programme *Meet the Press*, and came up with an unforgettable line to defend their position that there were more people at the Trump inauguration than any in history. When the presenter suggested the White House wasn't telling the truth, she replied: 'You're saying it's a falsehood … Sean Spicer, our press secretary, gave alternative facts.'

Alternative facts: the most genius euphemism for an untruth that has ever been minted. It was newspeak. Oh. And what became the Amazon bestselling book in the United States the week after the 2017 inauguration? A book written by a British author 68 years earlier. George Orwell's *1984*.

Leabharlanna Fhine Gall

Index

JS indicates Jon Sopel.